MathFlare

Name: ___________________________

Class: ___________

Teacher: ___________________________

Introduction

As parents and educators, we recognize the pivotal role mathematics plays in shaping a child's academic journey and future success. Yet, the path to mathematical proficiency can often seem daunting, fraught with challenges and complexities. That's where the transformative power of MathFlare Workbooks shine through, illuminating the way forward with clarity, precision, and purpose.

Introducing MathFlare Workbooks – a beacon of guidance, a testament to excellence, and a catalyst for achievement. Crafted with meticulous care and expertise, MathFlare Workbooks stand as paragons of educational excellence, designed to nurture young minds, ignite a passion for learning, and develop a deep-rooted understanding of mathematical concepts.

Picture this: your child eagerly delves into the pages of Mathflare Workbook, greeted by a step-by-step guide illuminated with vivid examples that demystify complex mathematical concepts. With each turn of the page, they embark on a journey of discovery, encountering thoughtfully curated practice questions that reinforce learning and hone problem-solving skills. And when they unveil the answers to those very questions, a sense of accomplishment blossoms within them – a tangible reward for their hard work and dedication.

But MathFlare Workbooks are more than just tools for learning; they are pathways to comprehension, fostering a deep-seated understanding of mathematical concepts through a sequential, logical flow. From fundamental principles to advanced problem-solving strategies, every chapter builds upon the last, ensuring a robust foundation upon which future knowledge can be constructed.

As parents, we yearn for nothing more than to see our children thrive, to witness the spark of inspiration ignited within them as they conquer academic challenges with confidence and poise. MathFlare Workbooks serve as partners in this noble endeavor, offering not just practice questions, but the keys to unlocking a world of opportunity.

And for teachers, MathFlare Workbooks stand as invaluable allies in the quest to cultivate mathematical proficiency in the classroom. With answers readily available, instructors can focus on guiding and nurturing their students, confident in the knowledge that MathFlare Workbooks provide a solid framework upon which to build.

In the pages of MathFlare Workbooks, we find not just the promise of academic excellence, but the seeds of a brighter tomorrow. So let us embrace the power of mathematics, let us champion the journey of learning, and let us pave the way for a generation of young minds poised to shape the world. With MathFlare Workbooks as our guide, the possibilities are infinite, and the future, bright.

Table of Contents

MathFlare
MATH
WORKBOOK
5
Step by Step Guide
and Essential Practice
with Answers
Multiplication
Division
Place Value and
Expanded
Notations
Fractions
and Geometry
Unit
Conversion
MathFlare Publishing

MathFlare
MATH
WORKBOOK
5-6
Step by Step Guide
and Essential Practice
with Answers
Multiplication
Division
Place Value and
Expanded
Notations
Fractions
and Geometry
Units and
Statistics
MathFlare Publishing

MathFlare
MATH
WORKBOOK
6
Step by Step Guide
and Essential Practice
with Answers
Integers and
Statistics
Arithmetic and
Pre-Algebra
Fractions
and Geometry
Ratio and
Percentage
MathFlare Publishing

MathFlare
MATH
WORKBOOK
6-7
Step by Step Guide
and Essential Practice
with Answers
Arithmetic and
Pre-Algebra
Ratio, Percent
Proportion
Geometry
Statistics
MathFlare Publishing

MathFlare
MATH
WORKBOOK
7
Step by Step Guide
and Essential Practice
with Answers
Pre-Algebra
Ratio, Percent
Proportion
Geometry
Statistics
MathFlare Publishing

MathFlare
MATH
WORKBOOK
7-8
Step by Step Guide
and Essential Practice
with Answers
Pre-Algebra
Ratio, Percent
Proportion
Geometry and
Cartesian
Plane
Statistics
MathFlare Publishing

MathFlare
MATH
WORKBOOK
8-9
Step by Step Guide
and Essential Practice
with Answers
Pre-Algebra
Ratio, Proportion
and Percentage
Linear
Equations
Geometry and
Cartesian Plane
MathFlare Publishing

MathFlare
MATH
WORKBOOK
8
Step by Step Guide
and Essential Practice
with Answers
Pre-Algebra
Percentage
Linear
Equations
Geometry

<h1 style="text-align:center">Chapter. 01</h1>

<h1 style="text-align:center">Multiplication and Division</h1>

Multiplication

Multiplication is an easy way of adding numbers together quickly. Instead of adding the same number repeatedly, we use multiplication to find the total much faster.

For instance, rather than adding 2 + 2 + 2 + 2 + 2, we can multiply 2 by 5 to get the same result: 2 x 5 = 10.

Here, the first number (2) is called the multiplicand, second number (5) is the multiplier. The answer we get, in this case, 10, is called the product.

Let's think of multiplication as repeated addition.

Take 2 x 5, for example. It means adding 2 together five times, which we can illustrate as: 2 + 2 + 2 + 2 + 2 = 10

Multiplication can also be visualized as groups of objects. Imagine we have 2 groups, each containing 5 oranges.

To find the total number of oranges, we multiply the number of groups (2) by the number of oranges in each group (5):

2 groups of 5 oranges = 10 oranges

Expressed as multiplication: 2 x 5 = 10

In summary, multiplication offers various ways to approach it: through repeated addition or by envisioning groups of objects. It's a powerful tool that makes solving math problems much quicker and more efficient!

We can also use the following table to quickly remember multiplication facts. The intersection of two points shows the product of two numbers.

For instance, the product of 5 x 6 = 30, or 6 x 5 = 30.

	1	2	3	4	5	6	7	8	9	10
1	1	2	3	4	5	6	7	8	9	10
2	2	4	6	8	10	12	14	16	18	20
3	3	6	9	12	15	18	21	24	27	30
4	4	8	12	16	20	24	28	32	36	40
5	5	10	15	20	25	30	35	40	45	50
6	6	12	18	24	30	36	42	48	54	60
7	7	14	21	28	35	42	49	56	63	70
8	8	16	24	32	40	48	56	64	72	80
9	9	18	27	36	45	54	63	72	81	90
10	10	20	30	40	50	60	70	80	90	100

Long Division and Remainders

Division is like the opposite of multiplication. It's all about sharing or distributing items equally among a certain number of groups or people.

When we divide one number by another, we're essentially splitting a number into equal parts. We're figuring out how many groups of a certain size can be made from that number.

For instance, let's divide 20 by 4.

When we divide 20 by 4, we're essentially asking, "How many groups of size 4 can we make from 20?"

Now, there are several parts or terms involved in the division process:

- **Dividend:** This is the number being divided, which in this case, is 20.

- **Divisor:** This is the number we're dividing by, which is 4.

- **Quotient:** This is the answer we get after dividing. It tells us how many groups of divisors can be made from the dividend. In this case, the answer is 5.

- **Remainder:** when the divisor doesn't evenly divide the dividend, we get the remainder.

So, when we divide 20 by 4, we found out that 5 groups of 4 can be made from 20.

Let's solve problems from exercises:

                          08,464.6
                   10) 84,646
                         - 0
                          84
                         - 80
                           46
        8,965 R1   - 40
     9) 80,686   64
        - 72   - 60
          86   46
        - 81   - 40
          58   60
        - 54   - 60
          46   0
        - 45
           1

Multi Digit Multiplication

                    93,369
               ×   755
            +   466845
            + 466845
            + 653583
            = 70493595

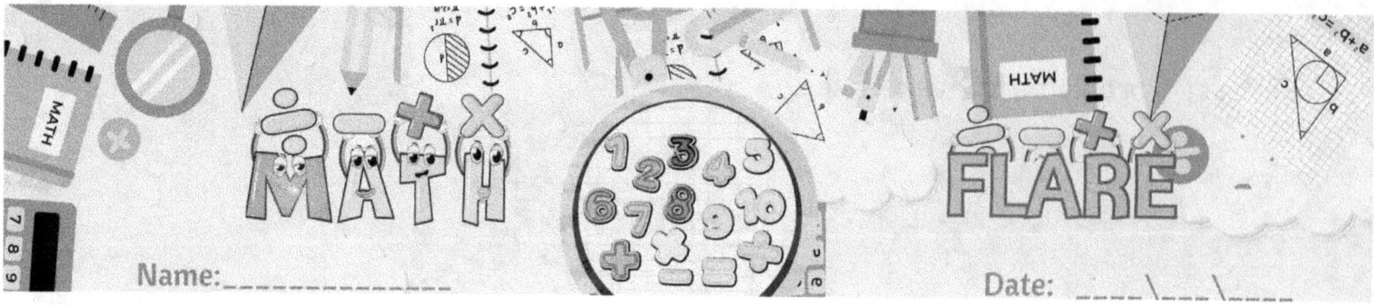

Long Division

Find the quotient.

1)

08,464.6
10 ⟌ 84,646

-0
84
-80
46
-40
64
-60

46
-40
60
-60
0

2)

8 ⟌ 69,368

3)

10 ⟌ 92,865

4)

9 ⟌ 89,318

5)

6 ⟌ 44,361

6)

4 ⟌ 81,839

7)

$$3\overline{)58{,}139}$$

8)

$$9\overline{)68{,}469}$$

9)

$$7\overline{)64{,}908}$$

10)

$$4\overline{)91{,}897}$$

11)

$$7\overline{)70{,}483}$$

12)

$$6\overline{)75{,}902}$$

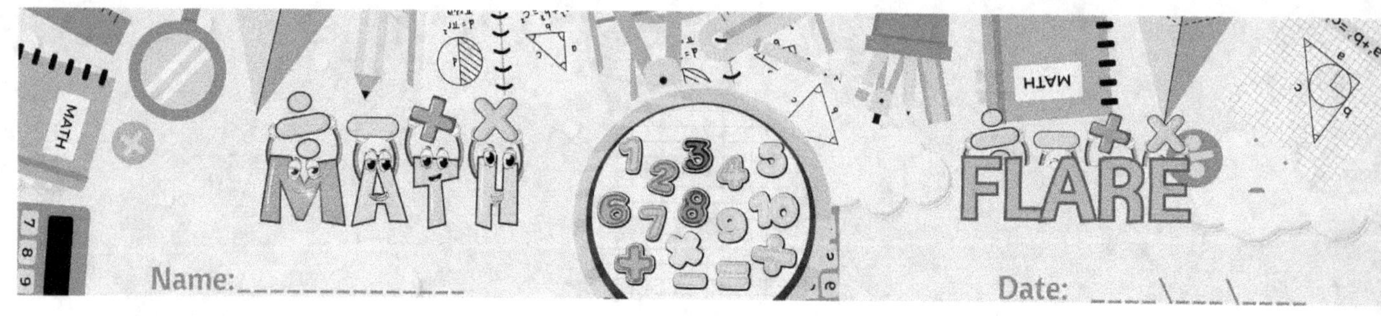

13)

$$4 \overline{)\ 65{,}981}$$

14)

$$5 \overline{)\ 23{,}249}$$

15)

$$6 \overline{)\ 59{,}032}$$

16)

$$6 \overline{)\ 62{,}244}$$

17)

$$4 \overline{)\ 27{,}172}$$

18)

$$5 \overline{)\ 64{,}271}$$

19)

$$3 \overline{) 97{,}366}$$

20)

$$10 \overline{) 46{,}786}$$

21)

$$6 \overline{) 24{,}030}$$

22)

$$8 \overline{) 38{,}333}$$

23)

$$6 \overline{) 53{,}767}$$

24)

$$8 \overline{) 98{,}301}$$

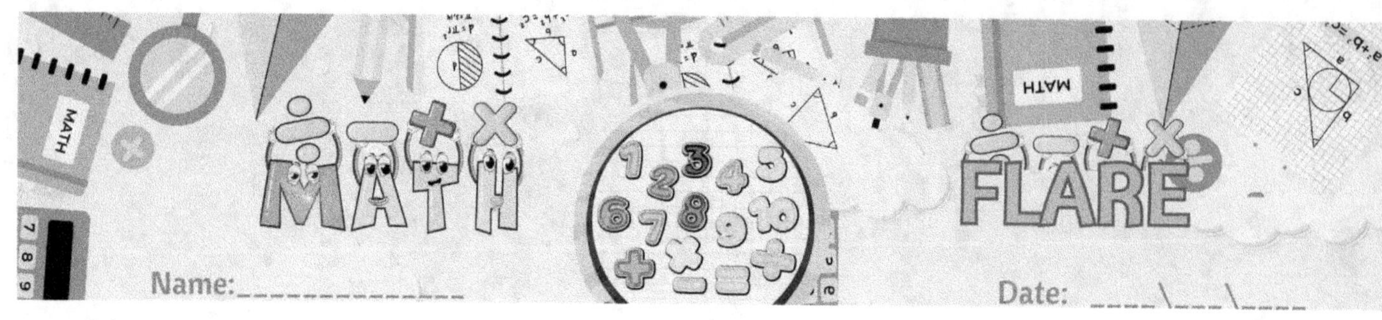

25)

$$5\overline{)20{,}873}$$

26)

$$6\overline{)20{,}878}$$

27)

$$5\overline{)17{,}702}$$

28)

$$4\overline{)40{,}173}$$

29)

$$3\overline{)31{,}628}$$

30)

$$7\overline{)25{,}500}$$

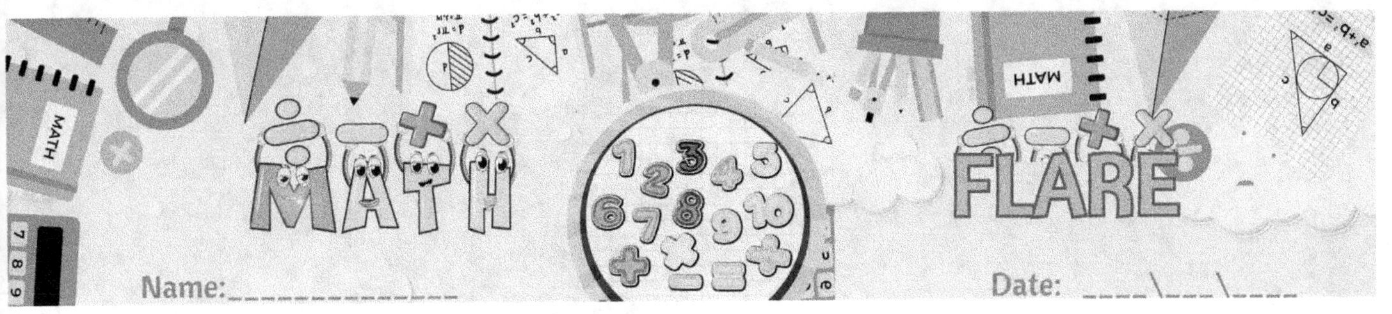

Long Division: Remainders

Find the quotient.

1)

$$19 \overline{)76{,}285}$$

2)

$$20 \overline{)63{,}673} \quad 3{,}183 \ R13$$

$$-0$$
$$63$$
$$-60$$
$$36$$
$$-20$$
$$167$$
$$-160$$
$$73$$
$$-60$$
$$13$$

3)

$$2 \overline{)35{,}578}$$

4)

$$20 \overline{)71{,}268}$$

5)

$$11 \overline{)\,97{,}172}$$

6)

$$4 \overline{)\,88{,}844}$$

7)

$$8 \overline{)\,67{,}780}$$

8)

$$6 \overline{)\,85{,}338}$$

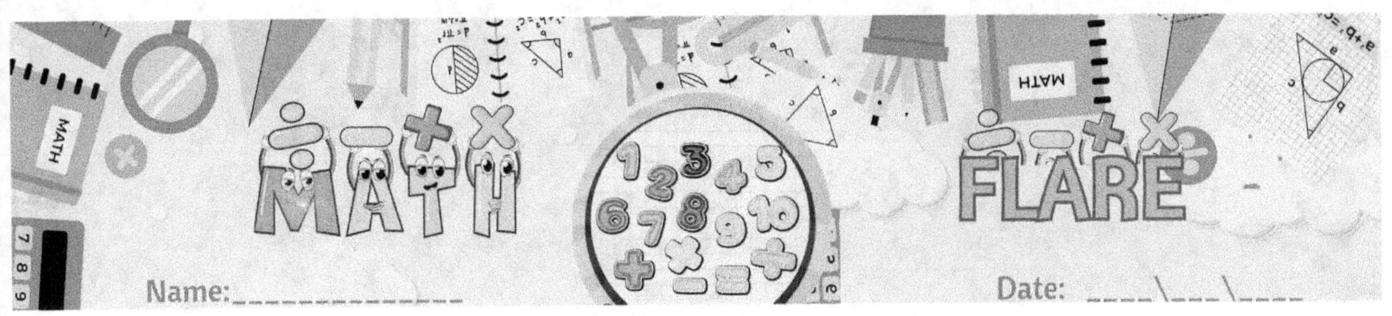

9)

$$13\overline{)55{,}460}$$

10)

$$14\overline{)94{,}867}$$

11)

$$11\overline{)75{,}751}$$

12)

$$18\overline{)11{,}169}$$

13)

$$2\overline{)12{,}117}$$

14)

$$17\overline{)96{,}115}$$

15)

$$7\overline{)27{,}016}$$

16)

$$6\overline{)36{,}443}$$

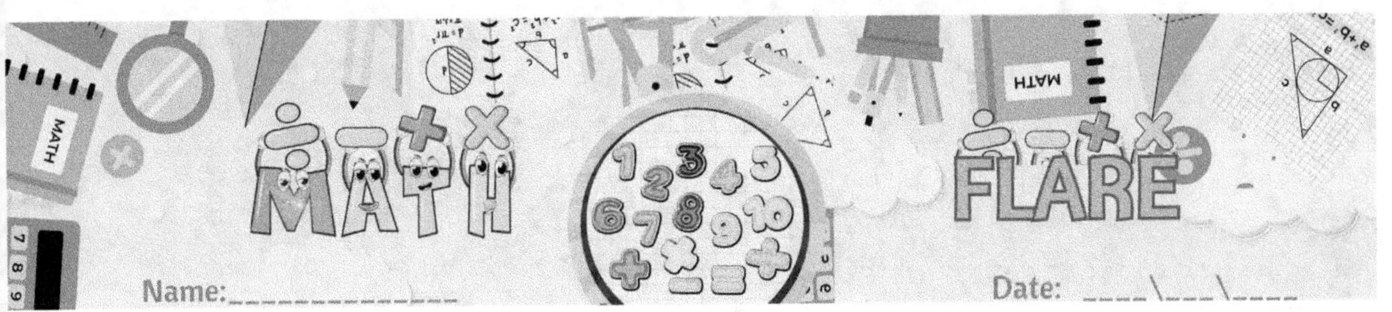

17)

$$14\overline{)66,043}$$

18)

$$20\overline{)39,883}$$

19)

$$17\overline{)37,959}$$

20)

$$18\overline{)26,224}$$

21)

13$\overline{)21{,}445}$

22)

17$\overline{)11{,}127}$

23)

19$\overline{)74{,}064}$

24)

7$\overline{)94{,}854}$

25)

20 ⟌ 26,852

26)

10 ⟌ 82,000

27)

9 ⟌ 76,202

28)

6 ⟌ 36,959

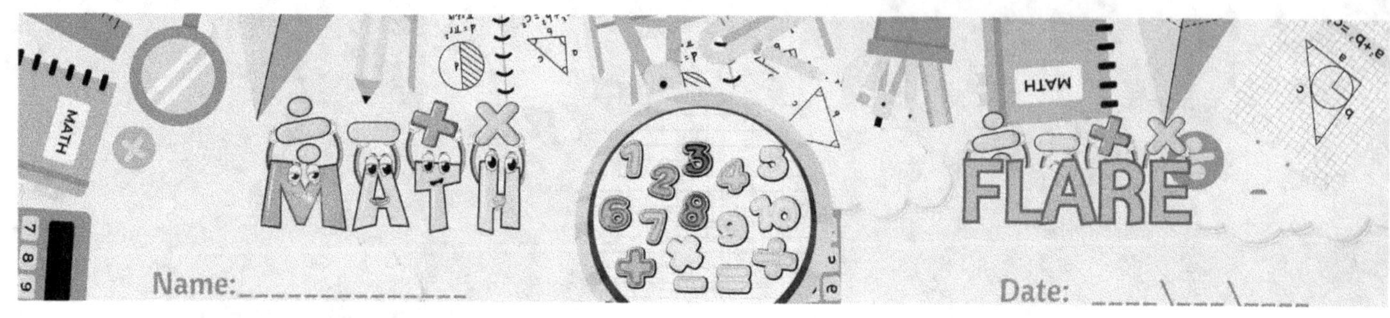

Multi Digit Multiplication

Find the product.

1)   93,369
  ×   755

+ 466845
+466845
+653583
=70493595

2)   96,773
  ×   336

3)   15,779
  ×   841

4)   82,338
  ×   709

5)   28,447
  ×   663

6)   55,840
  ×   988

7)   98,642
  ×   868

8)   92,075
  ×   711

9)   48,911
  ×   134

10) 57,003
   ×   200

11) 53,727
   ×   243

12) 24,014
   ×   147

13) 17,092
   ×   692

14) 70,189
   ×   287

15) 54,163
   ×   845

16) 56,269
   ×   326

17) 41,919
   ×   184

18) 15,113
   ×   623

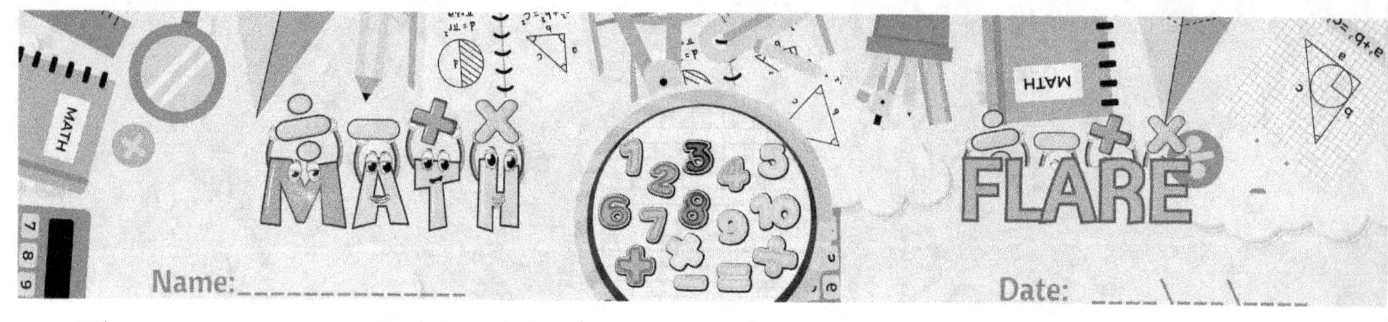

19)   87,469
  ×   925

20)   85,673
  ×   372

21)   83,356
  ×   401

22)   68,394
  ×   177

23)   51,528
  ×   959

24)   38,177
  ×   400

25)   16,178
  ×   208

26)   12,955
  ×   727

27)   86,402
  ×   269

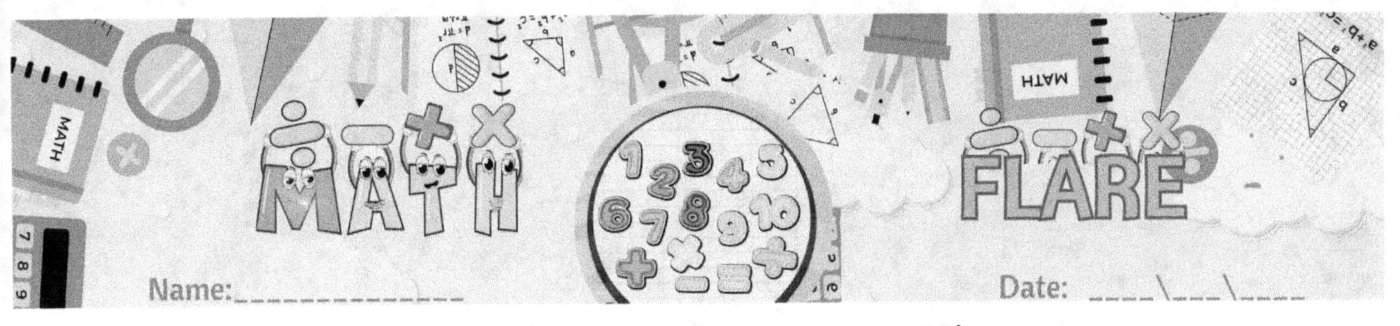

28)   77,694
  ×   790

29)   61,571
  ×   920

30)   26,529
  ×   464

31)   24,028
  ×   635

32)   26,837
  ×   438

33)   20,094
  ×   332

34)   66,974
  ×   901

35)   81,732
  ×   397

36)   83,720
  ×   563

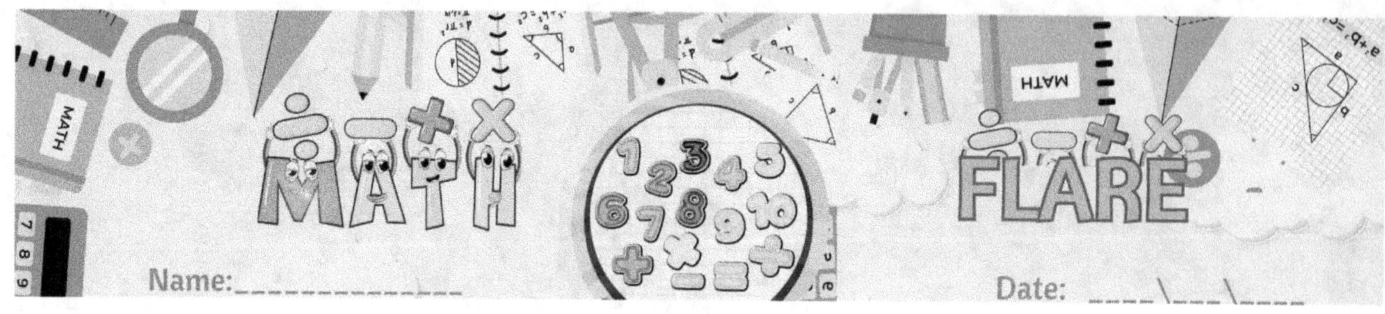

Multiplication Word Problems

1) If a boat travels at five miles per hour for 20 hours, how far will it go?

$$
\begin{array}{r}
5 \\
\times\ 20 \\
\hline
+0 \\
+10 \\
\hline
= 100
\end{array}
$$

a boat travels 5 miles per hour

in 20 minutes, how far it

will go?

So, a boat can travel 100 miles in 20 minutes

2) Joshua can solve 18 math problems in one hour. How many problems can Joshua solve in nine hours?

3) A bookshelf can hold 12 books. If there are eight bookshelves in a room, how many books can the room hold in total?

4) If a train travels at 10 miles per hour for six hours, how far will it go?

5) Aurora has seven vases of flowers. Each vase has three flowers. How many flowers does Aurora have in all?

6) If a bicycle travels at 11 miles per hour for 13 hours, how far will it go?

7) There are five pencils in each pack. If Ariana buys 19 packs, how many pencils will Ariana have?

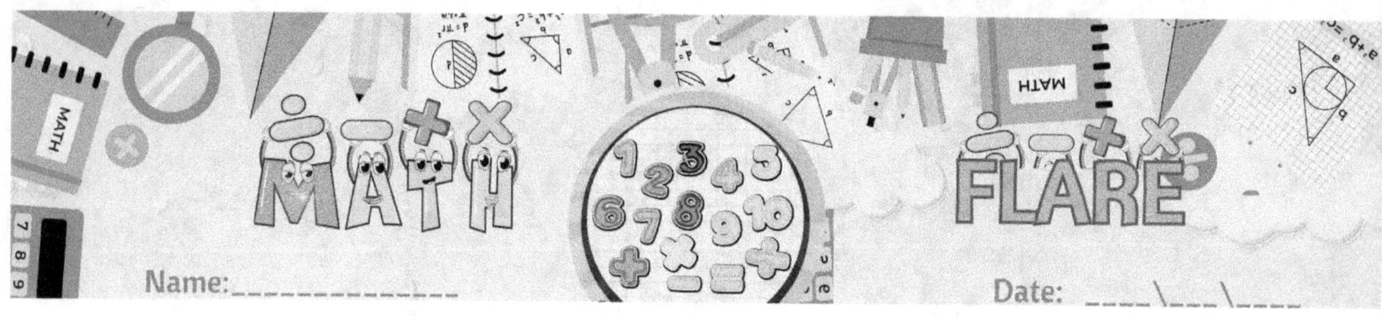

8) If a car travels at eight miles per hour for 15 hours, how far will it go?

9) There are 11 medicines in each bag. If Brielle buys nine bags, how many medicines will Brielle have?

10) Evelyn wants to make six flower arrangements, and each arrangement requires 12 flowers. How many flowers does Evelyn need in total?

11) Robert can solve six math problems in one hour. How many math problems can Robert solve in seven hours?

12) A garden has 10 rows of flowers and 17 flowers in each row. How many flowers are there in total?

13) If Lincoln can paint nine square feet of wall in one hour, how many square feet of wall can he paint in 16 hours?

14) There are 17 seats on a bus. If 13 buses are needed to transport a group of people, how many people can the group consist of at most?

15) A recipe for a cake calls for 11 cups of flour. How many cups of flour are needed to make 12 cakes?

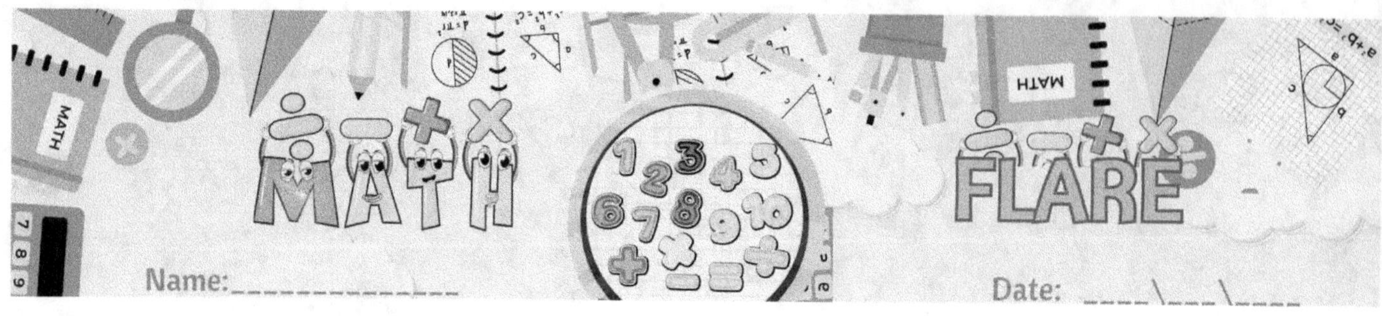

16) Roman can type seven words per minute. How many words can Roman type in 15 minutes?

17) Jackson can run eight laps in 1 hour. How many laps can Jackson run in 18 hour?

18) If there are nine students in each classroom and there are seven classrooms, how many students are there in total?

19) Kai can catch 17 fish per hour. How many fish can Kai catch in 13 hours?

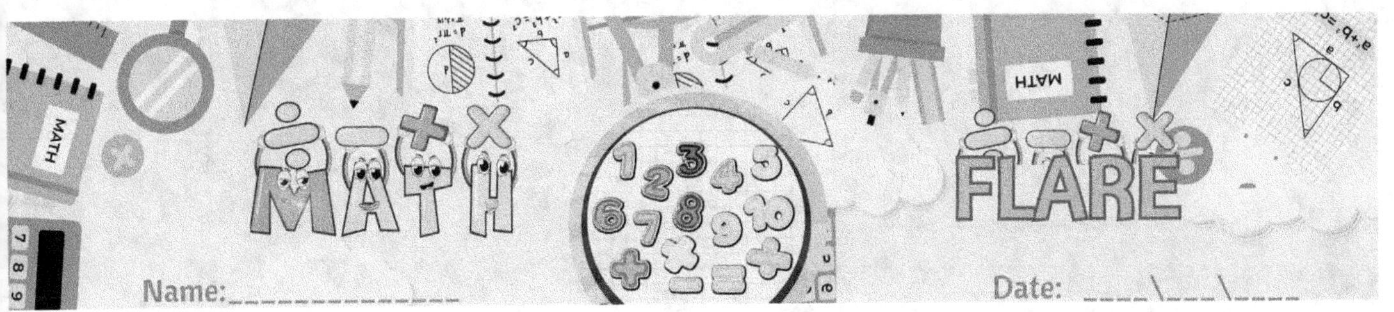

20) Chase can lift 12 kilograms of weight. How many kilograms of weight can he lift in 18 lifts?

21) Logan sells 18 cakes each day at his bakery. If he works three days, how many cakes does he sell?

22) Hazel baked five batches of cakes. Each batch had 18 cakes. How many cakes did Hazel bake in all?

23) Diego runs three miles per week. How many miles will Diego run in three weeks?

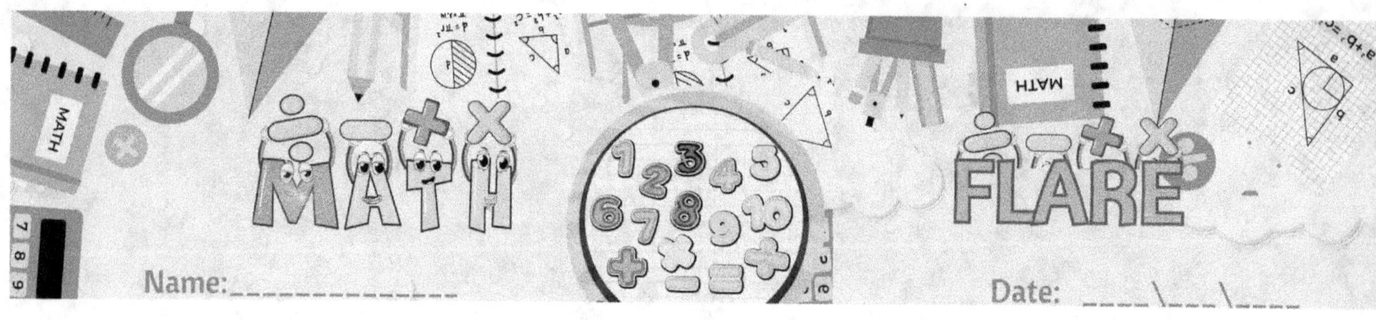

24) There are 16 pages in a book. If two books are needed for a class, how many pages are there in total?

25) Gabriella has 12 containers of paint. Each container holds two liters of paint. How many liters of paint does Gabriella have in total?

26) Harper has 17 jars of jam. Each jar has nine ounces of jam. How many ounces of jam does Harper have in all?

27) There are 19 flowers in each bouquet. If Sadie has 14 bouquets, how many flowers does Sadie have in all?

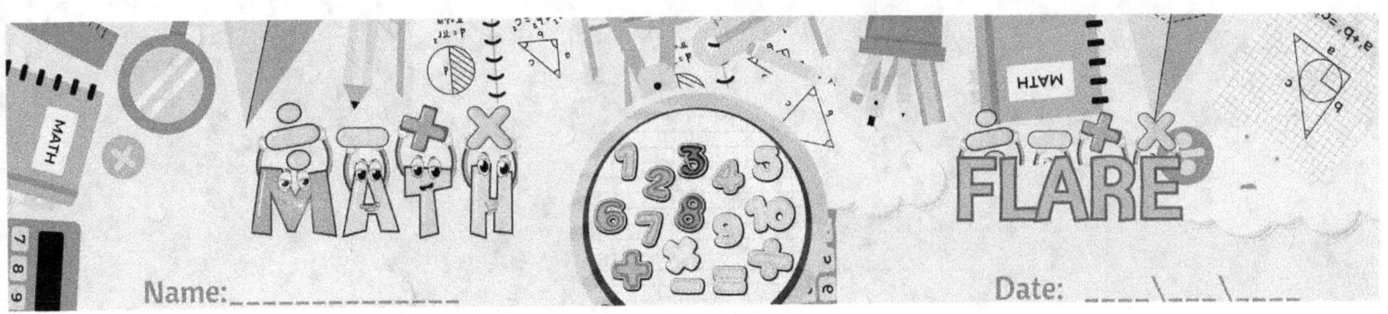

28) Dylan can lift five pounds of weight. How many pounds of weight can he lift in 19 repetitions?

29) Nicholas can lift 12 pounds of weight. How many pounds of weight can Nicholas lift in total if he lifts for three sets?

30) Claire has 20 boxes of flosses. Each box has 17 flosses. How many flosses does Claire have in all?

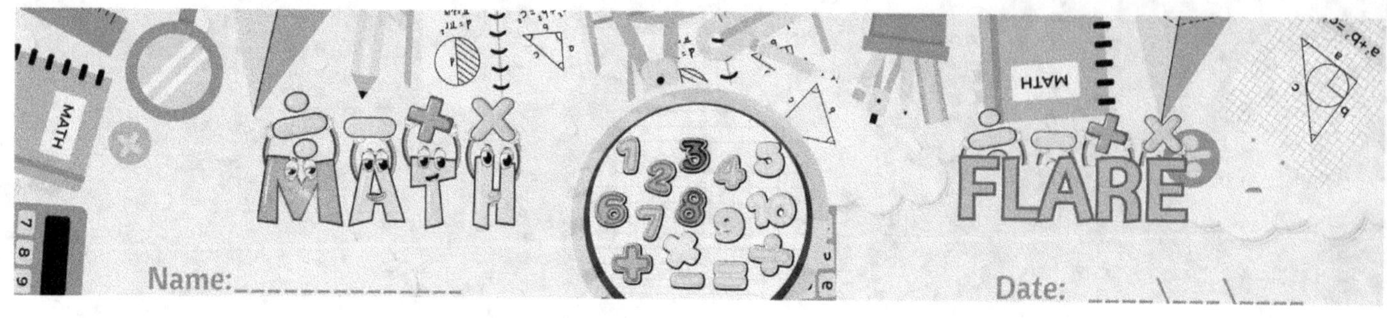

Division Word Problems

1) A book has 140 chapters. If you want to read the book in 20 days, how many chapters do you need to read per day?

$$\begin{array}{r} 7 \\ 20\overline{)140} \\ -140 \\ \hline 0 \end{array}$$

7 chapters

2) A box contains 1,309 candy bars. If each candy bar has 17 calories, how many calories are there in the box?

3) If Madelyn has 660 pens and wants to distribute them equally to 10 students, how many pens will each student get?

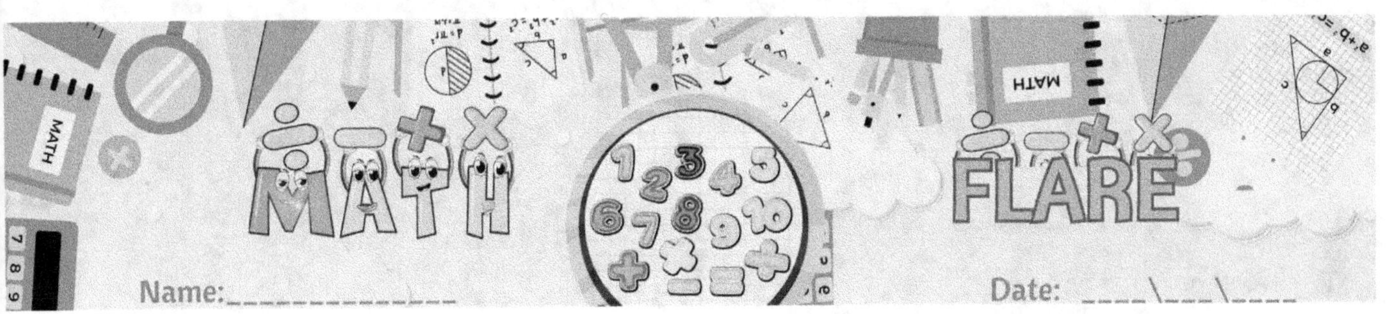

4) Maverick drove 338 miles in 13 hours. What was Maverick's average speed in miles per hour?

5) If Emilia has 1,067 papers and wants to distribute them equally to 11 students, how many papers will each student get?

6) Kennedy made 1,224 cookies for a bake sale. She put the cookies in bags, with 18 cookies in each bag. How many bags did she have for the bake sale?

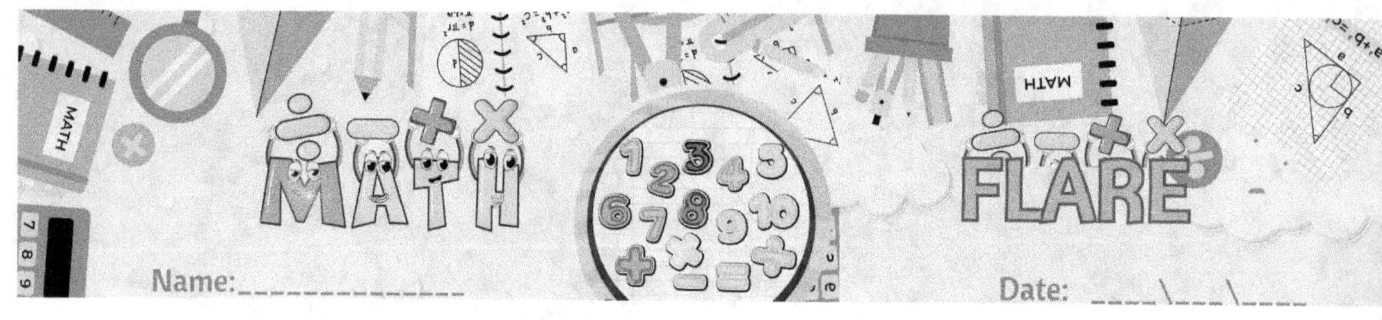

7) If Leah has 120 Markers and wants to divide them equally among five friends, how many Markers will each friend get?

8) A box of glasses weighs 95 pounds. If one glass weighs 19 pounds, how many glasses are there in the box?

9) At a restaurant, six friends decided to divide the bill equally. If each person paid $73, then what was the total bill?

10) Nova has 480 pears and wants to divide them equally among eight children. How many pears will each child get?

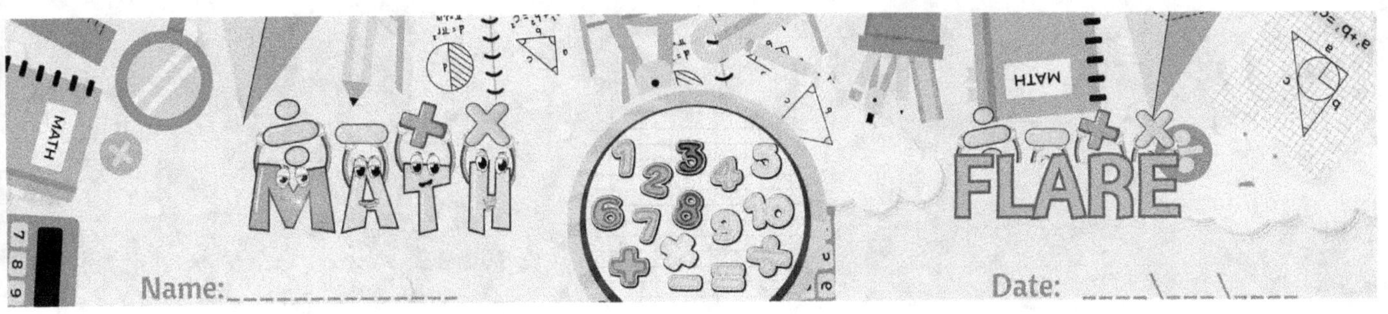

11) If a box contains 170 chocolates and each person can have five chocolates, how many people can be served from that box?

12) Brooklyn has 435 Clocks and wants to divide them equally among five people. How many Clocks will each person get?

13) If a field is 324 acres and it is divided into 18 equal parts, how many acres is each part?

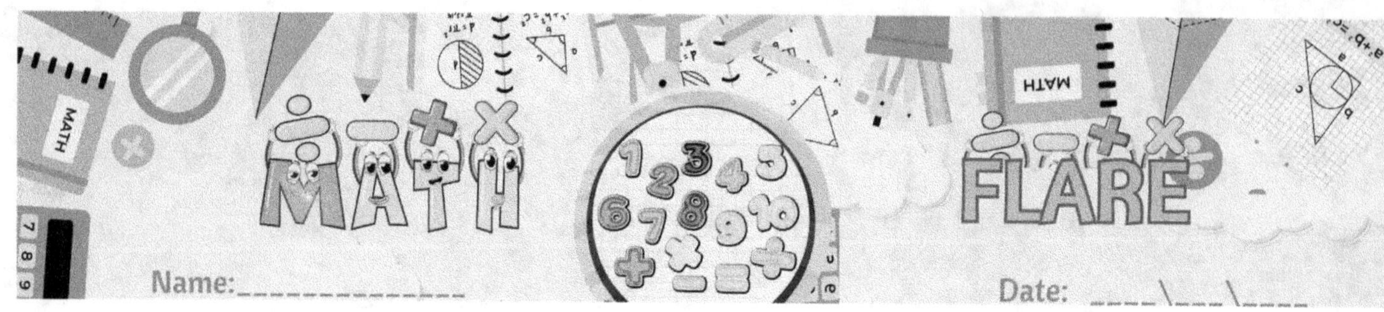

Name:_________________   Date: __________

14) A roll of tape is 260 feet long. If Caroline needs to cut the tape into four pieces that are all the same length, how long will each piece be?

15) Zara bought 10 Hairbrushes for a total of $350. How much did each Hairbrushes cost?

16) Wesley is reading a book with 630 pages. If Wesley wants to read the same number of pages every day, how many pages would Wesley have to read each day to finish in 15 days?

17) A pool is 1,027 meters long. If it is divided into 13 equal parts, how long is each part?

18) Oliver has 1,296 dollars and wants to buy 18 soaps. How much can he spend on each soaps?

19) A recipe calls for 444 cups of sugar to make six cookies. How much sugar is needed to make 1 cookie?

20) How many 14 cm pieces of rope can you cut from a rope that is 728 cm long?

21) Lila has 204 cookies and wants to divide them equally into 12 bags. How many cookies will be in each bag?

22) A rope is 377 meters long. If you cut it into 13 equal pieces, how long is each piece?

23) How many 17 cm pieces of pipe can you cut from a pipe that is 1,445 cm long?

24) Luna has $1,144 and she wants to buy 13 Rocks that cost the same amount. How much does each Rocks cost?

Chapter. 02

Place Value and Expanded Notations

Place value tells us the value of a digit in a number based on where it's placed.

Imagine we have the number 5,987,647.52843. It has 12 digits.

Now, each digit holds a special place. Let's break down the number 5,987,647.52843:

- The digit 5 is in the millions place. Its value is 5 × 1,000,000=5,000,000.

- The digit 9 is in the hundred thousands place. Its value is 9×100,000=900,000.

- The digit 8 is in the ten thousands place. Its value is 8×10,000=80,000.

- The digit 7 is in the thousands place. Its value is 7×1,000=7,000.

- The digit 6 is in the hundreds place. Its value is 6×100=600.

- The digit 4 is in the tens place. Its value is 4×10=40.

- The digit 7 is in the ones place. Its value is 7×1=7.

- The digit 5 is in the tenths place. Its value is $5 \times \frac{1}{10} = 0.5$.

- The digit 2 is in the hundredths place. Its value is $2 \times \frac{1}{100} = 0.02$.

- The digit 8 is in the thousandths place. Its value is $8 \times \frac{1}{1000} = 0.008$.

- The digit 4 is in the ten thousandths place. Its value is $4 \times \frac{1}{10,000} = 0.0004$.

- The digit 3 is in the hundred thousandths place. Its value is $3 \times \dfrac{1}{100,000} =$ 0.00003.

When we add these values together, we find the value of the entire number:

$$5,000,000 + 900,000 + 80,000 + 7,000 + 600 + 40 + 7 + 0.5 + 0.02 + 0.008$$
$$+ 0.0004 + 0.00003 = 5,987,647.52843$$

Let's solve some problems:

Place value of the underlined digit:

$$9,216.46795 = \underline{5 \text{ hundred thousandths}}$$

Expanded notations:

442,218.932 — 4 hundred thousands + 4 ten thousands + 2 thousands + 2 hundreds + 1 ten + 8 ones + 9 tenths + 3 hundredths + 2 thousandths

81,315,897.3 — 80,000,000 + 1,000,000 + 300,000 + 10,000 + 5,000 + 800 + 90 + 7 + 0.3

50,131,193.9 — 5 ten millions + 1 hundred thousand + 3 ten thousands + 1 thousand + 1 hundred + 9 tens + 3 ones + 9 tenths

Place Value

Determine the place value of the underlined digit.

1) 72,644,3<u>6</u>2 = _______6 tens_______

2) 219,784,<u>8</u>08 = _____________________

3) 9,216.4679<u>5</u> = _____________________

4) 472,39<u>3</u>,105 = _____________________

5) 215,624.1<u>6</u> = _____________________

6) 93,7<u>3</u>8.3143 = _____________________

7) 619,5<u>7</u>8,081 = _____________________

8) $\underline{6}5,677,206.2$ = _______________________

9) $807,1\underline{4}2,168$ = _______________________

10) $77,957,1\underline{4}6.3$ = _______________________

11) $661,628,1\underline{8}9$ = _______________________

12) $\underline{1}65,787,862$ = _______________________

13) $675,970.\underline{9}56$ = _______________________

14) $3,6\underline{7}0.81132$ = _______________________

15) $15,81\underline{5}.5789$ = _______________________

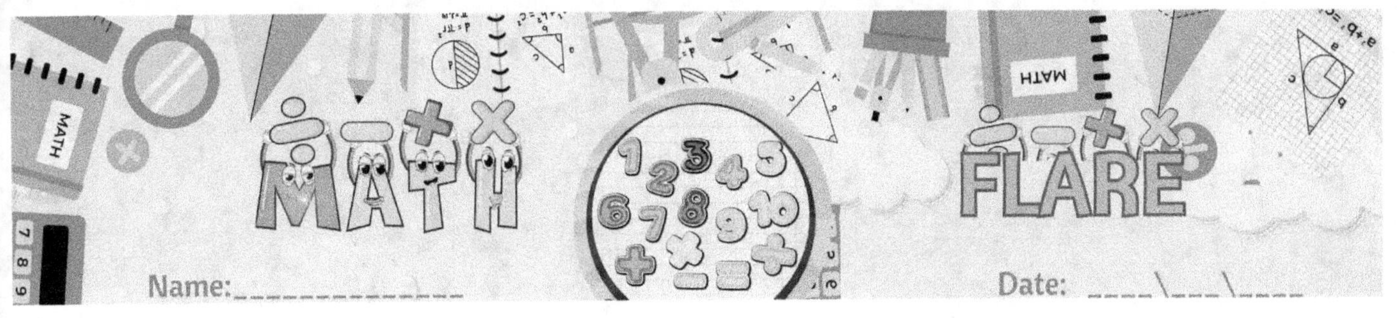

16) 5,974,508.02 = _________________________________

17) 5,481,171.74 = _________________________________

18) 4,311,279.16 = _________________________________

19) 355,908.667 = _________________________________

20) 41,046,574.8 = _________________________________

21) 794,677.619 = _________________________________

22) 7,461,557.99 = _________________________________

23) 61,478.0912 = _________________________________

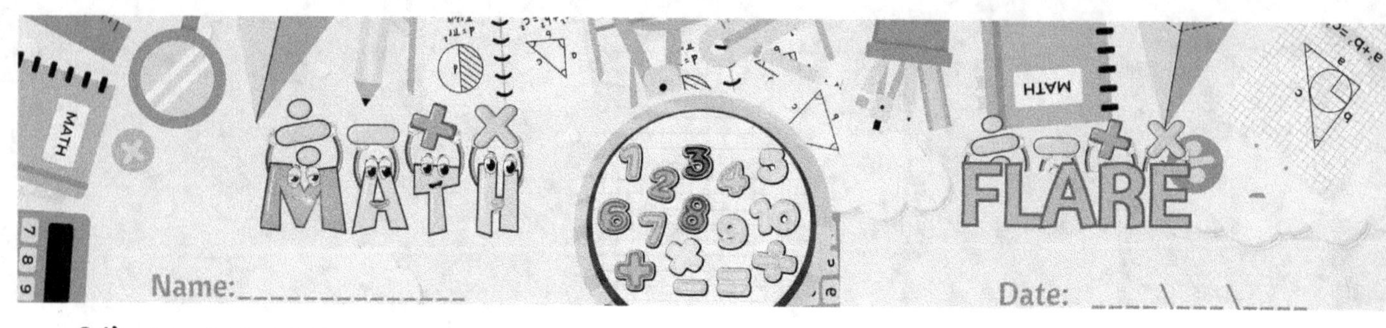

24) 60,41_3,853.1 = ______________________

25) 8_7,201,736.7 = ______________________

26) 76,381.78_32 = ______________________

27) _85,620.4055 = ______________________

28) 12,608.31_86 = ______________________

29) 79,560.48_01 = ______________________

30) _7,554,190.8 = ______________________

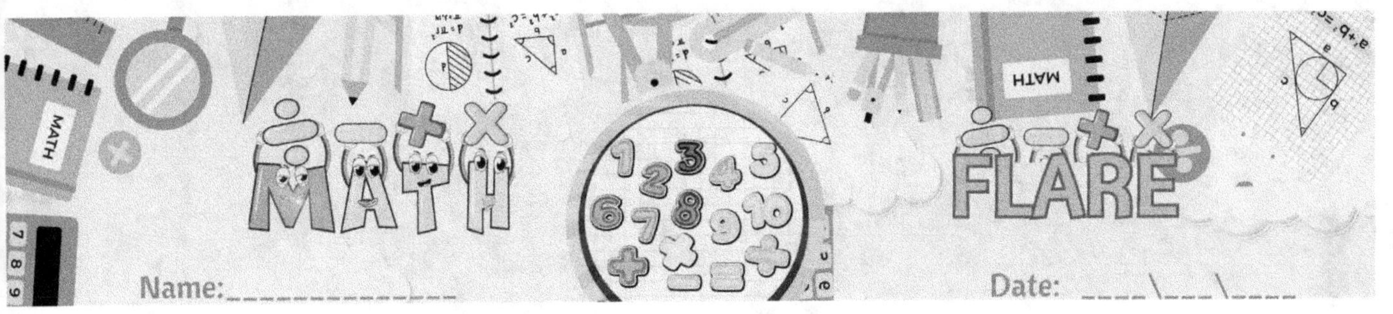

Place Value and Expanded Notation

1) _______442,218.932_______   4 hundred thousands + 4 ten thousands + 2 thousands + 2 hundreds + 1 ten + 8 ones + 9 tenths + 3 hundredths + 2 thousandths

2) _____________________   6 hundred millions + 8 ten millions + 4 millions + 3 hundred thousands + 1 ten thousand + 1 thousand + 1 hundred + 7 tens + 4 ones

3) _____________________   1 hundred thousand + 5 ten thousands + 8 thousands + 3 hundreds + 9 tens + 1 one + 5 tenths + 1 hundredth

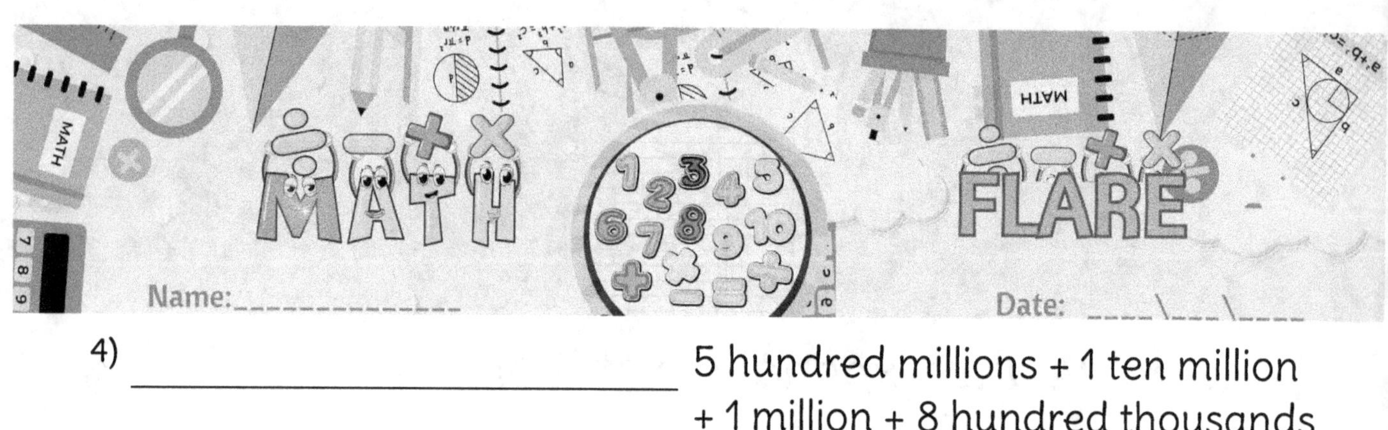

4) _________________________ 5 hundred millions + 1 ten million + 1 million + 8 hundred thousands + 1 thousand + 6 hundreds

5) _________________________ 8 hundred thousands + 8 ten thousands + 2 thousands + 7 hundreds + 7 tens + 6 ones + 8 tenths + 9 hundredths + 1 thousandth

6) _________________________ 4 ten millions + 7 millions + 2 hundred thousands + 2 ten thousands + 3 thousands + 6 hundreds + 1 ten + 1 one + 7 tenths

7) _________________________ 6 ten millions + 5 millions + 9 hundred thousands + 1 ten thousand + 4 thousands + 1 hundred + 3 tens + 9 ones + 5 tenths

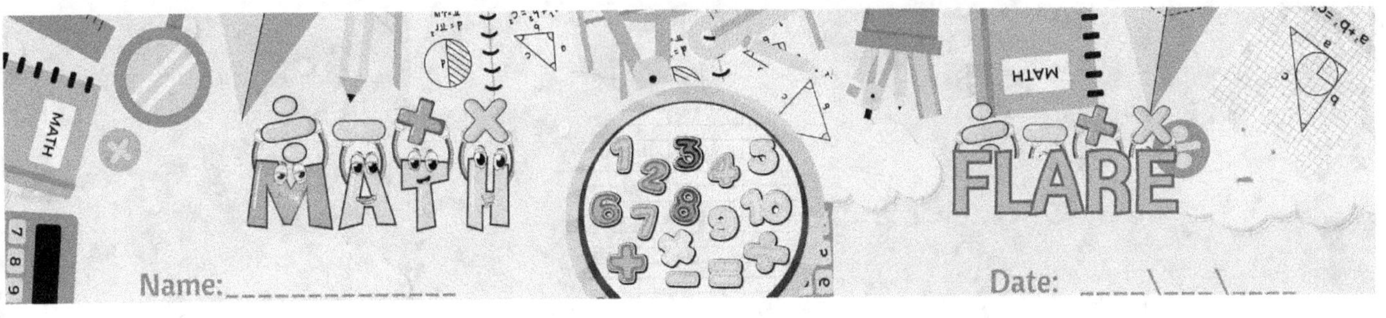

8) ________________________   8 hundred thousands + 9 ten thousands + 9 thousands + 9 hundreds + 8 tens + 3 ones + 6 tenths + 6 hundredths + 6 thousandths

9) ________________________   7 hundred millions + 3 ten millions + 7 millions + 9 hundred thousands + 7 thousands + 8 hundreds + 5 tens + 1 one

10) ________________________   9 hundred thousands + 2 ten thousands + 3 thousands + 9 tens + 5 ones + 5 hundredths + 1 thousandth

11) ________________________   8 millions + 2 hundred thousands + 7 ten thousands + 9 thousands + 8 hundreds + 8 tens + 5 tenths + 1 hundredth

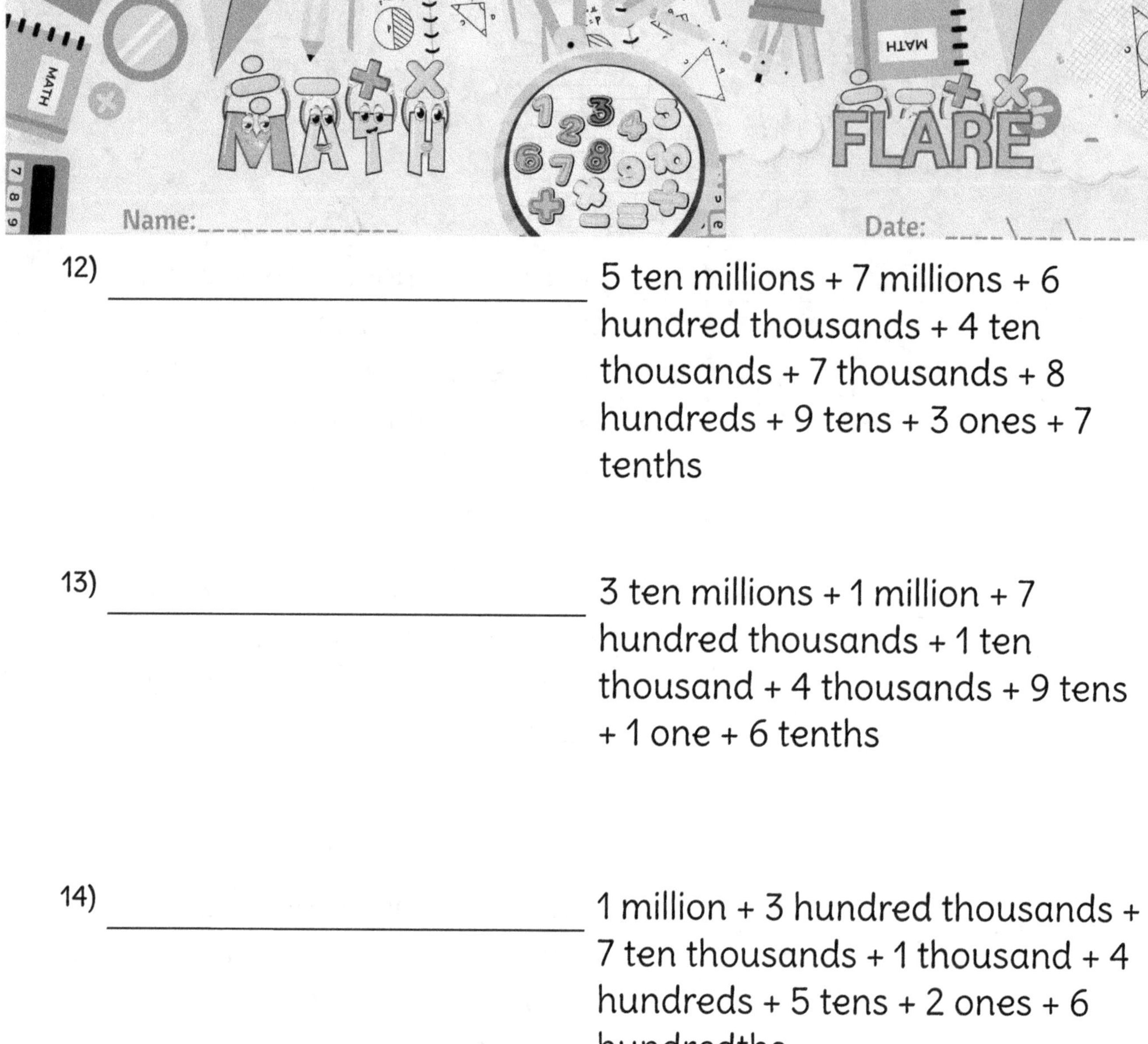

12) ________________________________ 5 ten millions + 7 millions + 6 hundred thousands + 4 ten thousands + 7 thousands + 8 hundreds + 9 tens + 3 ones + 7 tenths

13) ________________________________ 3 ten millions + 1 million + 7 hundred thousands + 1 ten thousand + 4 thousands + 9 tens + 1 one + 6 tenths

14) ________________________________ 1 million + 3 hundred thousands + 7 ten thousands + 1 thousand + 4 hundreds + 5 tens + 2 ones + 6 hundredths

15) ________________________________ 9 millions + 9 hundred thousands + 9 ten thousands + 6 thousands + 4 tens + 4 ones + 5 hundredths

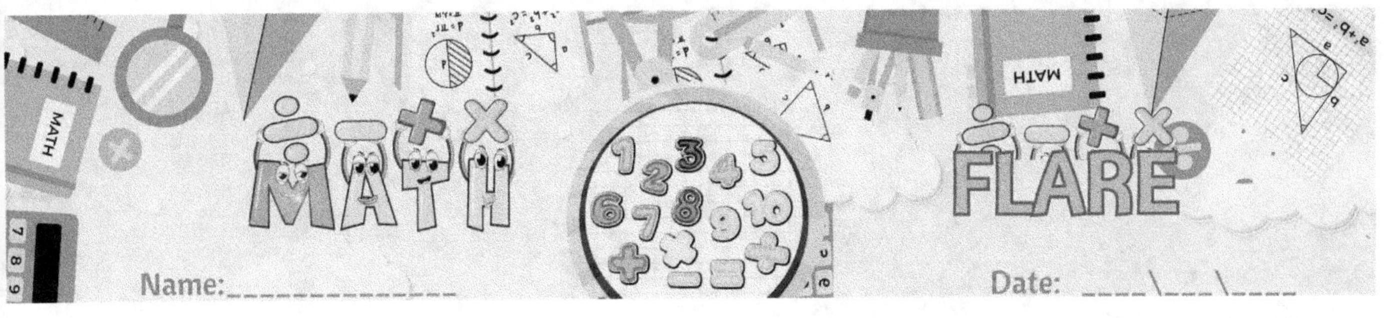

16) _______________________ 9 hundred millions + 6 ten millions + 4 millions + 6 hundred thousands + 8 ten thousands + 2 thousands + 9 hundreds + 3 tens + 6 ones

17) _______________________ 5 hundred thousands + 4 ten thousands + 2 thousands + 4 hundreds + 6 tens + 8 tenths + 2 hundredths + 4 thousandths

18) _______________________ 3 millions + 5 hundred thousands + 4 ten thousands + 2 thousands + 4 tens + 5 ones + 8 tenths + 6 hundredths

19) _______________________ 7 hundred millions + 4 ten millions + 5 millions + 7 hundred thousands + 4 thousands + 5 hundreds + 8 tens + 5 ones

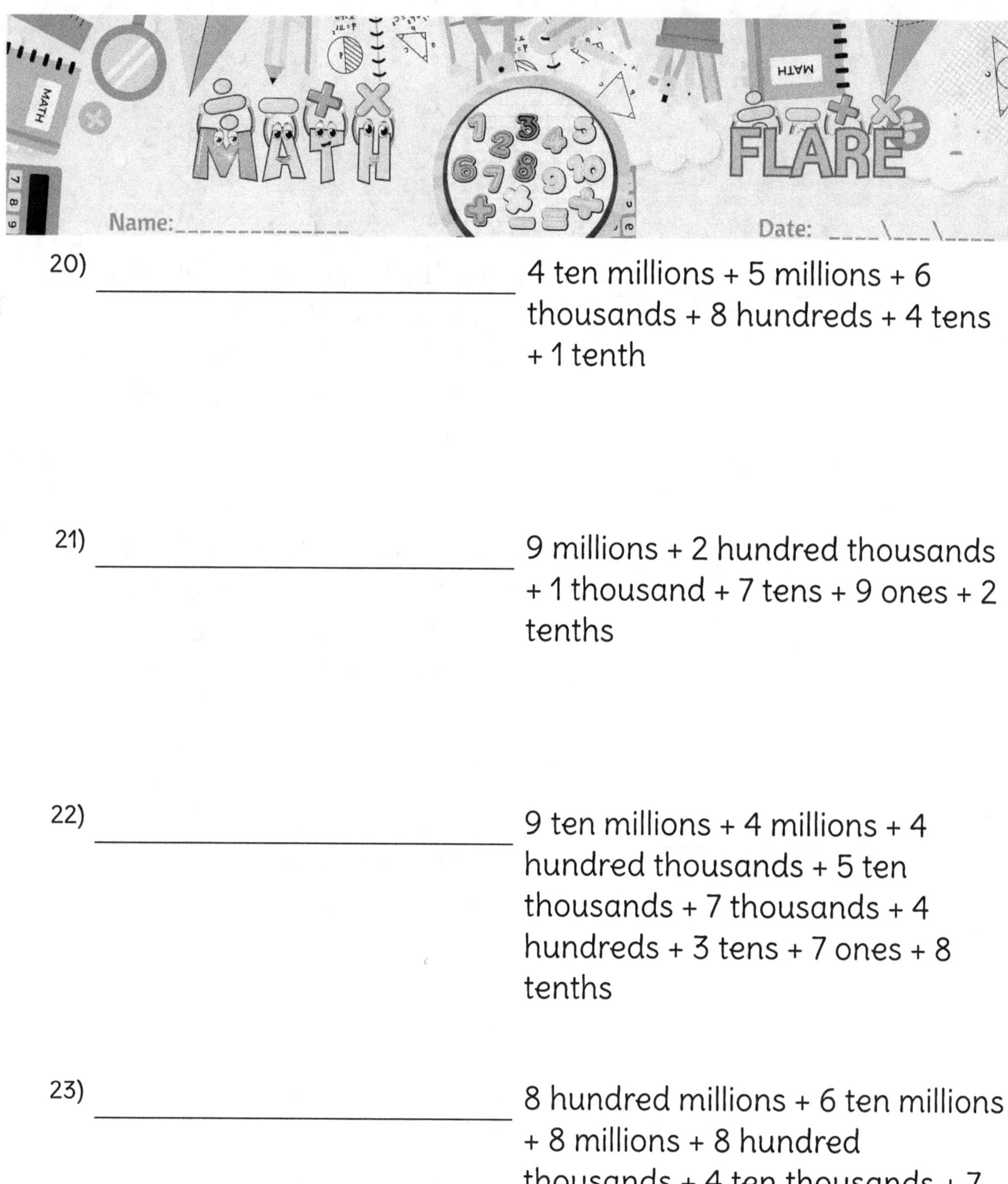

20) _________________________ 4 ten millions + 5 millions + 6 thousands + 8 hundreds + 4 tens + 1 tenth

21) _________________________ 9 millions + 2 hundred thousands + 1 thousand + 7 tens + 9 ones + 2 tenths

22) _________________________ 9 ten millions + 4 millions + 4 hundred thousands + 5 ten thousands + 7 thousands + 4 hundreds + 3 tens + 7 ones + 8 tenths

23) _________________________ 8 hundred millions + 6 ten millions + 8 millions + 8 hundred thousands + 4 ten thousands + 7 hundreds + 1 ten + 8 ones

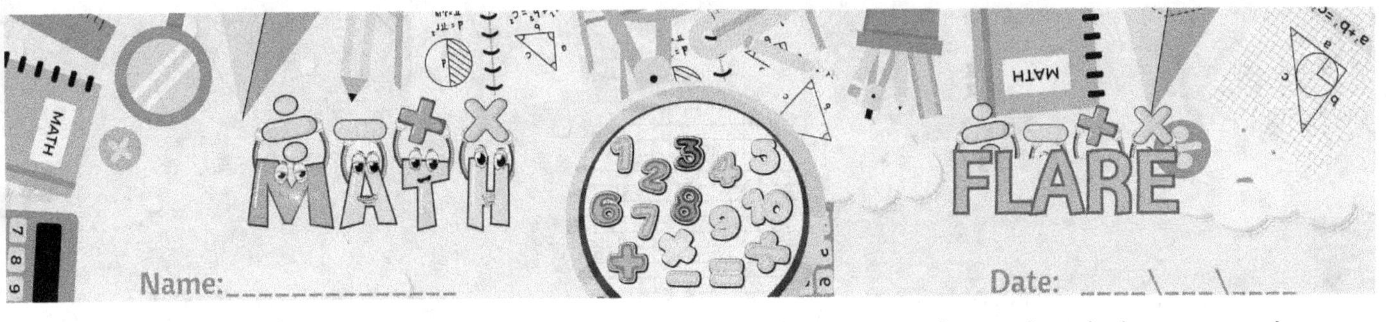

24) _______________________________ 2 millions + 2 hundred thousands + 1 ten thousand + 5 thousands + 5 hundreds + 1 ten + 2 tenths + 8 hundredths

25) _______________________________ 5 hundred millions + 3 ten millions + 5 millions + 9 hundred thousands + 3 ten thousands + 9 thousands + 8 hundreds + 3 tens + 6 ones

26) _______________________________ 1 ten million + 9 millions + 6 hundred thousands + 5 ten thousands + 4 thousands + 4 hundreds + 6 tens + 9 ones + 7 tenths

27) _______________________________ 8 hundred thousands + 2 thousands + 4 hundreds + 9 tens + 3 ones + 4 tenths + 6 hundredths + 1 thousandth

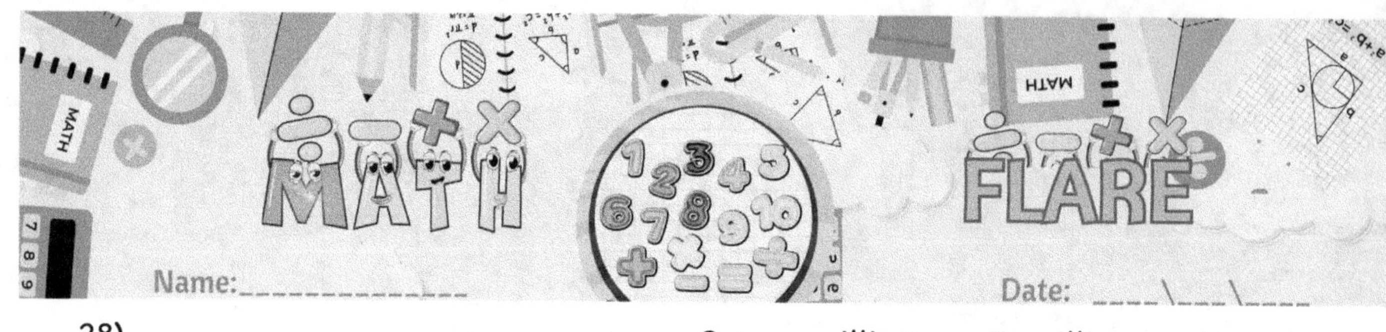

28) _______________________________ 2 ten millions + 5 millions + 7 hundred thousands + 8 ten thousands + 2 thousands + 9 hundreds + 4 tens + 5 ones + 6 tenths

29) _______________________________ 1 million + 3 hundred thousands + 3 ten thousands + 5 thousands + 2 hundreds + 6 tens + 6 ones + 9 tenths + 2 hundredths

30) _______________________________ 9 millions + 5 hundred thousands + 6 ten thousands + 5 thousands + 2 hundreds + 4 tens + 8 ones + 5 tenths + 8 hundredths

Place Value and Expanded Notation

1) 81,315,897.3 _______________________ 80,000,000 + 1,000,000 + 300,000 + 10,000 + 5,000 + 800 + 90 + 7 + 0.3

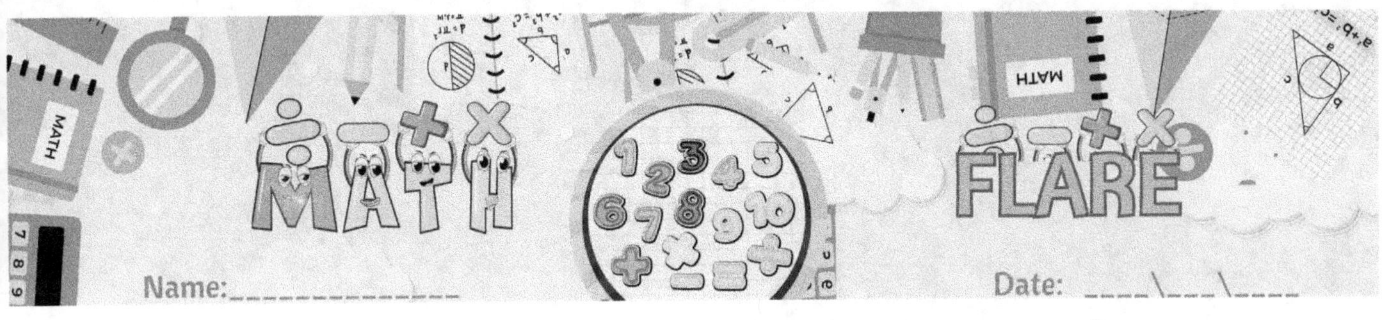

2) _______________________________

80,000,000 + 7,000,000 + 600,000 + 70,000 + 900 + 30 + 6 + 0.4

3) _______________________________

20,000,000 + 9,000,000 + 700,000 + 8,000 + 700 + 0.8

4) _______________________________

500,000 + 10,000 + 3,000 + 700 + 30 + 4 + 0.3 + 0.05 + 0.004

5) _______________________________

40,000,000 + 7,000,000 + 600,000 + 80,000 + 3,000 + 900 + 90 + 1 + 0.7

6) _______________________________

400,000,000 + 40,000,000 + 2,000,000 + 100,000 + 60,000 + 7,000 + 600 + 5

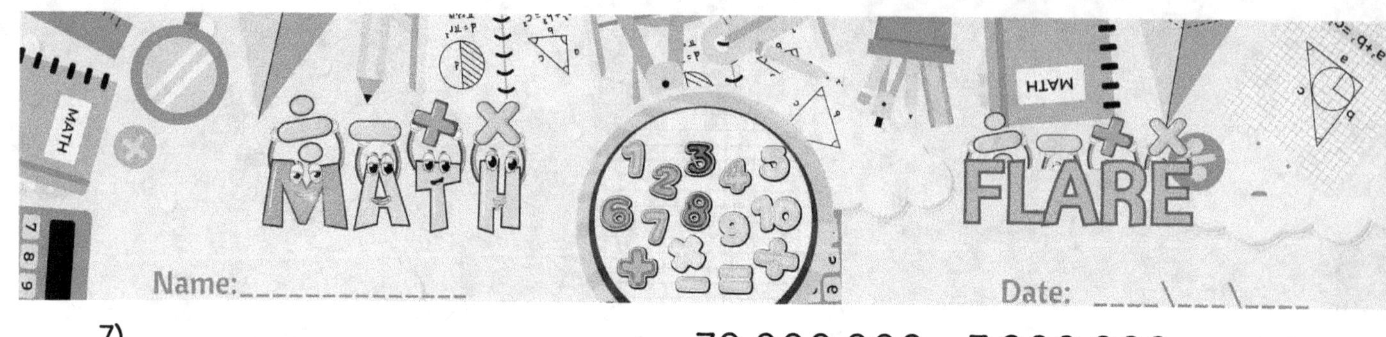

7) ___________________________ 70,000,000 + 7,000,000 + 200,000 + 50,000 + 3,000 + 30 + 5 + 0.4

8) ___________________________ 80,000,000 + 100,000 + 10,000 + 5,000 + 600 + 60 + 5 + 0.5

9) ___________________________ 70,000,000 + 6,000,000 + 400,000 + 6,000 + 300 + 9 + 0.8

10) ___________________________ 60,000,000 + 4,000,000 + 400,000 + 20,000 + 4,000 + 600 + 30 + 7 + 0.1

11) ___________________________ 900,000 + 50,000 + 8,000 + 100 + 20 + 6 + 0.6 + 0.04 + 0.002

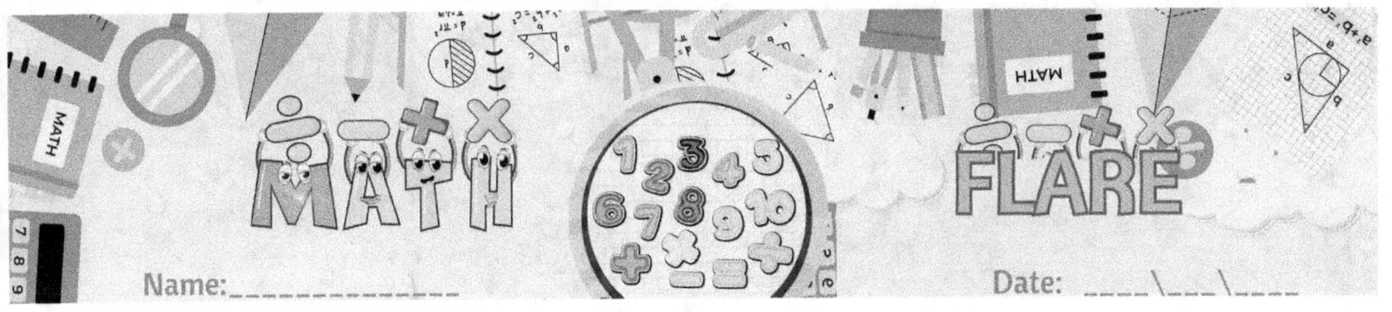

12) _________________________

800,000,000 + 20,000,000 +
2,000,000 + 900,000 + 30,000 +
6,000 + 800 + 5

13) _________________________

300,000,000 + 40,000,000 +
2,000,000 + 300,000 + 70,000 +
9,000 + 900 + 60 + 9

14) _________________________

600,000,000 + 80,000,000 +
1,000,000 + 900,000 + 8,000 +
800 + 40 + 3

15) _________________________

500,000,000 + 80,000,000 +
9,000,000 + 500,000 + 20,000 +
200 + 10 + 1

16) _________________________

100,000 + 20,000 + 3,000 + 800
+ 90 + 6 + 0.8

17) _______________________ 2,000,000 + 300,000 + 40,000 + 6,000 + 600 + 50 + 4 + 0.1

18) _______________________ 100,000 + 40,000 + 4,000 + 30 + 3 + 0.8 + 0.08 + 0.001

19) _______________________ 50,000,000 + 9,000,000 + 300,000 + 80,000 + 9,000 + 40 + 9

20) _______________________ 80,000,000 + 9,000,000 + 600,000 + 40,000 + 8,000 + 400 + 30 + 2 + 0.3

21) _______________________ 6,000,000 + 90,000 + 2,000 + 600 + 20 + 2 + 0.6 + 0.04

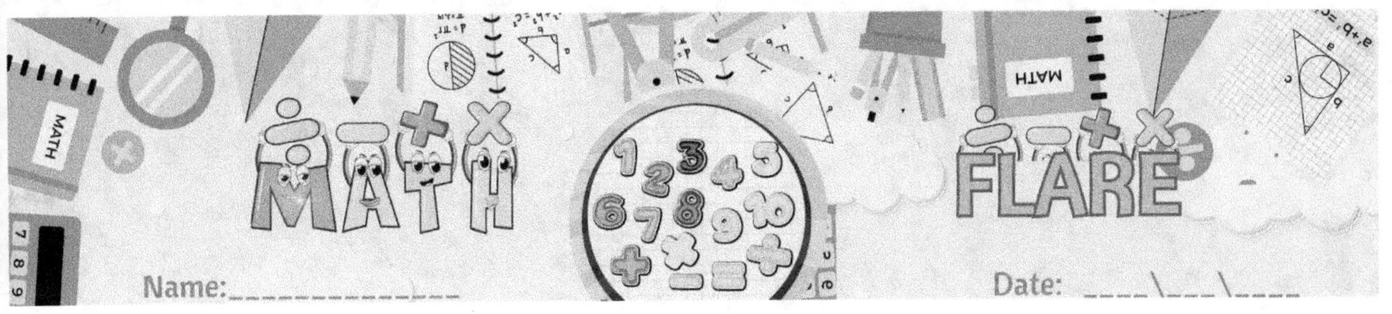

22) _______________________ 6,000,000 + 200,000 + 40,000 +
3,000 + 200 + 20 + 2 + 0.9 + 0.09

23) _______________________ 2,000,000 + 500,000 + 30,000 +
7,000 + 300 + 60 + 5 + 0.2 + 0.09

24) _______________________ 700,000 + 40,000 + 8,000 + 300
+ 80 + 3 + 0.02

25) _______________________ 200,000,000 + 10,000,000 +
2,000,000 + 800,000 + 30,000 +
4,000 + 600 + 40 + 1

26) _______________________ 4,000,000 + 900,000 + 70,000 +
6,000 + 400 + 40 + 5 + 0.5 + 0.02

27) _________________________ 80,000,000 + 1,000,000 + 500,000 + 40,000 + 7,000 + 40 + 5 + 0.5

28) _________________________ 9,000,000 + 300,000 + 60,000 + 8,000 + 400 + 4 + 0.8 + 0.02

29) _________________________ 900,000,000 + 70,000,000 + 5,000,000 + 800,000 + 60,000 + 1,000 + 700 + 60 + 3

30) _________________________ 700,000,000 + 80,000,000 + 6,000,000 + 200,000 + 30,000 + 2,000 + 100 + 90 + 4

31) _________________________ 600,000 + 60,000 + 9,000 + 700 + 40 + 2 + 0.6 + 0.05 + 0.005

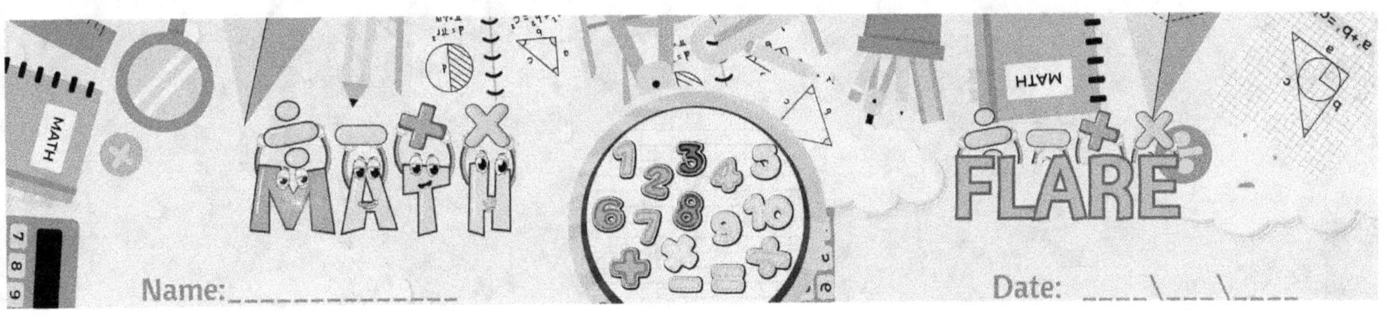

Place Value and Expanded Notation

1) 50,131,193.9   5 ten millions + 1 hundred thousand
+ 3 ten thousands + 1 thousand
+ 1 hundred + 9 tens + 3 ones + 9 tenths

2) 86,645,697.4 _______________________________

3) 781,382.992 _______________________________

4) 209,936.078 _______________________________

5) 951,278,686 _______________________________

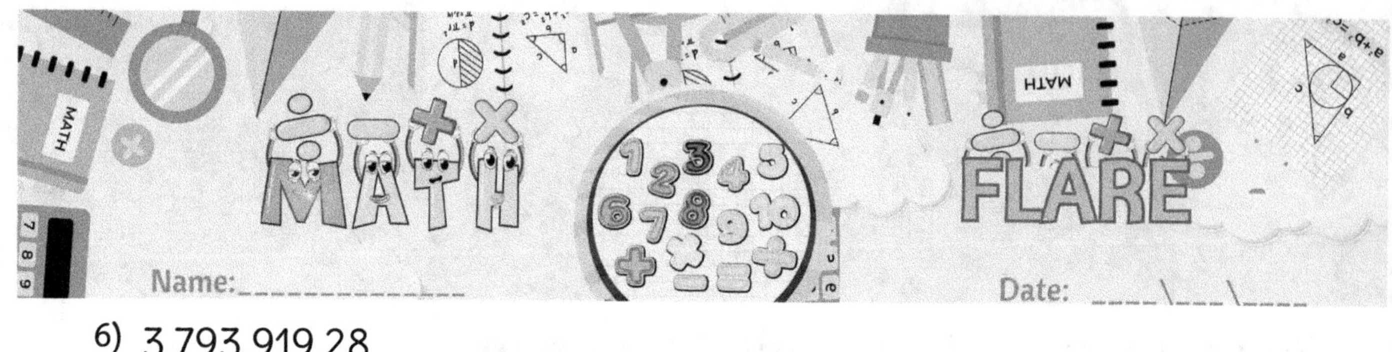

6) 3,793,919.28 _______________________________

7) 8,034,065.62 _______________________________

8) 660,305,288 _______________________________

9) 6,574,368.00 _______________________________

10) 29,215,258.1 _______________________________

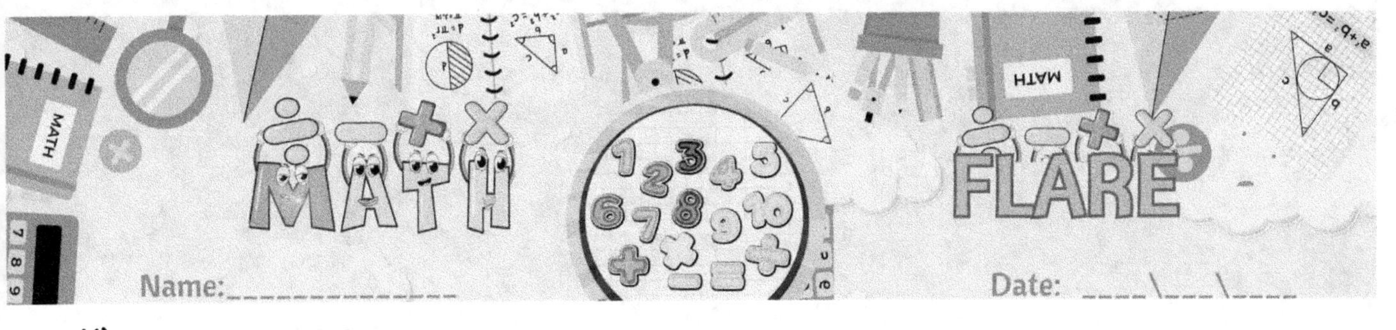

11) 74,130,416.8 ______________________________

12) 590,141.488 ______________________________

13) 2,014,582.13 ______________________________

14) 4,919,417.58 ______________________________

15) 197,171,115 ______________________________

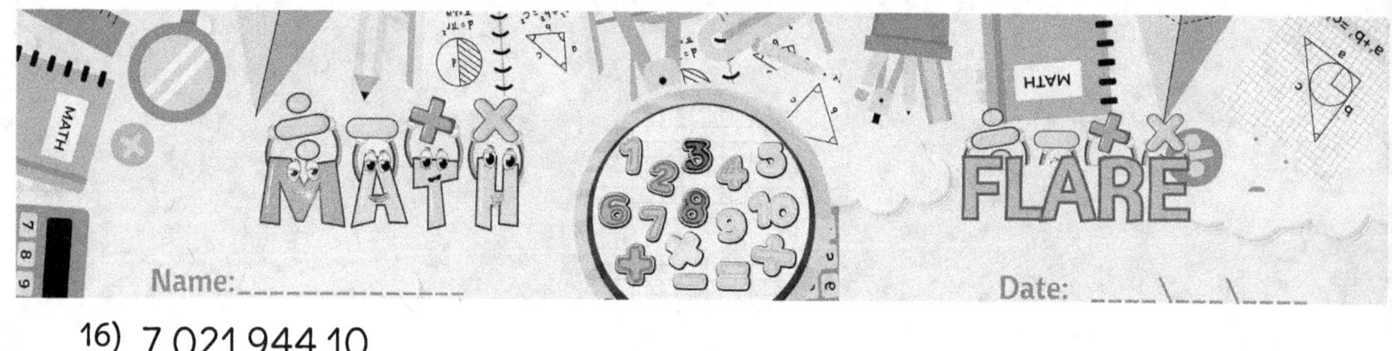

16) 7,021,944.10 _________________________________

17) 286,931,875 _________________________________

18) 632,030,816 _________________________________

19) 51,204,303.7 _________________________________

20) 9,618,792.86 _________________________________

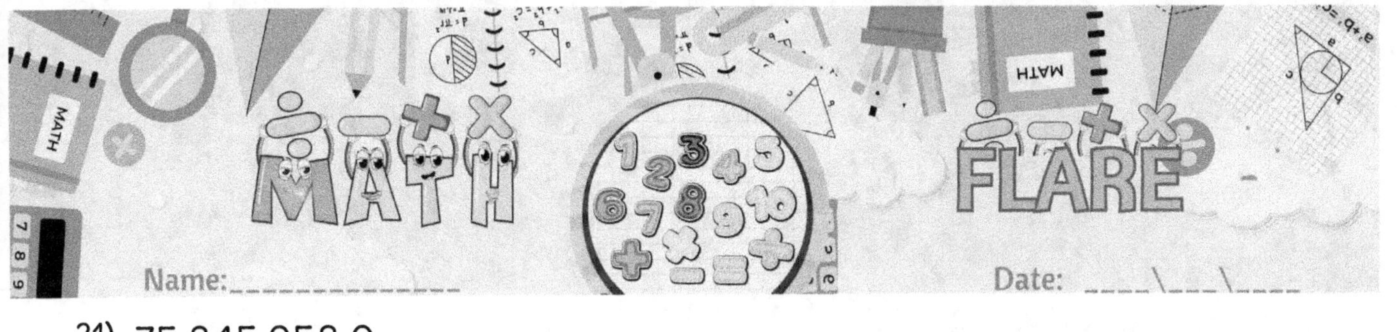

21) 75,845,958.0 ________________________

22) 66,393,896.6 ________________________

23) 23,704,236.7 ________________________

24) 4,472,625.94 ________________________

25) 2,888,366.74 ________________________

26) 7,229,728.35 _______________________________

27) 5,487,039.87 _______________________________

28) 4,008,997.13 _______________________________

29) 9,791,953.64 _______________________________

30) 626,697.148 _______________________________

Chapter. 03

Decimals

Adding Decimals

Adding decimals is like adding whole numbers, but we must align the decimal points carefully. For instance, when adding 49.88 and 45.78:

Step 1: Align the decimal points.

$$49.88$$
$$+\ 45.78$$

Step 2: Start adding from the rightmost digit (the ones place) and move to the left.

Add 8 and 8: 8 + 8 = 16. Write down 6 in the ones place and carry over 1 to the tenths place.

$$49.88$$
$$+\ 45.78$$
$$6$$

Step 3: Add the tenths place.

Add 1 (carried over from the previous step), 8, and 7: 1 + 8 + 7 = 16. Write down 6 in the tenths place and carry over 1 to the hundredths place.

$$49.88$$
$$+\ 45.78$$
$$66$$

Step 4: Continue adding digits to the left until you reach the leftmost digit:

$$49.88$$
$$+\ 45.78$$
$$9566$$

<u>Step 5: Finally, write the sum with the decimal point directly below the decimal points in the original numbers.</u>

$$49.88$$
$$+\ 45.78$$
$$95.66$$

Let's solve a problem:

$$835.68$$
$$+\ 825.29$$
$$1{,}660.97$$

Subtracting Decimals

Subtracting decimals follows a process like adding decimals, except instead of adding the numbers, we subtract them.

For example:

$$697.05$$
$$-\ 258.40$$
$$438.65$$

Multiplying Decimals

Multiplying decimals is a lot like multiplying whole numbers, but we need to be careful about where we put the decimal point in the answer.

Step 1: Start by multiplying the numbers together, just like we do with whole numbers. Ignore the decimals for now.

Step 2: Count how many decimal places there are in the numbers we're multiplying. This will tell us how many decimal places our answer should have.

Step 3: Put the decimal point in the answer by starting from the right side of the number. Move the decimal point to the left as many places as there are in the total number of decimal places.

For example, let's multiply 4.5 by 2.5:

Step 1: Multiply the numbers as if they were whole numbers:

$$25 \times 45 = 1125.$$

Step 2: There is one decimal place in 2.5 and one in 4.5, making a total of two decimal places.

Step 3: Starting from the right side of the answer, count two places to the left and put the decimal point there.

So, the final answer is 11.25.

Remember to pay close attention to where the decimal point goes in the answer.

Let's solve a problem:

$$
\begin{array}{r}
85.39 \\
\times \quad 1.44 \\
\hline
+ \;\; 34156 \\
+ \;\; 34156 \\
+ \;\; 8539 \\
\hline
= 122.9616
\end{array}
$$

Dividing Decimals

Dividing decimals is a lot like dividing whole numbers, but we need to be careful about placement of decimal point in the answer.

Steps to follow:

1. **Set up the division problem:** Write the dividend (the number being divided) and the divisor (the number you're dividing by) as you would in a long division problem.

$$1.7 \overline{)1.6}$$

2. **Move the decimal:** Move the decimal point to the right in the dividend and divisor by the same number of places.

$$17 \overline{)16}$$

3. **Perform the division:** Divide as you would with whole numbers.

```
      0 0.9 4
17 ) 1 6
    - 0
     1 6
    - 0
     1 6 0
   - 1 5 3
         7 0
       - 6 8
           2
```

4. **Place the decimal point:** Place the decimal point in the quotient directly above its position in the dividend.

So, the quotient is 0.94.

Let's solve another problem:

$$
\begin{array}{r}
4.567 \\
12\overline{)\,54.8} \\
-0 \\
\overline{54} \\
-48 \\
\overline{68} \\
-60 \\
\overline{80} \\
-72 \\
\overline{80} \\
-72 \\
\overline{8}
\end{array}
$$

Using the Power of 10

Using the powers of 10, 100, and 1000 makes multiplying and dividing by these numbers very convenient. Let's illustrate with examples:

Multiplying by Powers of 10:

- To multiply a number by 10, simply move the decimal point one place to the right.

$$5 \times 10 = 50$$

- To multiply a number by 100, move the decimal point two places to the right.

$$5 \times 100 = 500$$

- To multiply a number by 1000, move the decimal point three places to the right.

$$5 \times 1000 = 5000.$$

Dividing by Powers of 10:

- To divide a number by 10, simply move the decimal point one place to the left.

$$50 \div 10 = 5$$

- To divide a number by 100, move the decimal point two places to the left.

$$500 \div 100 = 5$$

- To divide a number by 1000, move the decimal point three places to the left.

$$5000 \div 1000 = 5$$

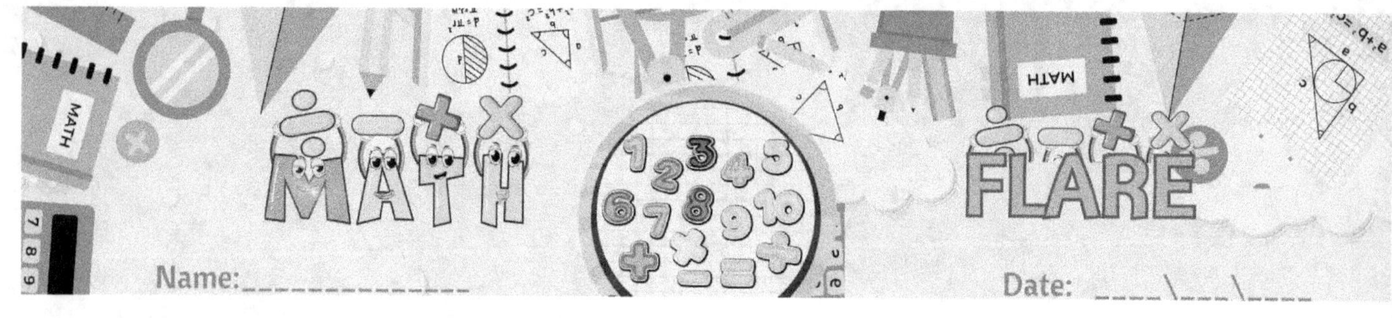

Adding Decimals

Find the sum.

1) 835.68
  + 825.29
  ─────────
    1,660.97

2) 977.82
  + 974.49
  ─────────

3) 556.81
  + 956.47
  ─────────

4) 560.99
  + 571.97
  ─────────

5) 638.24
  + 744.50
  ─────────

6) 431.26
  + 483.72
  ─────────

7) 936.44
  + 704.33
  ─────────

8) 867.95
  + 134.18
  ─────────

9) 152.28
  + 356.44
  ─────────

10) 115.66
  + 795.44
  ─────────

11) 628.53
  + 404.81
  ─────────

12) 563.81
  + 824.34
  ─────────

13) 911.27
  + 837.36
  ─────────

14) 729.41
  + 434.12
  ─────────

15) 921.09
  + 328.30
  ─────────

16) 830.68
  + 502.50
  ─────────

17) 681.10
  + 130.74
  ─────────

18) 456.46
  + 916.00
  ─────────

19) 612.30
  + 226.95
  ─────────

20) 935.12
  + 240.69
  ─────────

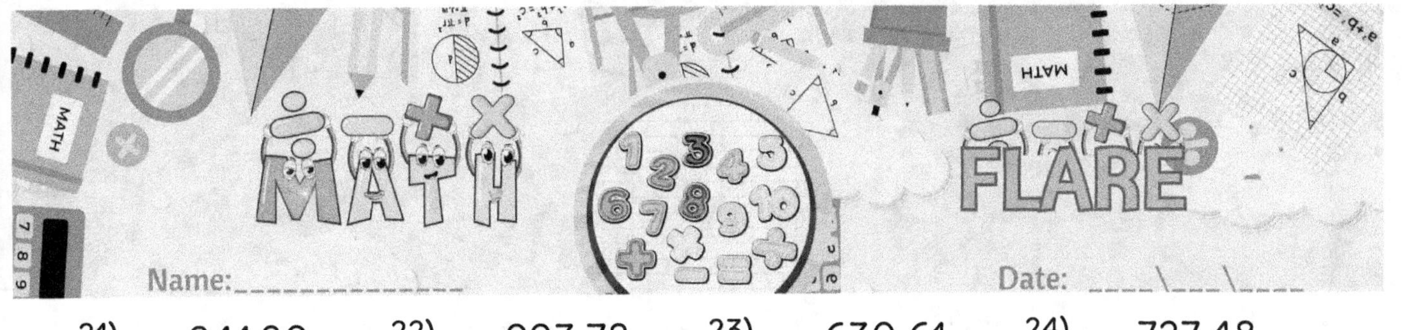

21) 241.20 + 714.95	22) 993.78 + 767.53	23) 630.61 + 374.73	24) 727.48 + 532.71
25) 579.30 + 254.65	26) 670.69 + 292.26	27) 385.23 + 283.74	28) 998.15 + 530.88
29) 361.47 + 253.48	30) 163.22 + 719.43	31) 327.06 + 226.88	32) 650.87 + 409.93
33) 913.81 + 928.74	34) 802.61 + 905.71	35) 347.87 + 951.94	36) 521.87 + 925.31
37) 421.31 + 874.96	38) 654.25 + 913.57	39) 411.02 + 796.27	40) 293.73 + 636.55

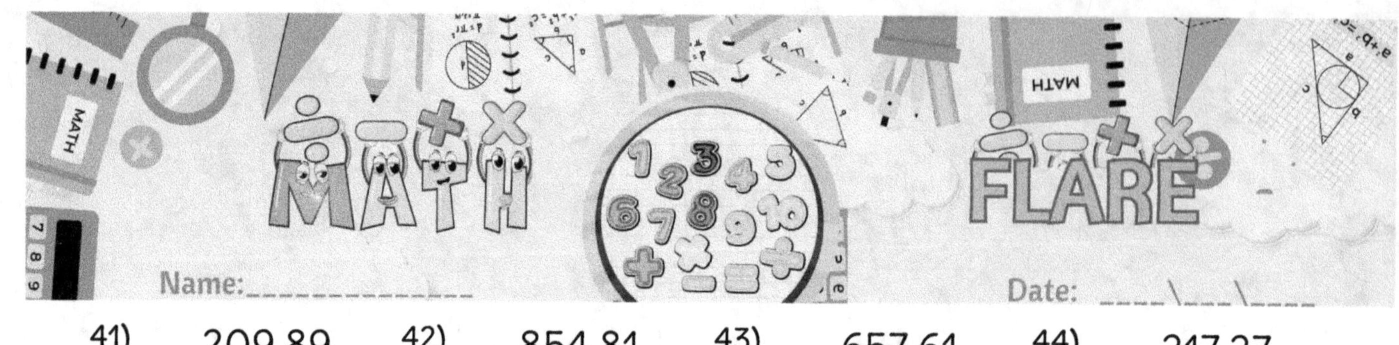

41)   209.89
    + 296.70
    ____

42)   854.81
    + 766.44
    ____

43)   657.61
    + 638.42
    ____

44)   217.27
    + 497.36
    ____

45)   132.58
    + 925.57
    ____

46)   654.53
    + 458.83
    ____

47)   163.73
    + 315.68
    ____

48)   913.62
    + 114.32
    ____

49)   164.09
    + 683.85
    ____

50)   853.71
    + 701.86
    ____

51)   572.11
    + 821.76
    ____

52)   284.84
    + 627.35
    ____

53)   732.78
    + 745.36
    ____

54)   870.94
    + 510.26
    ____

55)   629.49
    + 184.58
    ____

56)   219.86
    + 565.19
    ____

57)   959.74
    + 526.66
    ____

58)   609.55
    + 130.36
    ____

59)   372.06
    + 884.42
    ____

60)   752.32
    + 375.39
    ____

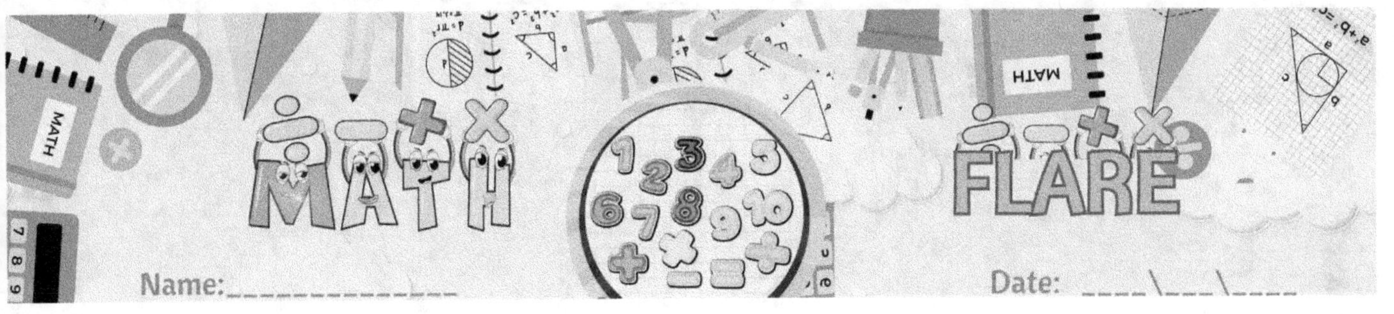

Subtracting Decimals

Find the difference.

1)   697.05
− 258.40
438.65

2)   766.40
− 564.64

3)   881.95
− 869.18

4)   811.62
− 605.75

5)   946.38
− 659.06

6)   312.21
− 303.53

7)   741.37
− 632.74

8)   149.69
− 114.80

9)   313.31
− 300.01

10)   786.41
− 147.67

11)   715.97
− 408.29

12)   839.52
− 170.41

13)   811.29
− 142.46

14)   609.56
− 351.02

15)   965.87
− 171.42

16)   869.41
− 259.13

17)   872.64
− 264.54

18)   587.55
− 433.08

19)   512.06
− 317.74

20)   649.43
− 398.93

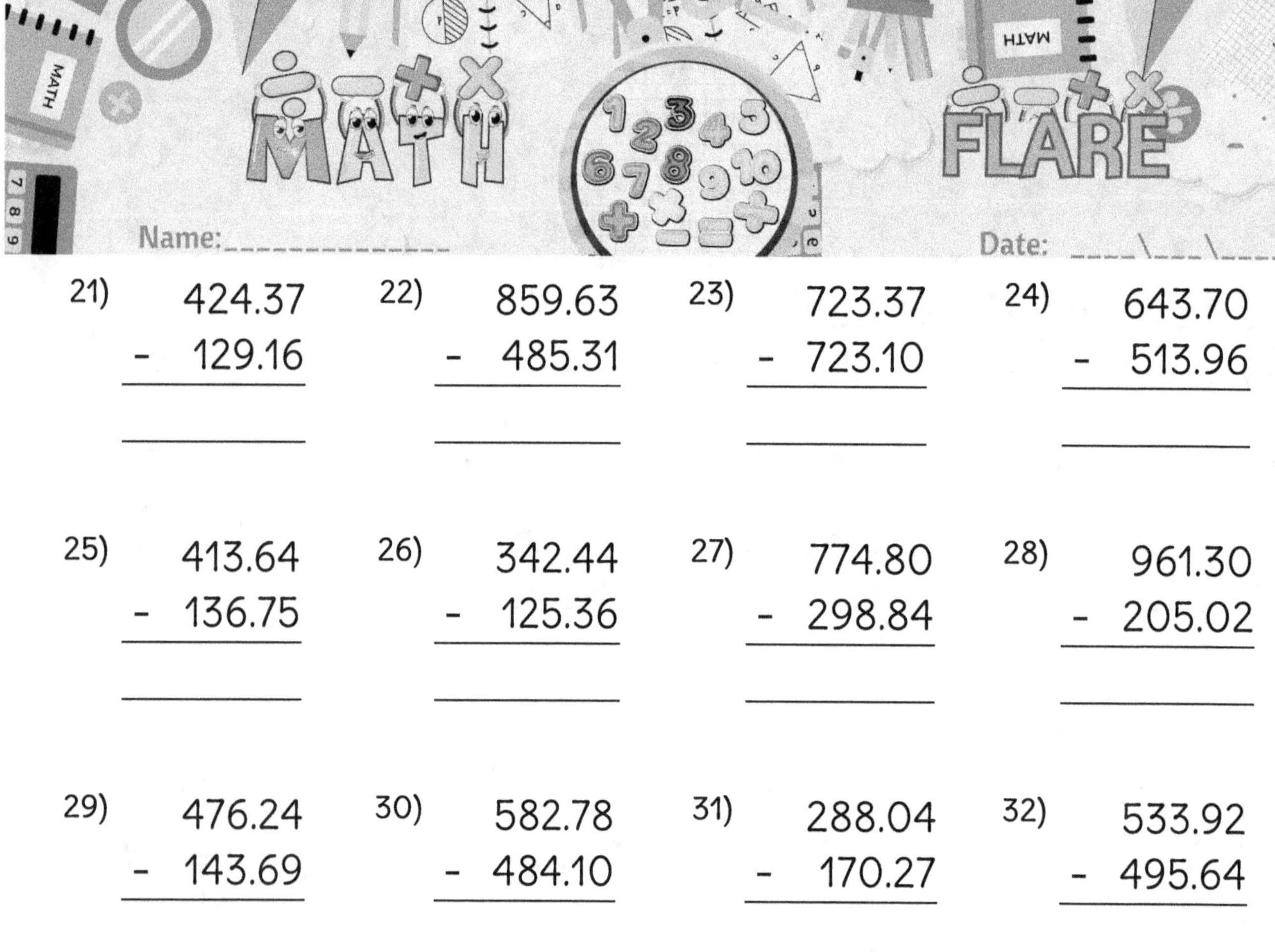

21) 424.37 − 129.16	22) 859.63 − 485.31	23) 723.37 − 723.10	24) 643.70 − 513.96
25) 413.64 − 136.75	26) 342.44 − 125.36	27) 774.80 − 298.84	28) 961.30 − 205.02
29) 476.24 − 143.69	30) 582.78 − 484.10	31) 288.04 − 170.27	32) 533.92 − 495.64
33) 879.94 − 689.56	34) 739.15 − 214.80	35) 454.61 − 211.13	36) 751.73 − 272.17
37) 639.70 − 281.52	38) 398.90 − 103.38	39) 799.05 − 728.47	40) 399.89 − 363.36

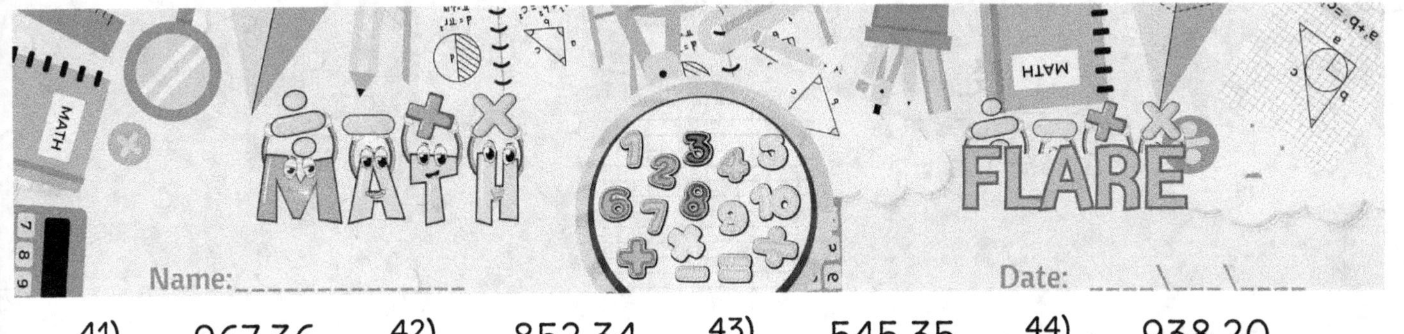

41) 967.36
   - 616.07
   ____

42) 852.34
   - 715.51
   ____

43) 545.35
   - 282.74
   ____

44) 938.20
   - 479.93
   ____

45) 706.76
   - 460.00
   ____

46) 815.89
   - 172.05
   ____

47) 705.84
   - 561.40
   ____

48) 373.39
   - 211.54
   ____

49) 893.65
   - 362.42
   ____

50) 880.60
   - 376.91
   ____

51) 304.80
   - 123.63
   ____

52) 934.50
   - 718.61
   ____

53) 251.03
   - 183.54
   ____

54) 910.22
   - 570.95
   ____

55) 786.62
   - 589.93
   ____

56) 834.89
   - 312.83
   ____

57) 492.52
   - 312.18
   ____

58) 275.12
   - 134.68
   ____

59) 525.49
   - 197.28
   ____

60) 921.02
   - 142.09
   ____

Multiplying Decimals
Find the product.

1)
$$
\begin{array}{r}
85.39 \\
\times\ \ 1.44 \\
\hline
+\ 34156 \\
+\ 34156 \\
+\ 8539 \\
\hline
=122.9616
\end{array}
$$

2)
$$
\begin{array}{r}
20.86 \\
\times\ \ 6.47 \\
\hline
\end{array}
$$

3)
$$
\begin{array}{r}
82.48 \\
\times\ \ 6.00 \\
\hline
\end{array}
$$

4)
$$
\begin{array}{r}
34.55 \\
\times\ \ 1.72 \\
\hline
\end{array}
$$

5)
$$
\begin{array}{r}
71.11 \\
\times\ \ 4.35 \\
\hline
\end{array}
$$

6)
$$
\begin{array}{r}
59.41 \\
\times\ \ 7.96 \\
\hline
\end{array}
$$

7)
$$
\begin{array}{r}
91.62 \\
\times\ \ 1.29 \\
\hline
\end{array}
$$

8)
$$
\begin{array}{r}
40.67 \\
\times\ \ 9.68 \\
\hline
\end{array}
$$

9)
$$
\begin{array}{r}
99.84 \\
\times\ \ 5.63 \\
\hline
\end{array}
$$

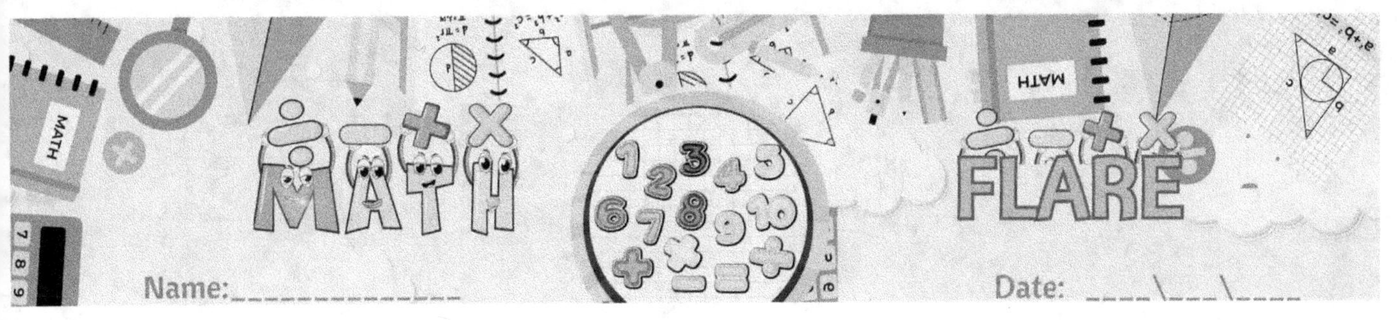

10)   40.87
  ×   7.46

11)   40.75
  ×   4.82

12)   85.27
  ×   5.07

13)   46.33
  ×   8.40

14)   34.97
  ×   1.15

15)   53.05
  ×   4.63

16)   29.76
  ×   4.61

17)   37.24
  ×   2.27

18)   39.88
  ×   3.08

19) 19.91
   × 2.81

20) 44.22
   × 8.46

21) 25.97
   × 7.60

22) 43.56
   × 9.65

23) 45.32
   × 2.13

24) 56.32
   × 2.19

25) 25.72
   × 6.93

26) 28.64
   × 6.95

27) 14.52
   × 2.12

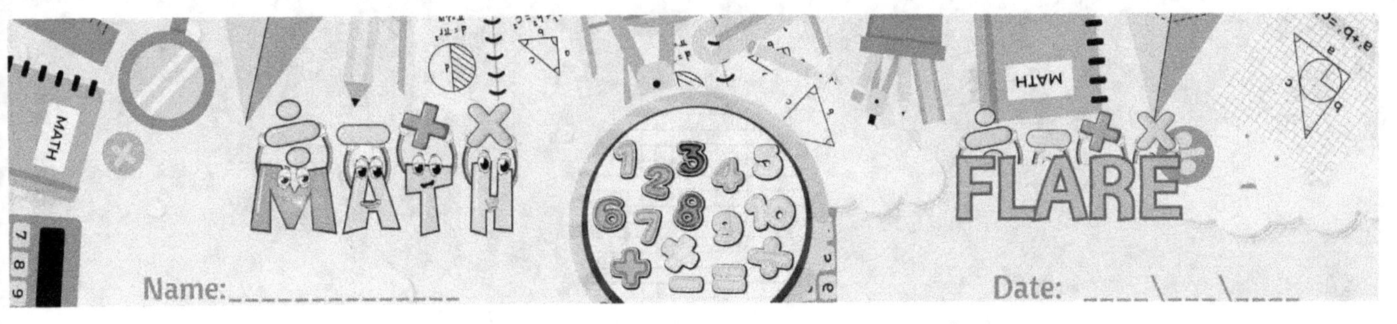

28)   62.64
  ×   4.71

29)   29.13
  ×   7.01

30)   28.38
  ×   9.83

31)   35.08
  ×   3.31

32)   64.17
  ×   3.47

33)   23.82
  ×   2.32

34)   52.47
  ×   7.88

35)   73.06
  ×   1.99

36)   86.98
  ×   8.16

37) 22.17
× 5.61

38) 58.71
× 6.47

39) 14.65
× 8.86

40) 15.39
× 3.50

41) 37.80
× 2.30

42) 85.74
× 8.36

43) 27.74
× 6.01

44) 41.64
× 2.60

45) 60.10
× 9.26

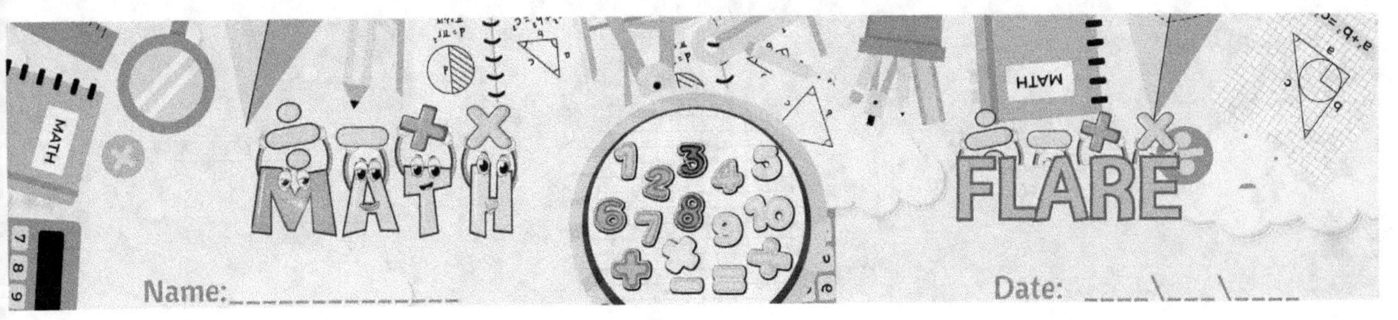

46)   11.67
  × 4.97

47)   99.78
  × 4.58

48)   59.62
  × 9.28

49)   21.84
  × 1.88

50)   82.80
  × 3.21

51)   68.87
  × 7.74

52)   48.84
  × 1.59

53)   82.35
  × 4.69

54)   57.43
  × 5.83

55)   62.48
  ×   9.78

56)   42.52
  ×   4.05

57)   64.74
  ×   9.33

58)   70.56
  ×   2.20

59)   47.33
  ×   8.04

60)   17.00
  ×   6.36

61)   81.60
  ×   3.64

62)   28.78
  ×   8.03

63)   18.19
  ×   4.72

Dividing Decimals

Find the quotient.

1)

$$12\overline{)54.8}$$

$$
\begin{array}{r}
-0 \\
\hline
54 \\
-48 \\
\hline
68 \\
-60 \\
\hline
80 \\
-72 \\
\hline
80 \\
-72 \\
\hline
8
\end{array}
$$

2)

$$15\overline{)45.0}$$

3)

$$7\overline{)71.0}$$

4)

$$9\overline{)42.5}$$

5)

$$9\overline{)31.8}$$

6)

$$16\overline{)92.2}$$

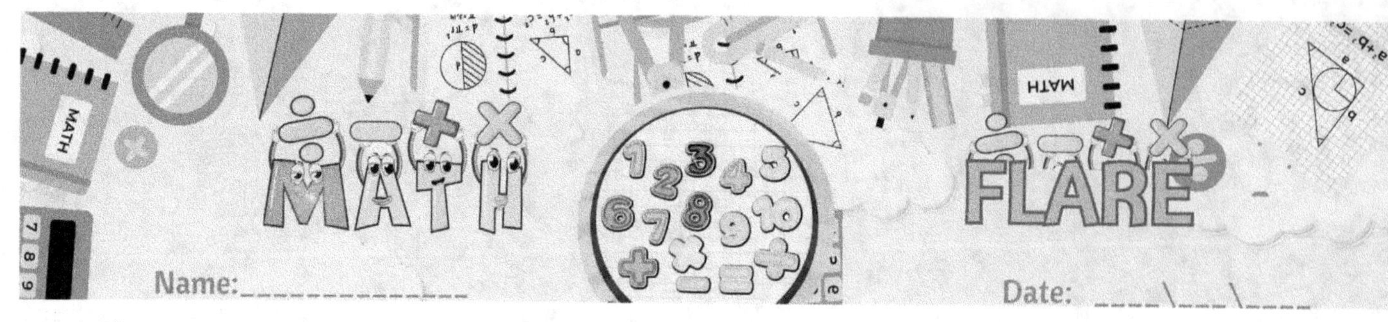

7)

16)‾51.2

8)

3)‾83.4

9)

20)‾96.3

10)

17)‾32.7

11)

8)‾94.9

12)

16)‾98.2

13)

16)‾10.2

14)

20)‾48.7

15)

5)‾72.4

16)

$$4\overline{)40.1}$$

17)

$$14\overline{)28.2}$$

18)

$$4\overline{)62.3}$$

19)

$$4\overline{)81.2}$$

20)

$$9\overline{)75.4}$$

21)

$$17\overline{)74.5}$$

22)

$$10\overline{)35.9}$$

23)

$$7\overline{)56.9}$$

24)

$$14\overline{)39.5}$$

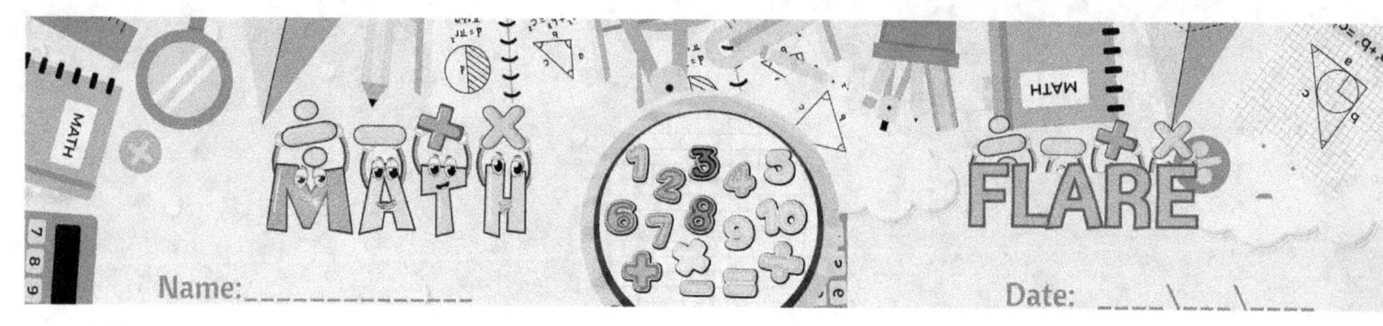

25) $5\overline{)43.5}$

26) $19\overline{)60.3}$

27) $10\overline{)35.5}$

28) $4\overline{)77.1}$

29) $13\overline{)64.1}$

30) $18\overline{)74.1}$

31) $8\overline{)90.9}$

32) $1\overline{)76.5}$

33) $16\overline{)18.7}$

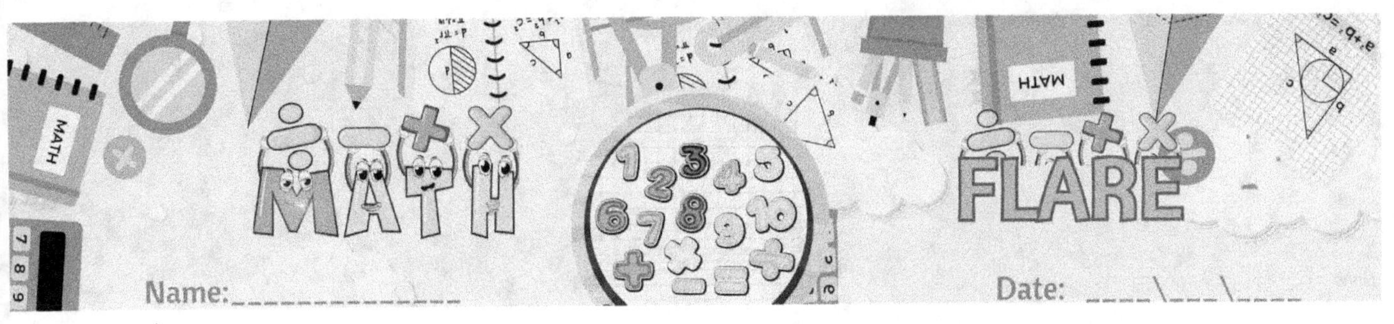

34)

16)62.5

35)

16)37.9

36)

16)34.0

37)

3)21.8

38)

10)15.6

39)

14)33.0

40)

15)52.8

41)

10)64.7

42)

8)69.8

Chapter. 04

Fractions

Fractions represent parts of a whole. They consist of a numerator (the number on top) and a denominator (the number on the bottom).

For example: we have an orange, and we divide it into 5 equal slices. Each slice represents $\frac{1}{5}$ of the orange. Now, if we take 3 of those slices, we have taken $\frac{3}{5}$ of the orange.

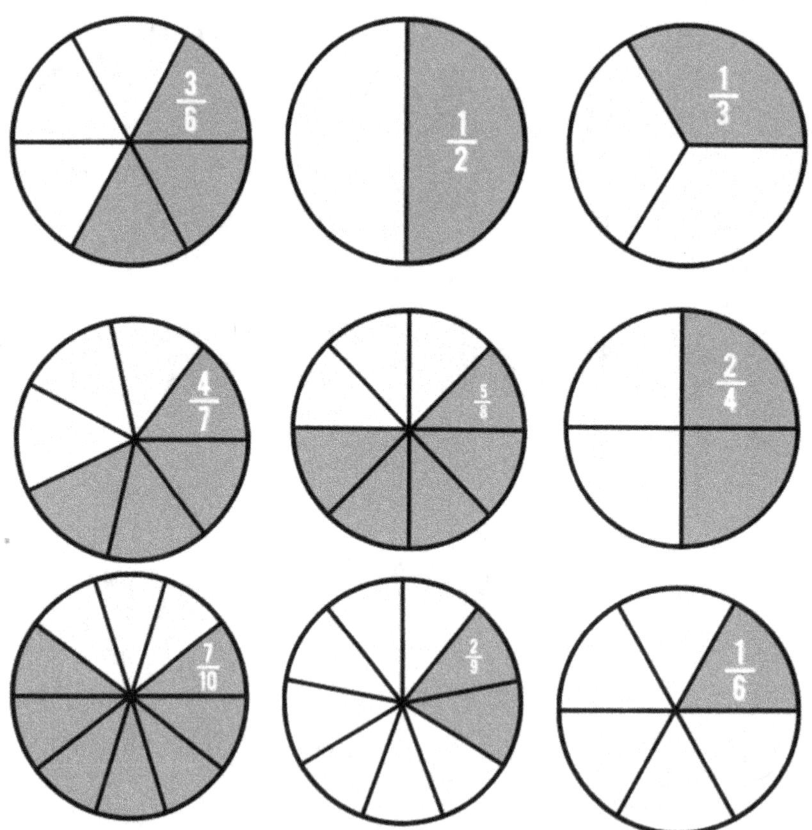

Equivalent Fractions

Equivalent fractions are fractions that represent the same value or part of a whole, even though they may look different.

To find equivalent fractions, you can:

- Multiply or divide both the numerator and denominator by the same nonzero number.
- Simplify fractions to their simplest form.

$\frac{1}{2}$ and $\frac{2}{4}$ are equivalent fractions because if you multiply the numerator and denominator of $\frac{1}{2}$ by 2, you get $\frac{2}{4}$. Similarly, if you divide both the numerator and denominator of $\frac{2}{4}$ by 2, you get $\frac{1}{2}$.

Let's solve a problem:

$$\frac{}{8} = \frac{15}{40}$$

To solve the missing numerator, we can cross multiply.

$$40x = 8 \times 15$$

$$40x = 120$$

$$x = \frac{120}{40} = x = 3$$

$$\frac{3}{8} = \frac{15}{40}$$

Convert Fractions and Decimals

To transform a fraction into a decimal, we divide the numerator by the denominator.

For instance, $\frac{1}{4}$ equals 0.25 because when we divide 1 by 4, we get 0.25.

In certain cases, the resulting decimal repeats infinitely, like $\frac{1}{3}$, which equals 0.3333...

In such instances, we round the decimal to a specific number of decimal places.

Let's solve a problem:

$$\frac{52}{100} = \underline{\ \ 0.52\ \ }$$

Least Common Multiple (LCM)

The Lowest Common Multiple (LCM) of two or more numbers is the smallest multiple that is divisible by each of the numbers.

There are several methods to find the LCM; however, we will focus on only two:

Listing Multiples: List the multiples of each number until you find a common multiple. For example:

$$
\begin{array}{l|l}
8 & 8,\ 16,\ 24,\ 32,\ 40,\ 48,\ 56 \\
\hline
7 & 7,\ 14,\ 21,\ 28,\ 35,\ 42,\ 49,\ 56
\end{array}
$$
, LCM = $\underline{56}$

Division Method: Divide each number with the smallest prime number that divides at least one of the numbers evenly. The product of all the divisors and quotients is the LCM. For example:

$$
\begin{array}{c|cc}
2 & 7 & 8 \\
\hline
2 & 7 & 4 \\
\hline
2 & 7 & 2 \\
\hline
7 & 7 & 1 \\
\hline
 & 1 & 1
\end{array}
$$

$$\text{LCM} = 2 \times 2 \times 2 \times 7 = \underline{56}$$

Both methods have their advantages. For big numbers, using the division way is usually faster. But if we are working with smaller numbers or like seeing patterns, listing multiples might make more sense.

Fractions Multiplication

To multiply fractions, we simply multiply the numerators together to get the new numerator and multiply the denominators together to get the new denominator.

For example, let's multiply: $\frac{2}{4} \times \frac{1}{4}$

$$\text{Numerator: } 2 \times 1 = 2$$

$$\text{Denominator: } 4 \times 4 = 16$$

$$\text{Therefore, } \frac{2}{16}$$

$$\text{we can simplify the resulting fraction: } \frac{1}{8}$$

Let's solve a problem:

$$\frac{4}{5} \times \frac{4}{5} = \frac{4 \times 4}{5 \times 5} = \frac{16}{25}$$

Fractions Division

To divide fractions, we multiply by the reciprocal of the divisor.

For example, let's divide:

$$\frac{6}{8} \div \frac{4}{8}$$

$$\frac{6}{8} \times \frac{8}{4} = \frac{48}{32} = \frac{3}{2}$$

<u>Mixed Numbers: Mixed into Improper</u>

Mixed numbers and improper fractions are two different ways to represent the same value of a fraction.

1. **Mixed Number:** A mixed number is a combination of a whole number and a proper fraction. For example, $2\frac{1}{3}$ is a mixed number, where 2 is the whole number part and $\frac{1}{3}$ is the fraction part.

2. **Improper Fraction:** An improper fraction is a fraction where the numerator is greater than or equal to the denominator. For example, $\frac{7}{3}$ is an improper fraction because 6 is greater than 3.

To convert a mixed number to an improper fraction, you multiply the whole number by the denominator of the fraction, add the numerator, and then write the result over the original denominator. For example:

$$2\frac{1}{3} = \frac{2 \text{ x } 3 + 1}{3} = \frac{7}{3}$$

To convert an improper fraction to a mixed number, we divide the numerator by the denominator. The quotient becomes the whole number part, and the remainder becomes the numerator of the fraction. For example:

$$\frac{7}{3} = 2\frac{1}{3}$$

Let's solve some problems:

$$2\frac{10}{20} = \frac{\begin{array}{c}20 \times 2 = 40\\ 40 + 10 = 50\end{array}}{} = \frac{50}{20} = \frac{5}{2}$$

$$\frac{41}{16} = \frac{2\frac{9}{16}}{}$$

$$41 \div 16 = 2 \text{ with a remainder of } 9$$

Mixed Numbers: Addition and Subtraction

To add or subtract mixed numbers, we follow similar steps as when adding or subtracting regular fractions. For instance:

Addition:

- <u>Add the whole numbers:</u> Add the whole number parts of the mixed numbers together.
- <u>Add the fractions:</u> Add the fractions parts of the mixed numbers together.
- <u>Simplify (if needed):</u> If the fraction part of the sum is an improper fraction, simplify it by converting it to a mixed number.

Subtraction:

- <u>Subtract the whole numbers:</u> Subtract the whole number part of the second mixed number from the whole number part of the first mixed number.
- <u>Subtract the fractions:</u> Subtract the fraction part of the second mixed number from the fraction part of the first mixed number.
- <u>Simplify (if needed):</u> If the fraction part of the difference is a negative fraction, borrow from the whole number part or simplify it by converting it to a mixed number.

Let's solve some problems:

$$3\frac{4}{8} + 7\frac{1}{3} = \frac{4}{8} + \frac{1}{3} = \frac{4\times3 + 8\times1}{8\times3} = \frac{12 + 8}{24} = \frac{20}{24} = 10\frac{5}{6}$$

$$3 + 7 = 10$$

$$7\frac{4}{6} - 2\frac{3}{8} = \frac{4}{6} - \frac{3}{8} = \frac{4\times8 - 6\times3}{6\times8} = \frac{32 - 18}{48} = \frac{14}{48} = 5\frac{7}{24}$$

$$7 - 2 = 5$$

Mixed Numbers: Multiplication and Division

To multiply or divide mixed numbers, we follow these steps:

Multiplication:

- <u>Convert the mixed numbers to improper fractions:</u> Multiply the whole number by the denominator of the fraction, then add the numerator. Write the result over the original denominator.
- <u>Multiply the fractions:</u> Multiply the numerators together to get the new numerator and multiply the denominators together to get the new denominator.
- <u>Simplify (if needed):</u> If the result is an improper fraction, simplify it by converting it back to a mixed number.

Division:

- <u>Convert the mixed numbers to improper fractions:</u>
- <u>Invert the divisor:</u> Flip the second fraction (the one you're dividing by) so that the division becomes multiplication.
- <u>Multiply the fractions:</u> Multiply the numerators together to get the new numerator and multiply the denominators together to get the new denominator.

- <u>Simplify (if needed):</u> If the result is an improper fraction, simplify it by converting it back to a mixed number.

Let's solve some problems:

$$1\frac{2}{4} \times 3\frac{1}{6} = \frac{3}{2} \times \frac{19}{6} = \frac{3 \times 19}{2 \times 6} = \frac{57}{12} = 4\frac{3}{4}$$

1 x 4 + 2 = 6 = $\frac{6}{2}$ = $\frac{3}{2}$ 3 x 8 + 1 = $\frac{19}{6}$

$$2\frac{6}{10} \div 6\frac{6}{7} = \frac{13}{5} \times \frac{7}{48} = \frac{13 \times 7}{5 \times 48} = \frac{91}{240}$$

2 x 10 + 6 = 26 = $\frac{26}{10}$ = $\frac{13}{5}$ 6 x 7 + 6 = $\frac{48}{7}$

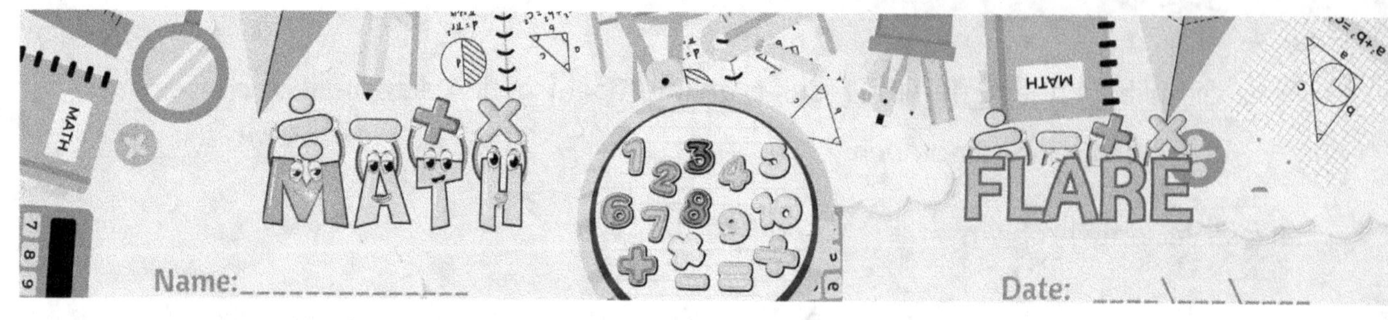

Convert Fractions and Decimals

Convert Fractions to Decimals and Decimals to Fractions.

1) $0.5 = \dfrac{0.5}{1} = \dfrac{0.5 \times 6}{1 \times 6} = \dfrac{3}{6} = \dfrac{1}{2}$

2) $0.25 = $ ___________________

3) $\dfrac{9}{20} = $
$$20\overline{)9} \quad \begin{array}{r} 0.45 \\ -0 \\ \hline 90 \\ -80 \\ \hline 10 \end{array} = 0.45$$

4) $0.92 = $ ___________________

5) $\dfrac{1}{5} = $ ___________________

6) $0.257 = $ ___________________

7) $0.5 = $ ___________________

8) $\dfrac{6}{12} = $ ___________________

9) $0.16 = $ ___________________

10) $0.95 = $ ___________________

11) $\dfrac{4}{11} = $ ___________________

12) $0.5 = $ ___________________

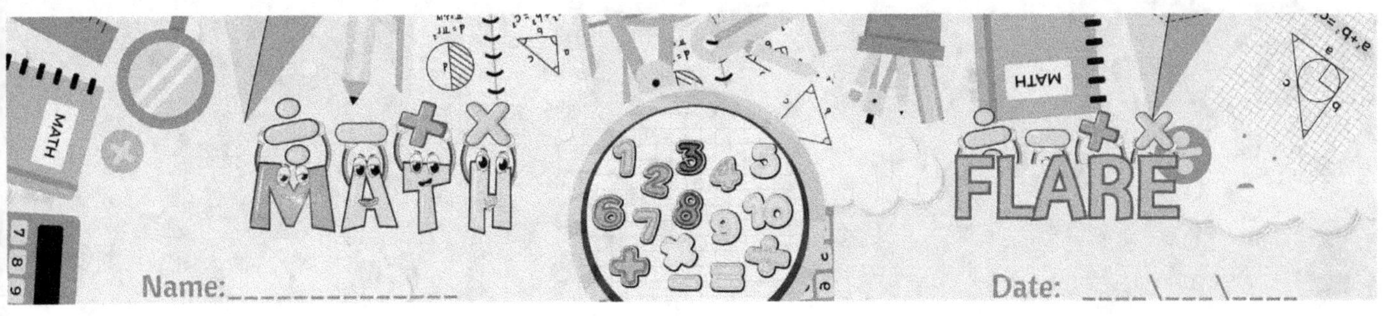

Name:_______________ Date: _______________

13) 0.8 = _______________________

14) $\dfrac{3}{22}$ = _______________________

15) $\dfrac{2}{17}$ = _______________________

16) $\dfrac{4}{19}$ = _______________________

17) $\dfrac{1}{8}$ = _______________________

18) 0.694 = _______________________

19) 0.609 = _______________________

20) $\dfrac{5}{24}$ = _______________________

21) $\dfrac{24}{30}$ = _______________________

22) 0.455 = _______________________

23) $\dfrac{57}{100}$ = _______________________

24) $\dfrac{15}{25}$ = _______________________

25) $\frac{14}{18}$ = _____________

26) 0.4 = _____________

27) 0.333 = _____________

28) $\frac{4}{7}$ = _____________

29) $\frac{11}{13}$ = _____________

30) $\frac{22}{23}$ = _____________

31) $\frac{52}{70}$ = _____________

32) 0.594 = _____________

33) 0.083 = _____________

34) 0.6 = _____________

35) $\frac{66}{75}$ = _____________

36) $\frac{13}{16}$ = _____________

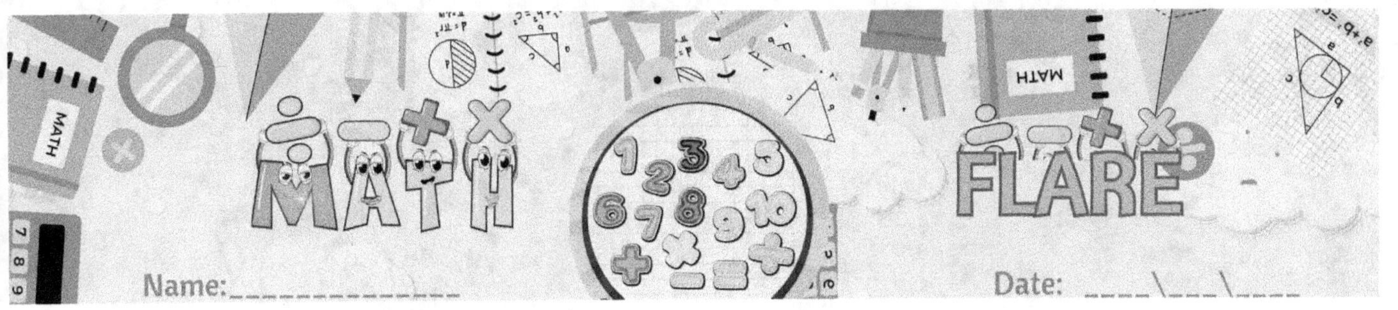

Fractions Multiplication

Find the product.

1) $\dfrac{4}{5} \times \dfrac{1}{5} =$ _______ $\dfrac{4}{25}$

$\dfrac{4 \times 1}{5 \times 5}$

2) $\dfrac{4}{5} \times \dfrac{1}{9} =$ _______________

3) $\dfrac{6}{11} \times \dfrac{2}{3} =$ _______________

4) $\dfrac{1}{2} \times \dfrac{1}{4} =$ _______________

5) $\dfrac{1}{3} \times \dfrac{7}{12} =$ _______________

6) $\dfrac{6}{7} \times \dfrac{1}{3} =$ _______________

7) $\dfrac{1}{4} \times \dfrac{2}{3} =$ _______________

8) $\dfrac{7}{9} \times \dfrac{5}{7} =$ _______________

9) $\dfrac{1}{2} \times \dfrac{3}{10} =$ _______________

10) $\dfrac{8}{9} \times \dfrac{7}{8} =$ _______________

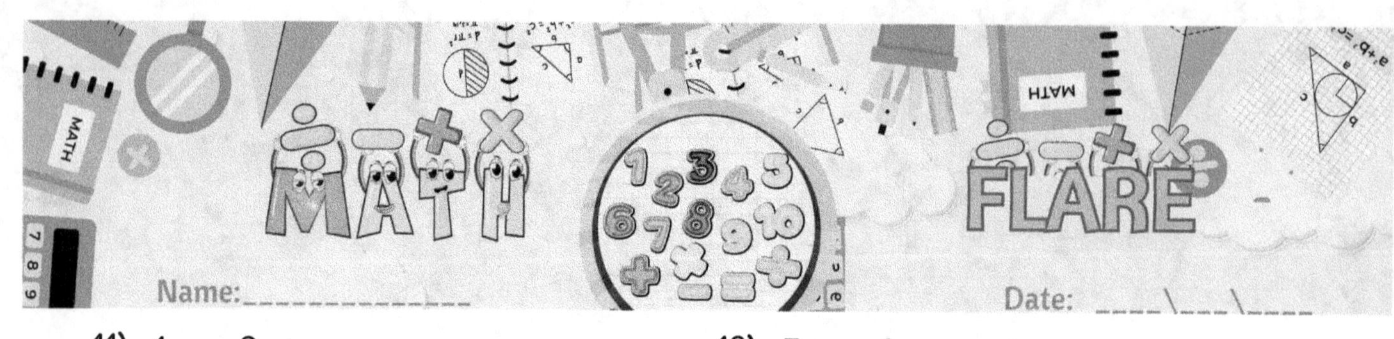

Name: ___________________   Date: _______________

11) $\dfrac{1}{5} \times \dfrac{9}{11} =$ _______________

12) $\dfrac{3}{11} \times \dfrac{4}{9} =$ _______________

13) $\dfrac{1}{4} \times \dfrac{1}{7} =$ _______________

14) $\dfrac{3}{8} \times \dfrac{2}{5} =$ _______________

15) $\dfrac{1}{3} \times \dfrac{5}{11} =$ _______________

16) $\dfrac{5}{6} \times \dfrac{3}{4} =$ _______________

17) $\dfrac{1}{2} \times \dfrac{1}{8} =$ _______________

18) $\dfrac{1}{11} \times \dfrac{3}{5} =$ _______________

19) $\dfrac{2}{5} \times \dfrac{5}{6} =$ _______________

20) $\dfrac{1}{8} \times \dfrac{1}{11} =$ _______________

21) $\dfrac{3}{5} \times \dfrac{3}{7} =$ _______________

22) $\dfrac{2}{3} \times \dfrac{3}{10} =$ _______________

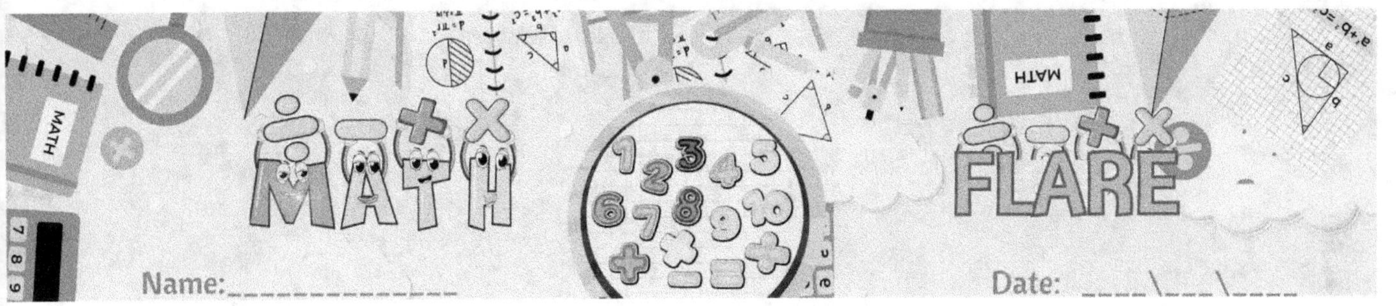

23) $\dfrac{1}{2} \times \dfrac{1}{12} =$ _______________

24) $\dfrac{8}{11} \times \dfrac{3}{4} =$ _______________

25) $\dfrac{1}{4} \times \dfrac{1}{5} =$ _______________

26) $\dfrac{7}{8} \times \dfrac{7}{8} =$ _______________

27) $\dfrac{4}{9} \times \dfrac{2}{3} =$ _______________

28) $\dfrac{5}{11} \times \dfrac{1}{9} =$ _______________

29) $\dfrac{4}{5} \times \dfrac{1}{2} =$ _______________

30) $\dfrac{11}{12} \times \dfrac{1}{2} =$ _______________

31) $\dfrac{1}{3} \times \dfrac{1}{2} =$ _______________

32) $\dfrac{11}{12} \times \dfrac{4}{5} =$ _______________

33) $\dfrac{2}{3} \times \dfrac{1}{5} =$ _______________

34) $\dfrac{3}{8} \times \dfrac{2}{11} =$ _______________

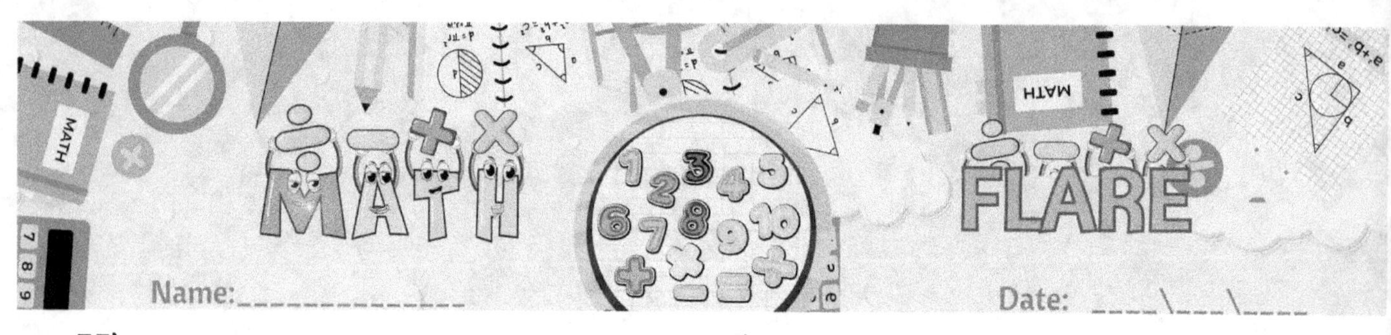

35) $\dfrac{2}{3} \times \dfrac{1}{3} =$ ______________

36) $\dfrac{1}{2} \times \dfrac{5}{9} =$ ______________

37) $\dfrac{1}{3} \times \dfrac{3}{4} =$ ______________

38) $\dfrac{1}{3} \times \dfrac{10}{11} =$ ______________

39) $\dfrac{9}{10} \times \dfrac{1}{6} =$ ______________

40) $\dfrac{3}{11} \times \dfrac{1}{2} =$ ______________

41) $\dfrac{1}{4} \times \dfrac{3}{11} =$ ______________

42) $\dfrac{4}{7} \times \dfrac{5}{6} =$ ______________

43) $\dfrac{1}{3} \times \dfrac{4}{5} =$ ______________

44) $\dfrac{3}{5} \times \dfrac{1}{4} =$ ______________

45) $\dfrac{2}{3} \times \dfrac{2}{3} =$ ______________

46) $\dfrac{1}{6} \times \dfrac{1}{2} =$ ______________

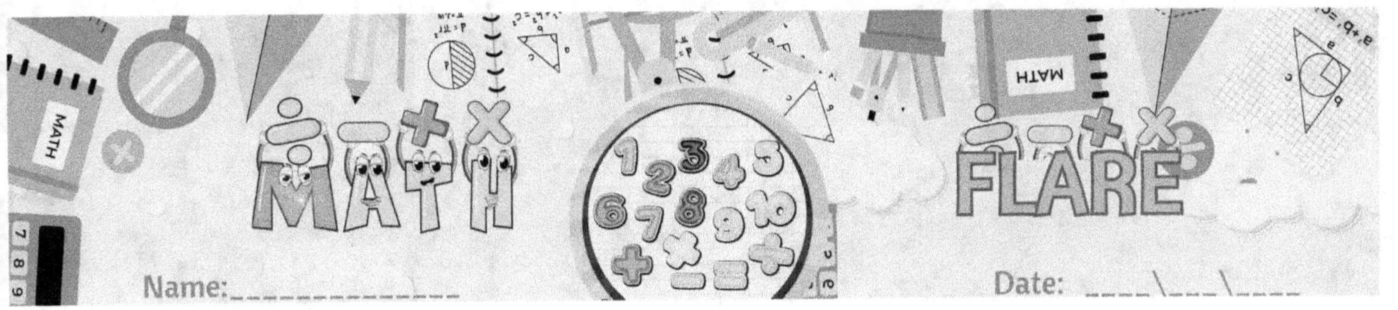

Fractions Division

Find the quotient.

1) $\dfrac{2}{3} \div \dfrac{1}{2} =$ $\quad 1\dfrac{1}{3}$

$\dfrac{2}{3} \times \dfrac{2}{1} = \dfrac{2 \times 2}{3 \times 1} = \dfrac{4}{3}$

2) $\dfrac{5}{11} \div \dfrac{4}{6} =$ _______________

3) $\dfrac{5}{9} \div \dfrac{3}{8} =$ _______________

4) $\dfrac{1}{2} \div \dfrac{5}{9} =$ _______________

5) $\dfrac{1}{8} \div \dfrac{11}{12} =$ _______________

6) $\dfrac{7}{10} \div \dfrac{3}{6} =$ _______________

7) $\dfrac{4}{7} \div \dfrac{2}{4} =$ _______________

8) $\dfrac{3}{5} \div \dfrac{8}{12} =$ _______________

9) $\dfrac{7}{12} \div \dfrac{9}{11} =$ _______________

10) $\dfrac{1}{6} \div \dfrac{5}{7} =$ _______________

11) $\dfrac{2}{9} \div \dfrac{4}{5} =$ _______________

12) $\dfrac{7}{12} \div \dfrac{7}{10} =$ _______________

13) $\dfrac{1}{4} \div \dfrac{5}{7} =$ _______________

14) $\dfrac{7}{10} \div \dfrac{2}{3} =$ _______________

15) $\dfrac{2}{3} \div \dfrac{3}{5} =$ _______________

16) $\dfrac{3}{7} \div \dfrac{2}{6} =$ _______________

17) $\dfrac{2}{5} \div \dfrac{6}{8} =$ _______________

18) $\dfrac{2}{7} \div \dfrac{9}{10} =$ _______________

19) $\dfrac{3}{10} \div \dfrac{2}{3} =$ _______________

20) $\dfrac{1}{6} \div \dfrac{4}{6} =$ _______________

21) $\dfrac{1}{4} \div \dfrac{6}{9} =$ _______________

22) $\dfrac{1}{3} \div \dfrac{2}{4} =$ _______________

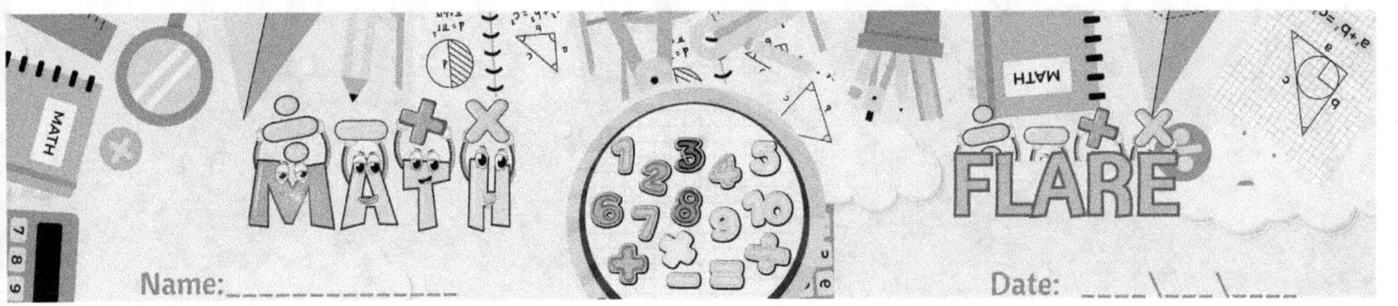

23) $\dfrac{1}{4} \div \dfrac{2}{11} =$ ______________

24) $\dfrac{1}{6} \div \dfrac{5}{6} =$ ______________

25) $\dfrac{1}{12} \div \dfrac{3}{4} =$ ______________

26) $\dfrac{1}{2} \div \dfrac{8}{9} =$ ______________

27) $\dfrac{3}{10} \div \dfrac{4}{12} =$ ______________

28) $\dfrac{1}{3} \div \dfrac{4}{5} =$ ______________

29) $\dfrac{1}{6} \div \dfrac{3}{4} =$ ______________

30) $\dfrac{3}{10} \div \dfrac{11}{12} =$ ______________

31) $\dfrac{3}{8} \div \dfrac{1}{2} =$ ______________

32) $\dfrac{1}{9} \div \dfrac{4}{11} =$ ______________

33) $\dfrac{1}{4} \div \dfrac{4}{8} =$ ______________

34) $\dfrac{10}{11} \div \dfrac{6}{8} =$ ______________

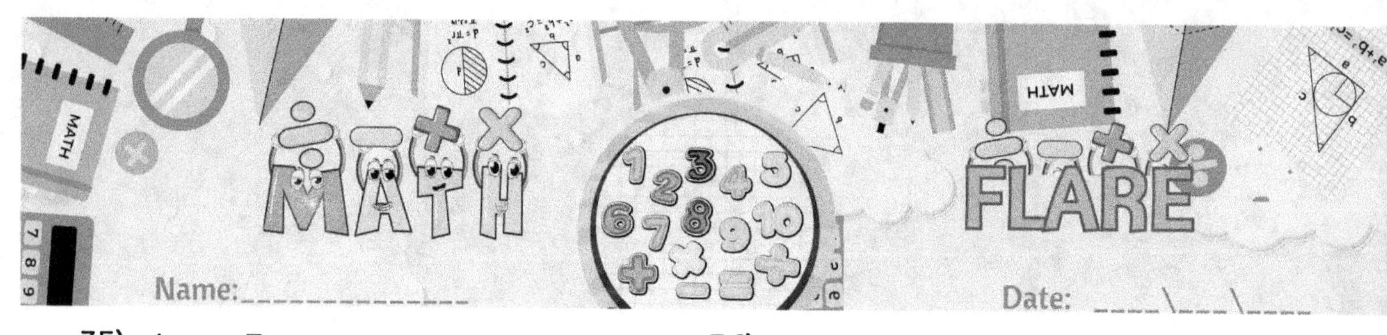

35) $\dfrac{1}{6} \div \dfrac{7}{12} =$ ______________

36) $\dfrac{2}{5} \div \dfrac{1}{6} =$ ______________

37) $\dfrac{4}{7} \div \dfrac{5}{7} =$ ______________

38) $\dfrac{1}{8} \div \dfrac{2}{3} =$ ______________

39) $\dfrac{1}{3} \div \dfrac{4}{8} =$ ______________

40) $\dfrac{1}{3} \div \dfrac{1}{3} =$ ______________

41) $\dfrac{2}{7} \div \dfrac{5}{6} =$ ______________

42) $\dfrac{1}{12} \div \dfrac{5}{9} =$ ______________

43) $\dfrac{3}{10} \div \dfrac{5}{10} =$ ______________

44) $\dfrac{7}{8} \div \dfrac{2}{11} =$ ______________

45) $\dfrac{3}{5} \div \dfrac{1}{2} =$ ______________

46) $\dfrac{3}{10} \div \dfrac{2}{5} =$ ______________

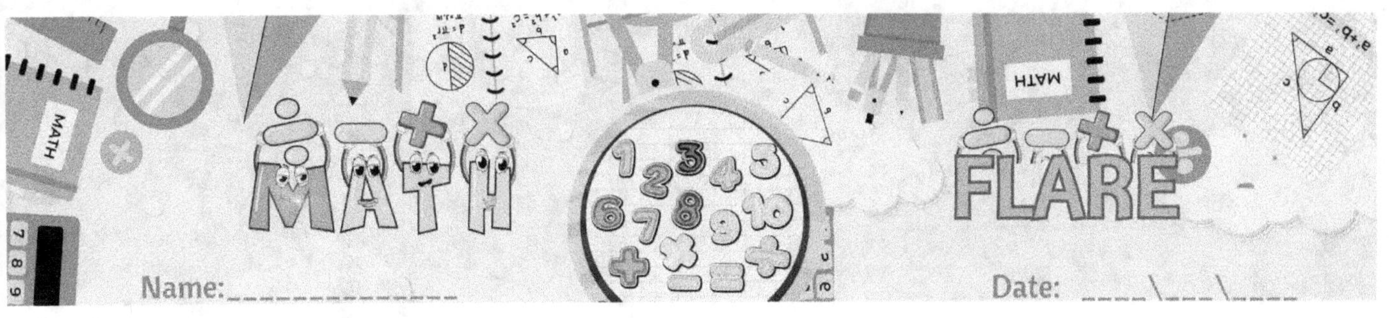

Mixed Numbers

Convert the Mixed numbers into improper fractions.

1) $2\frac{10}{20} = $ $20 \times 2 = 40$ $40 + 10 = 50$ $= \frac{50}{20} = \frac{5}{2}$

2) $6\frac{1}{6} = $ _______________

3) $8\frac{3}{4} = $ _______________

4) $2\frac{1}{2} = $ _______________

5) $5\frac{3}{5} = $ _______________

6) $6\frac{3}{16} = $ _______________

7) $4\frac{8}{12} = $ _______________

8) $1\frac{6}{10} = $ _______________

9) $3\frac{1}{16} = $ _______________

10) $4\frac{2}{18} = $ _______________

11) $6\frac{1}{3} = $ _______________

12) $8\frac{1}{2} = $ _______________

13) $9\frac{1}{12} = $ _______________

14) $5\frac{2}{3} = $ _______________

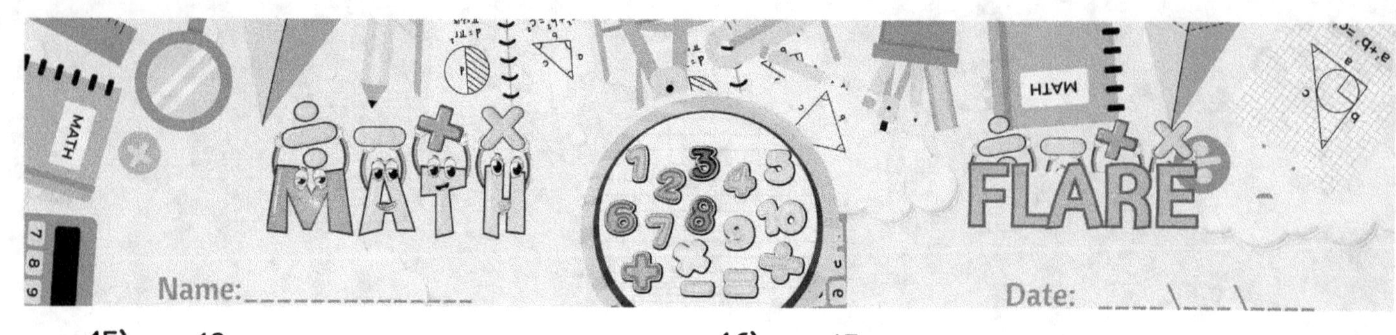

15) $2\frac{12}{14} =$ _______________

16) $3\frac{15}{20} =$ _______________

17) $8\frac{2}{18} =$ _______________

18) $6\frac{15}{20} =$ _______________

19) $1\frac{1}{3} =$ _______________

20) $7\frac{3}{7} =$ _______________

21) $9\frac{12}{20} =$ _______________

22) $5\frac{7}{14} =$ _______________

23) $9\frac{1}{3} =$ _______________

24) $2\frac{3}{10} =$ _______________

25) $2\frac{1}{18} =$ _______________

26) $2\frac{1}{3} =$ _______________

27) $8\frac{8}{12} =$ _______________

28) $6\frac{2}{18} =$ _______________

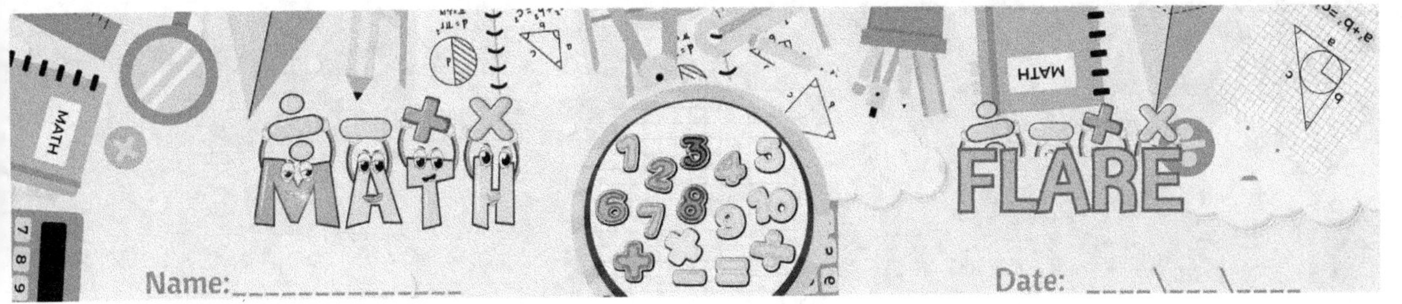

29) $2\frac{13}{16} =$ __________

30) $4\frac{3}{6} =$ __________

31) $4\frac{3}{4} =$ __________

32) $4\frac{1}{2} =$ __________

33) $1\frac{1}{4} =$ __________

34) $5\frac{1}{20} =$ __________

35) $3\frac{1}{9} =$ __________

36) $2\frac{1}{14} =$ __________

37) $9\frac{4}{12} =$ __________

38) $6\frac{5}{7} =$ __________

39) $9\frac{3}{9} =$ __________

40) $5\frac{1}{2} =$ __________

41) $7\frac{7}{8} =$ __________

42) $3\frac{8}{10} =$ __________

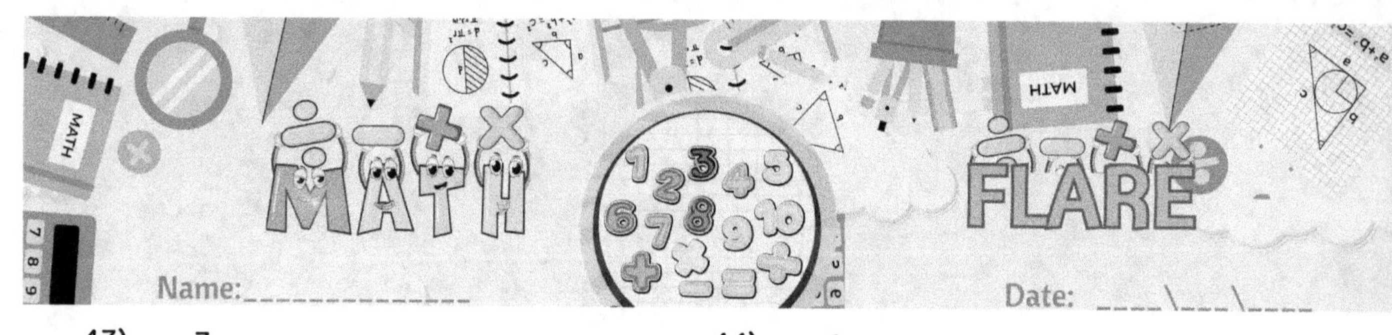

43) $2\frac{3}{4}$ = _______________

44) $2\frac{6}{7}$ = _______________

45) $9\frac{1}{2}$ = _______________

46) $1\frac{17}{20}$ = _______________

47) $8\frac{10}{12}$ = _______________

48) $2\frac{9}{10}$ = _______________

49) $1\frac{2}{10}$ = _______________

50) $1\frac{4}{6}$ = _______________

51) $7\frac{2}{6}$ = _______________

52) $5\frac{3}{7}$ = _______________

53) $9\frac{3}{18}$ = _______________

54) $9\frac{2}{6}$ = _______________

55) $8\frac{3}{6}$ = _______________

56) $1\frac{3}{10}$ = _______________

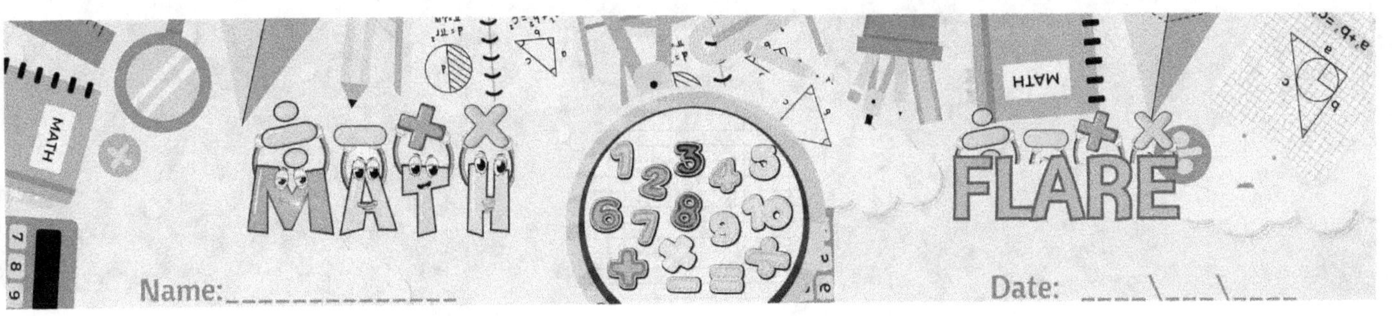

Mixed Numbers

Convert the Improper fractions into Mixed numbers.

1) $\dfrac{41}{16}$ = $2\dfrac{9}{16}$

$41 \div 16 = 2$ with a remainder of 9

2) $\dfrac{84}{10}$ =

3) $\dfrac{10}{6}$ =

4) $\dfrac{7}{6}$ =

5) $\dfrac{35}{10}$ =

6) $\dfrac{33}{4}$ =

7) $\dfrac{26}{10}$ =

8) $\dfrac{93}{14}$ =

9) $\dfrac{151}{16}$ =

10) $\dfrac{39}{7}$ =

11) $\dfrac{33}{12}$ =

12) $\dfrac{114}{20}$ =

13) $\dfrac{14}{8}$ =

14) $\dfrac{66}{10}$ =

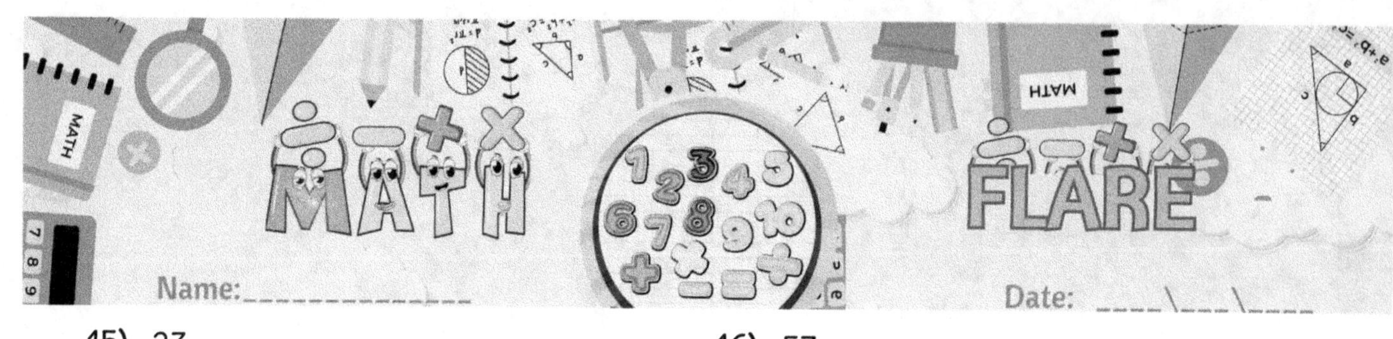

15) $\dfrac{23}{14} = $ ______________________

16) $\dfrac{57}{8} = $ ______________________

17) $\dfrac{17}{2} = $ ______________________

18) $\dfrac{95}{12} = $ ______________________

19) $\dfrac{29}{8} = $ ______________________

20) $\dfrac{12}{8} = $ ______________________

21) $\dfrac{107}{14} = $ ______________________

22) $\dfrac{5}{3} = $ ______________________

23) $\dfrac{136}{20} = $ ______________________

24) $\dfrac{65}{7} = $ ______________________

25) $\dfrac{116}{16} = $ ______________________

26) $\dfrac{23}{4} = $ ______________________

27) $\dfrac{31}{9} = $ ______________________

28) $\dfrac{10}{4} = $ ______________________

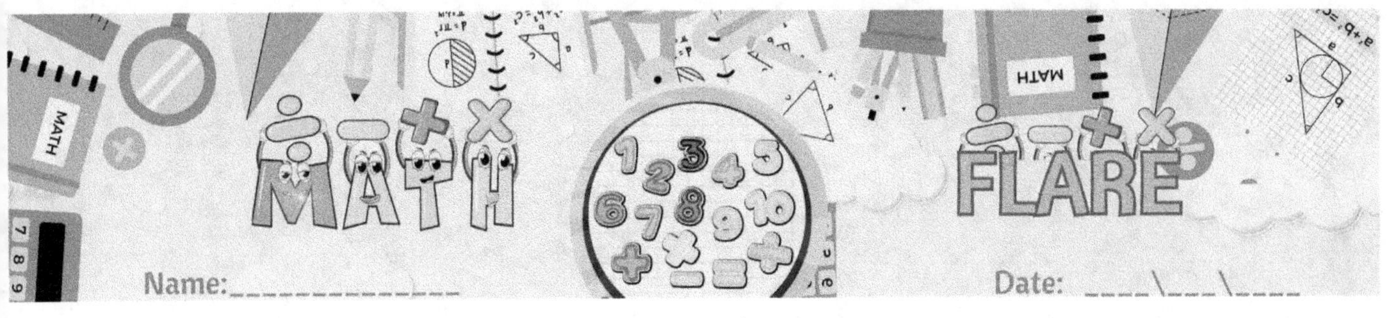

Name:_______________   Date: ____________

29) $\dfrac{12}{10}$ = _______________

30) $\dfrac{43}{10}$ = _______________

31) $\dfrac{12}{9}$ = _______________

32) $\dfrac{8}{5}$ = _______________

33) $\dfrac{35}{4}$ = _______________

34) $\dfrac{23}{7}$ = _______________

35) $\dfrac{174}{20}$ = _______________

36) $\dfrac{35}{8}$ = _______________

37) $\dfrac{59}{12}$ = _______________

38) $\dfrac{153}{18}$ = _______________

39) $\dfrac{60}{8}$ = _______________

40) $\dfrac{31}{14}$ = _______________

41) $\dfrac{66}{8}$ = _______________

42) $\dfrac{39}{4}$ = _______________

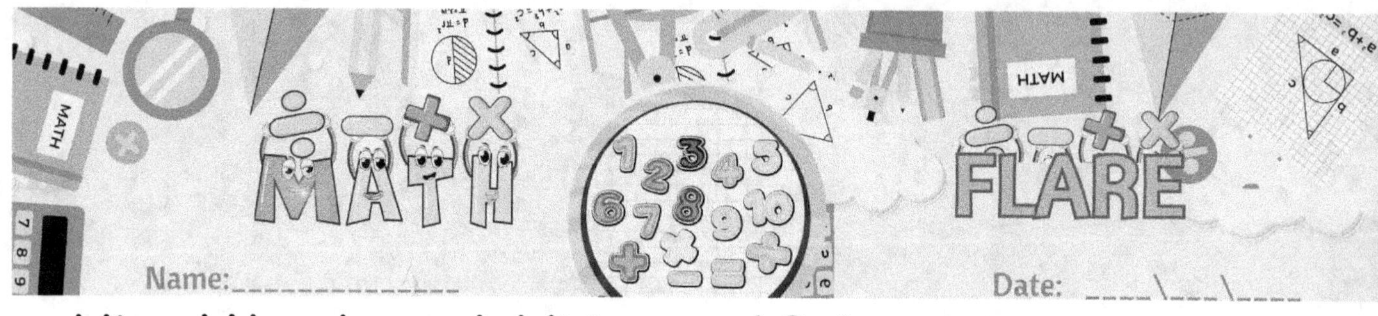

Mixed Numbers: Addition and Subtraction

Calculate.

1) $7\frac{4}{6} - 2\frac{3}{8} =$ $\dfrac{4}{6} - \dfrac{3}{8} = \dfrac{4\times8 - 6\times3}{6\times8} = \dfrac{32-18}{48} = \dfrac{14}{48} = 5\frac{7}{24}$

$7 - 2 = 5$

2) $8\frac{6}{7} - 7\frac{1}{2} =$

3) $3\frac{4}{8} + 7\frac{1}{3} =$

4) $7\frac{1}{4} - 5\frac{1}{2} =$

5) $8\frac{3}{7} - 5\frac{1}{10} =$

6) $8\frac{2}{5} - 7\frac{4}{6} =$

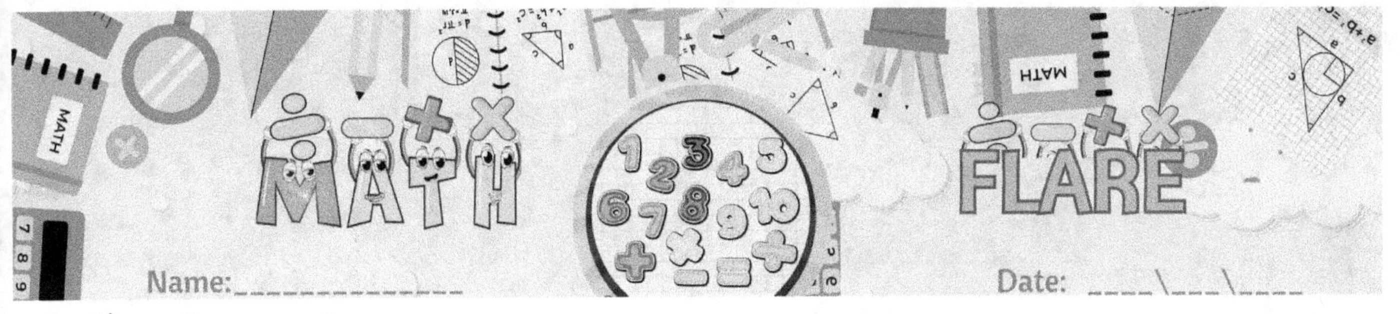

7) $7\frac{5}{9} - 5\frac{1}{10} =$ _______________________

8) $5\frac{3}{4} - 2\frac{1}{2} =$ _______________________

9) $4\frac{1}{7} + 4\frac{1}{9} =$ _______________________

10) $9\frac{1}{3} - 8\frac{6}{8} =$ _______________________

11) $7\frac{3}{5} - 3\frac{3}{6} =$ _______________________

12) $8\frac{7}{8} - 8\frac{8}{10} =$ _______________________

13) $1\frac{2}{4} + 2\frac{6}{9} =$ _______________

14) $2\frac{2}{7} + 8\frac{1}{2} =$ _______________

15) $3\frac{4}{6} - 1\frac{2}{3} =$ _______________

16) $2\frac{8}{10} - 2\frac{3}{5} =$ _______________

17) $3\frac{4}{8} - 2\frac{1}{4} =$ _______________

18) $9\frac{2}{9} - 8\frac{4}{7} =$ _______________

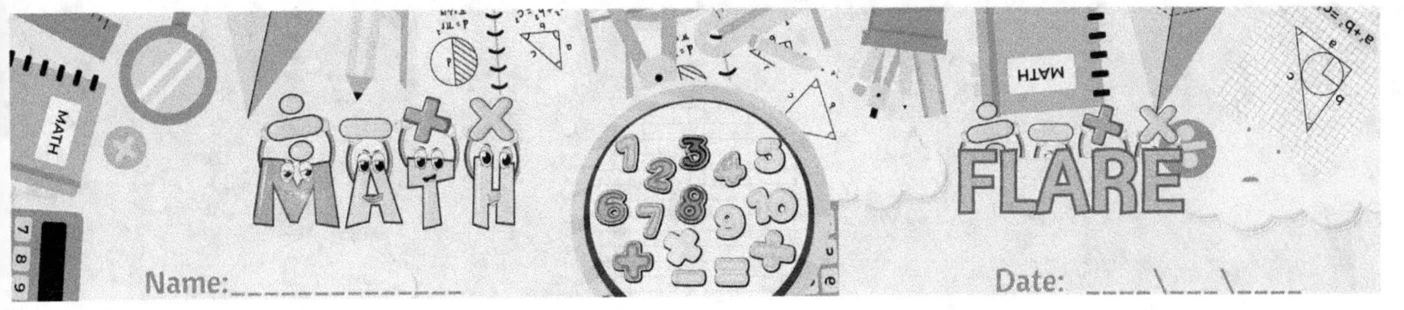

19) $4 \frac{1}{2} + 3 \frac{2}{3} =$ _______________

20) $9 \frac{4}{8} - 3 \frac{3}{7} =$ _______________

21) $9 \frac{6}{10} - 3 \frac{2}{6} =$ _______________

22) $4 \frac{3}{5} + 6 \frac{1}{4} =$ _______________

23) $9 \frac{8}{9} + 3 \frac{1}{2} =$ _______________

24) $8 \frac{2}{6} + 2 \frac{4}{7} =$ _______________

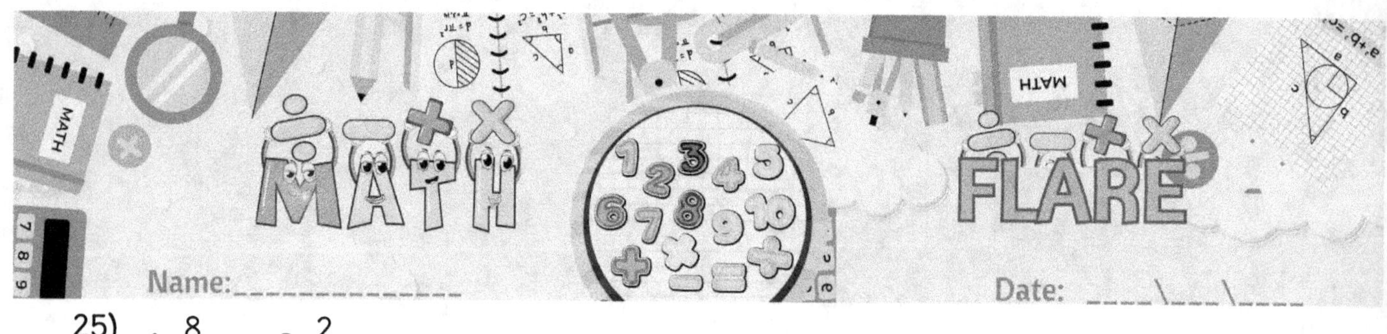

25) $1\frac{8}{10} + 9\frac{2}{3} =$ _______________

26) $3\frac{1}{4} + 9\frac{5}{8} =$ _______________

27) $7\frac{3}{5} - 4\frac{8}{9} =$ _______________

28) $7\frac{1}{4} - 4\frac{5}{7} =$ _______________

29) $4\frac{6}{9} + 7\frac{1}{3} =$ _______________

30) $4\frac{6}{8} - 2\frac{3}{6} =$ _______________

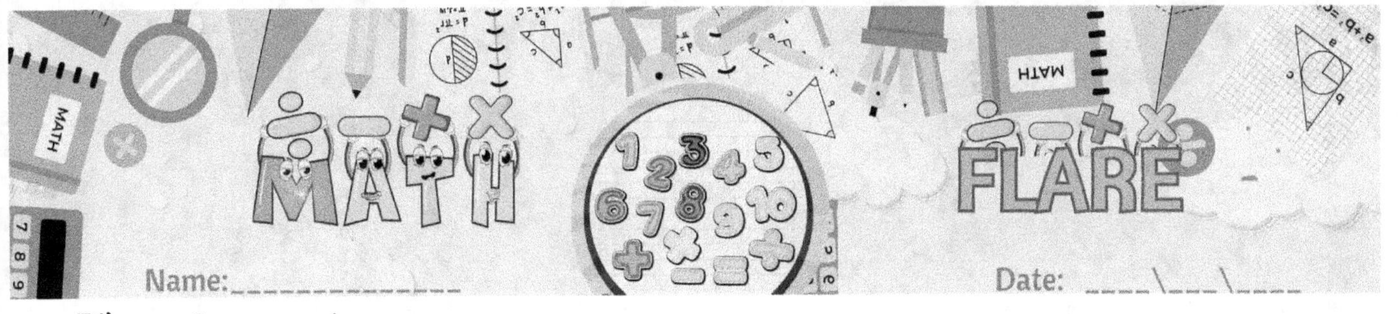

31) $6 \frac{2}{10} + 4 \frac{1}{2} =$ _______________

32) $9 \frac{4}{5} - 8 \frac{2}{9} =$ _______________

33) $1 \frac{1}{2} + 2 \frac{1}{3} =$ _______________

34) $8 \frac{1}{6} - 1 \frac{3}{7} =$ _______________

35) $9 \frac{4}{5} - 6 \frac{6}{8} =$ _______________

36) $6 \frac{8}{10} - 1 \frac{2}{4} =$ _______________

37) $4\frac{1}{6} - 3\frac{4}{9} =$ ______________________

38) $2\frac{5}{7} + 4\frac{1}{4} =$ ______________________

39) $4\frac{4}{5} + 1\frac{2}{3} =$ ______________________

40) $6\frac{1}{2} + 8\frac{6}{8} =$ ______________________

41) $3\frac{3}{10} + 9\frac{1}{7} =$ ______________________

42) $7\frac{1}{2} + 7\frac{2}{4} =$ ______________________

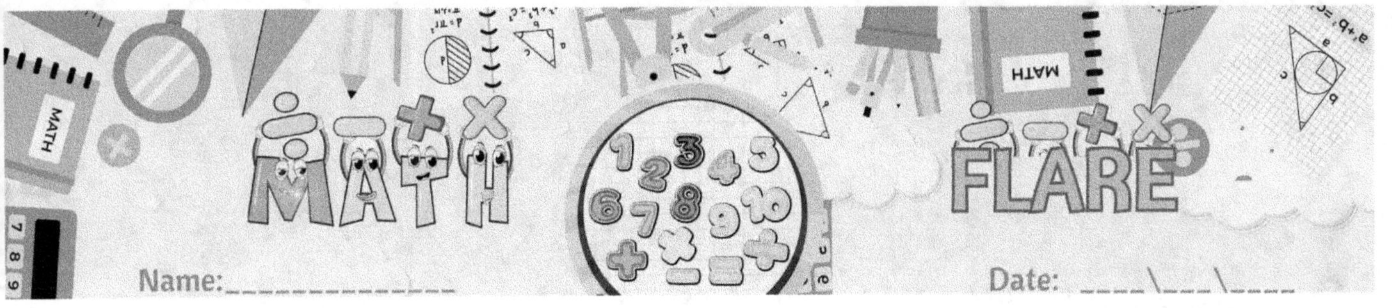

43) $3\frac{1}{3} + 4\frac{3}{8} =$ ______________________

44) $9\frac{9}{10} + 4\frac{3}{6} =$ ______________________

45) $8\frac{7}{9} - 7\frac{2}{5} =$ ______________________

46) $7\frac{8}{10} + 8\frac{6}{8} =$ ______________________

47) $8\frac{2}{3} - 6\frac{2}{9} =$ ______________________

48) $7\frac{1}{6} + 2\frac{1}{5} =$ ______________________

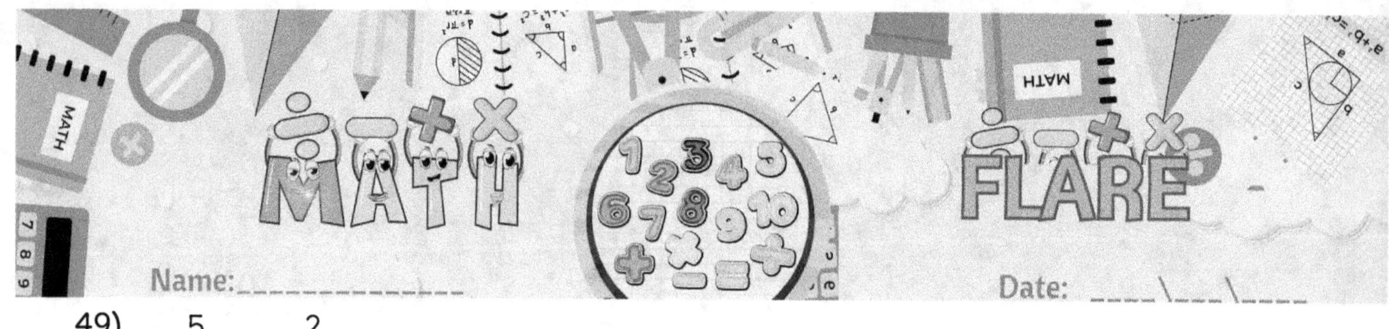

49) $2\frac{5}{7} + 7\frac{2}{4} =$ ___________________

50) $7\frac{1}{2} - 3\frac{5}{9} =$ ___________________

51) $8\frac{1}{7} - 5\frac{4}{10} =$ ___________________

52) $3\frac{1}{2} - 2\frac{4}{5} =$ ___________________

53) $4\frac{1}{4} - 2\frac{4}{8} =$ ___________________

54) $5\frac{2}{6} - 1\frac{1}{3} =$ ___________________

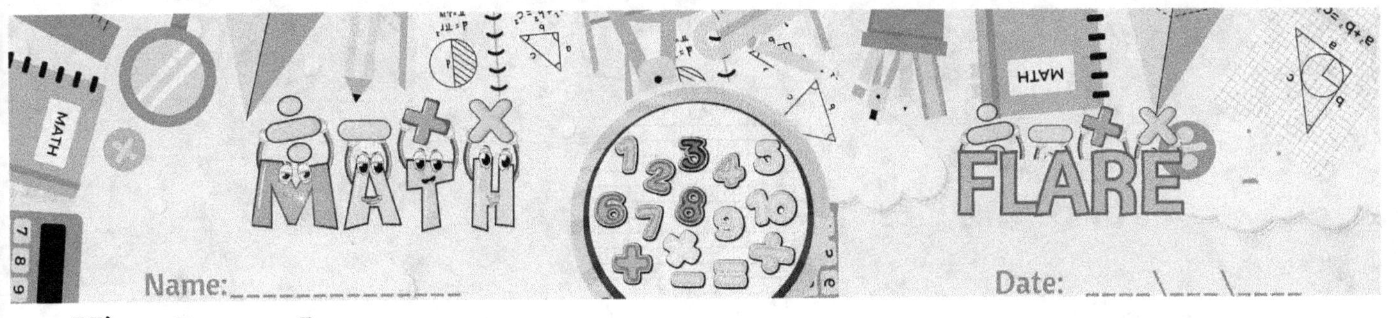

55) $1\frac{3}{8} + 8\frac{5}{9} =$ _______________

56) $6\frac{1}{3} + 3\frac{4}{7} =$ _______________

57) $8\frac{3}{4} + 3\frac{1}{6} =$ _______________

58) $7\frac{7}{10} + 1\frac{2}{7} =$ _______________

59) $6\frac{5}{9} - 1\frac{3}{5} =$ _______________

60) $9\frac{1}{3} + 9\frac{1}{2} =$ _______________

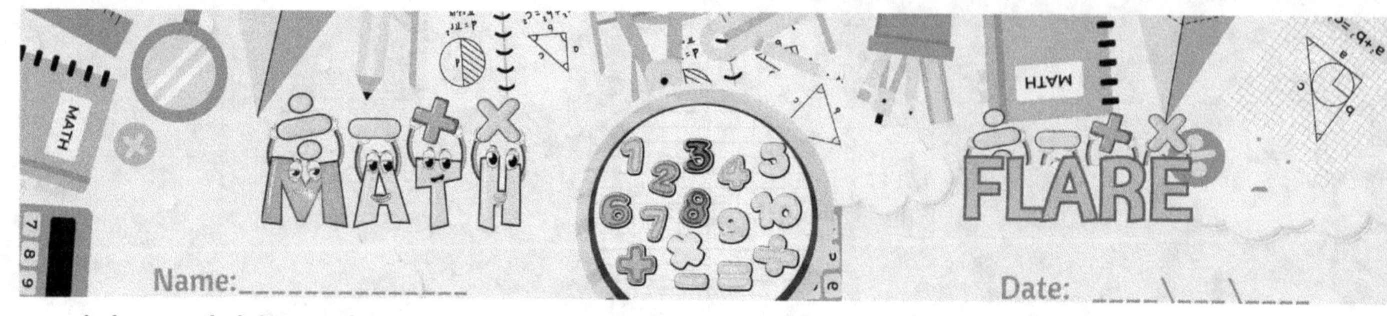

Mixed Numbers: Multiplication and Division

Calculate.

1) $1\frac{2}{4} \times 3\frac{1}{6} = \dfrac{3}{2} \times \dfrac{19}{6} = \dfrac{3 \times 19}{2 \times 6} = \dfrac{57}{12} = 4\frac{3}{4}$

$1 \times 4 + 2 = 6 = \dfrac{6}{2} = \dfrac{3}{2} \qquad 3 \times 8 + 1 = \dfrac{19}{6}$

2) $9\frac{3}{8} \times 1\frac{5}{7} =$ ___________________

3) $2\frac{6}{10} \div 6\frac{6}{7} = \dfrac{13}{5} \times \dfrac{7}{48} = \dfrac{13 \times 7}{5 \times 48} = \dfrac{91}{240}$

$2 \times 10 + 6 = 26 = \dfrac{26}{10} = \dfrac{13}{5} \qquad 6 \times 7 + 6 = \dfrac{48}{7}$

4) $1\frac{4}{9} \div 3\frac{2}{3} =$ ___________________

5) $4\frac{3}{8} \div 4\frac{4}{6} =$ ___________________

6) $5\frac{3}{4} \div 9\frac{1}{5} =$ ___________________

7) $8\frac{1}{2} \times 1\frac{3}{7} =$ _______________________

8) $3\frac{3}{5} \times 7\frac{1}{2} =$ _______________________

9) $1\frac{5}{6} \div 7\frac{3}{8} =$ _______________________

10) $7\frac{5}{9} \times 9\frac{3}{4} =$ _______________________

11) $9\frac{9}{10} \div 2\frac{1}{3} =$ _______________________

12) $5\frac{2}{6} \times 8\frac{1}{2} =$ _______________________

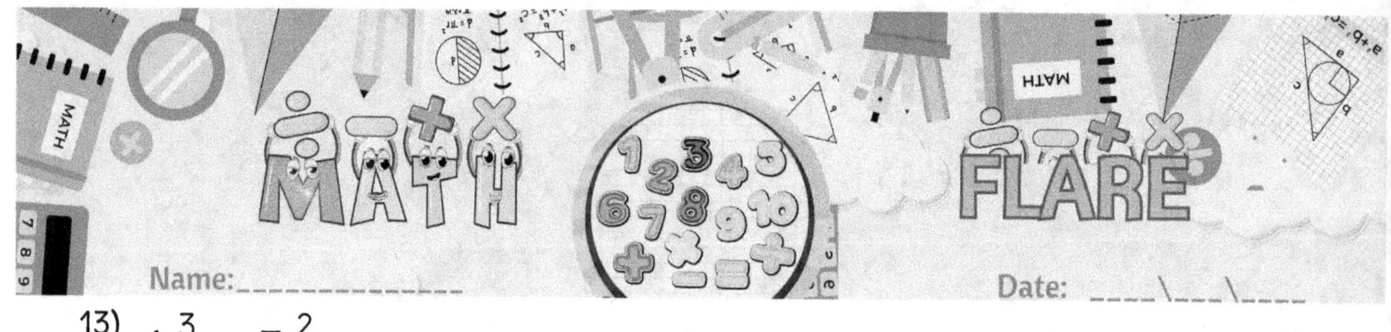

13) $1\frac{3}{9} \times 7\frac{2}{3} =$ ___________

14) $6\frac{2}{7} \times 4\frac{2}{10} =$ ___________

15) $4\frac{2}{8} \div 5\frac{3}{4} =$ ___________

16) $6\frac{2}{5} \times 8\frac{4}{7} =$ ___________

17) $1\frac{8}{9} \div 3\frac{2}{5} =$ ___________

18) $4\frac{2}{8} \times 2\frac{1}{2} =$ ___________

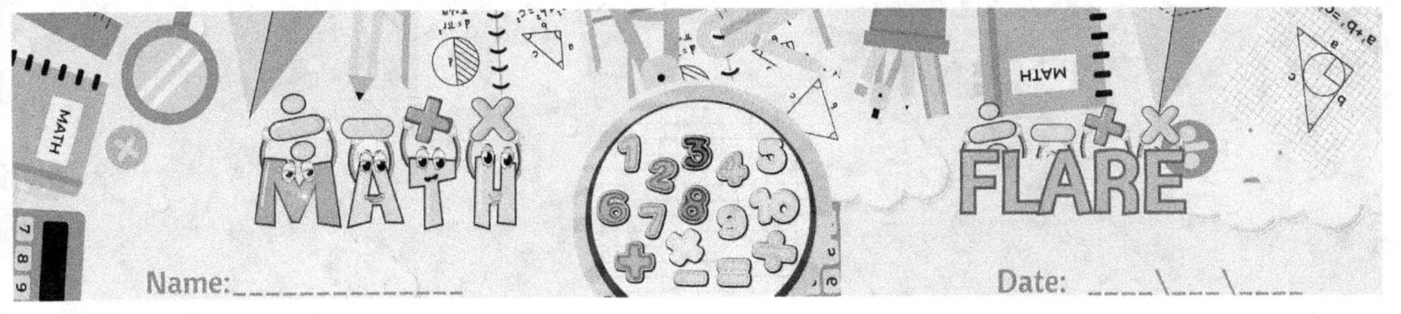

19) $8 \frac{2}{3} \times 7 \frac{1}{4} =$ _______________________

20) $1 \frac{3}{6} \times 8 \frac{1}{10} =$ _______________________

21) $7 \frac{1}{2} \times 6 \frac{4}{8} =$ _______________________

22) $4 \frac{3}{5} \times 1 \frac{2}{3} =$ _______________________

23) $5 \frac{8}{9} \times 7 \frac{2}{7} =$ _______________________

24) $7 \frac{1}{10} \div 6 \frac{1}{4} =$ _______________________

25) $8\frac{1}{6} \div 4\frac{2}{9} =$ _______________________

26) $9\frac{2}{5} \times 1\frac{7}{8} =$ _______________________

27) $6\frac{4}{6} \times 8\frac{3}{4} =$ _______________________

28) $6\frac{1}{2} \times 9\frac{2}{3} =$ _______________________

29) $9\frac{2}{10} \times 2\frac{1}{7} =$ _______________________

30) $4\frac{1}{5} \div 8\frac{9}{10} =$ _______________________

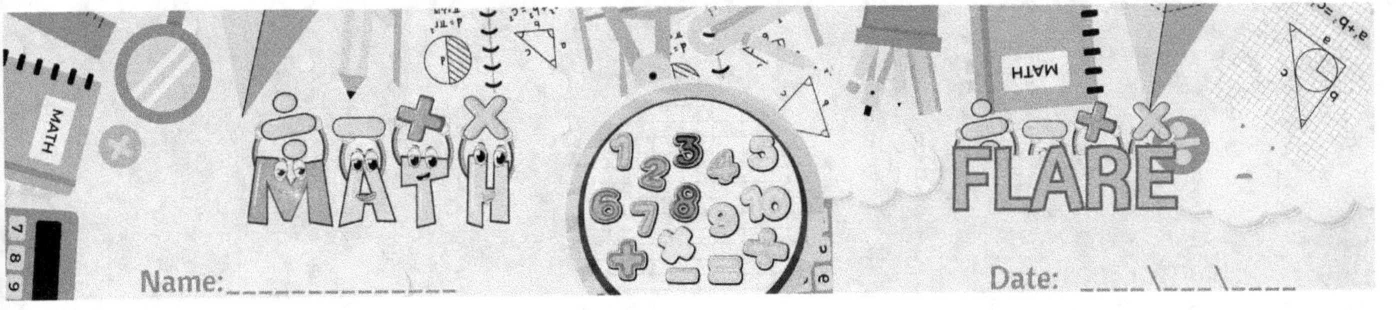

31) $6\frac{4}{6} \times 3\frac{3}{5} =$ ___________

32) $3\frac{6}{8} \div 9\frac{2}{9} =$ ___________

33) $6\frac{2}{4} \div 7\frac{1}{2} =$ ___________

34) $7\frac{1}{7} \times 5\frac{2}{3} =$ ___________

35) $2\frac{2}{3} \div 6\frac{3}{6} =$ ___________

36) $3\frac{1}{5} \div 8\frac{1}{2} =$ ___________

37) $6 \frac{2}{7} \times 3 \frac{4}{8} =$ ___________________

38) $5 \frac{5}{9} \div 9 \frac{3}{4} =$ ___________________

39) $3 \frac{5}{10} \times 1 \frac{2}{3} =$ ___________________

40) $3 \frac{5}{8} \div 7 \frac{2}{4} =$ ___________________

41) $1 \frac{1}{5} \times 6 \frac{8}{9} =$ ___________________

42) $4 \frac{1}{2} \div 5 \frac{3}{6} =$ ___________________

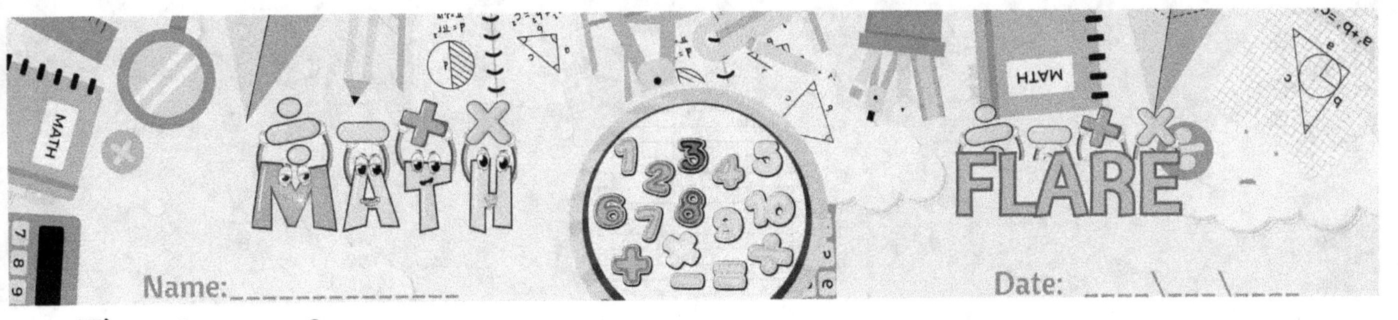

43) $1\frac{6}{7} \times 5\frac{8}{10} =$ _______________

44) $8\frac{3}{5} \times 5\frac{8}{10} =$ _______________

45) $3\frac{1}{7} \times 1\frac{1}{6} =$ _______________

46) $7\frac{1}{2} \div 2\frac{5}{8} =$ _______________

47) $1\frac{1}{3} \div 5\frac{2}{4} =$ _______________

48) $9\frac{4}{9} \times 5\frac{1}{2} =$ _______________

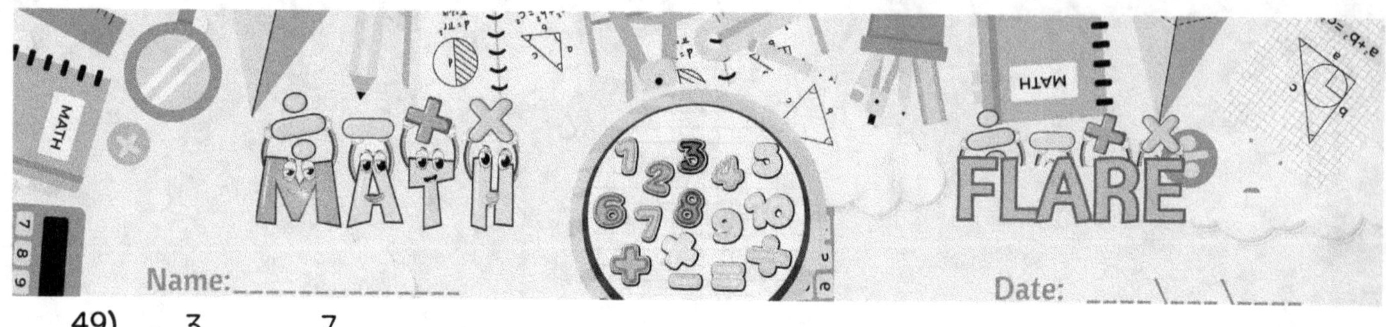

49) $9\frac{3}{6} \div 4\frac{7}{10} =$ ______________

50) $5\frac{2}{7} \times 1\frac{1}{4} =$ ______________

51) $4\frac{4}{9} \times 8\frac{4}{5} =$ ______________

52) $1\frac{1}{3} \times 7\frac{6}{8} =$ ______________

53) $5\frac{3}{6} \times 6\frac{2}{7} =$ ______________

54) $6\frac{4}{5} \times 6\frac{1}{2} =$ ______________

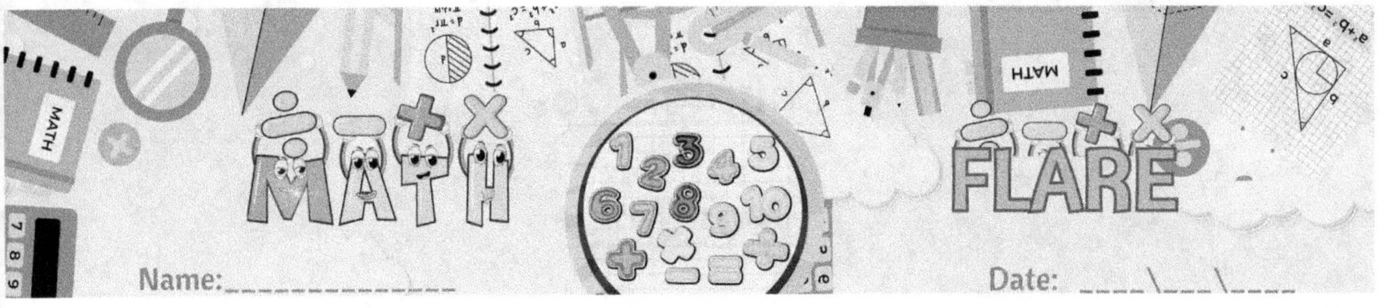

55) $9 \frac{2}{3} \div 6 \frac{8}{10} =$ ______________

56) $2 \frac{4}{9} \div 2 \frac{2}{4} =$ ______________

57) $1 \frac{7}{8} \div 5 \frac{4}{8} =$ ______________

58) $1 \frac{2}{7} \div 8 \frac{2}{9} =$ ______________

59) $8 \frac{2}{4} \div 9 \frac{4}{5} =$ ______________

60) $7 \frac{6}{10} \times 7 \frac{1}{2} =$ ______________

Chapter. 05

Geometry

Area and Perimeter

The area of a shape represents the amount of space it occupies. The perimeter of a shape is the total distance around its outer edge.

Area of Rectangle

For a square, since all four sides are equal, we only need to know the length of one side to find its area. We can calculate the area of a square by multiplying the length of one side by itself (squared). So, if the length of one side of the square is 's', then the area (A) is given by:

$$A = s \times s$$

4 in

4 in

$$A = 4 \times 4$$

$$A = 16$$

Perimeter of Rectangle

For a square, since all four sides are equal, we can find the perimeter by adding up the lengths of all four sides. If 's' represents the length of one side, then the perimeter (P) is given by:

$$P = 4 \times s$$

$$P = 4 \times 4$$

$$P = 16$$

Area of Triangle:

The area of a triangle represents the amount of space enclosed within its three sides. The formula for calculating the area of a triangle depends on the type of triangle. For a general triangle, we use the formula:

$$A = \frac{1}{2} \times base \times height$$

Where:

- A represents the area of the triangle.

- The base is the length of any one side of the triangle.

- The height is the perpendicular distance from the base to the opposite vertex.

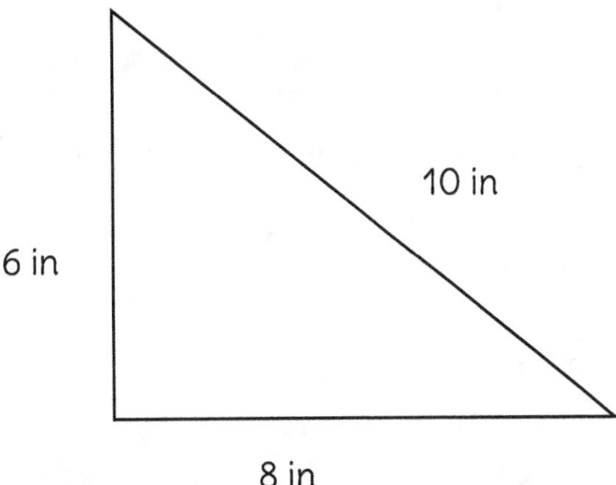

MathFlare - Math Workbook 5th Grade

$$A = \frac{1}{2} \times base \times height$$

$$A = \frac{1}{2} \times 6 \times 8$$

$$A = \frac{1}{2} \times 48$$

$$A = 24$$

Perimeter of Triangle:

The perimeter of a triangle is the total length of its three sides. To find the perimeter, we simply add the lengths of all three sides together:

$$P = side1 + side2 + side3$$

$$P = 6 + 8 + 10$$

$$P = 24$$

Equilateral Triangle

An equilateral triangle is a triangle in which all three sides are equal in length. To find the area and perimeter of an equilateral triangle, we can use the following formulas:

- Area (A): $\frac{\sqrt{3}}{4} \times a^2$ where a is the length of one side of the equilateral triangle.

- Perimeter (P): $P = 3a$ where a is the length of one side of the equilateral triangle.

Let's solve a problem:

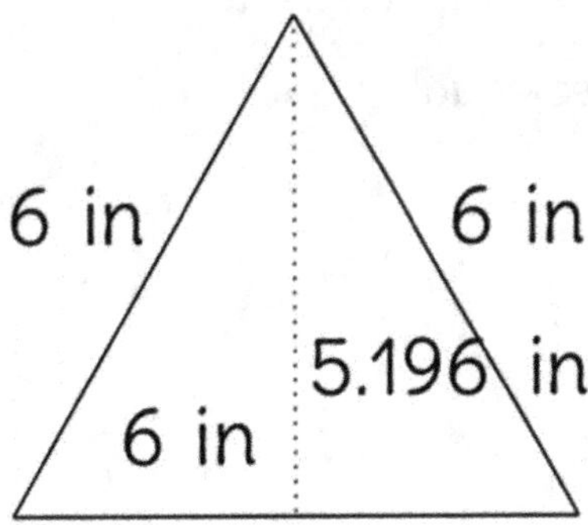

Area of Equilateral Triangle:

$$\text{Area (A): } \frac{\sqrt{3}}{4} \times (6)^2$$

$$\text{Area (A): } \frac{\sqrt{3}}{4} \times 36$$

$$\text{Area (A): } \frac{36\sqrt{3}}{4}$$

$$\text{Area (A): } \frac{36(1.73)}{4}$$

$$\text{Area (A): } \frac{62.35}{4}$$

$$\text{Area (A): } 15.59 \text{ in}^2$$

Perimeter of Equilateral Triangle:

$$P = 3a$$

$$P = 3(6) = 18$$

Isosceles Triangle

An isosceles triangle is a triangle with at least two sides of equal length. The angles opposite the equal sides are also equal.

Area of Isosceles Triangle

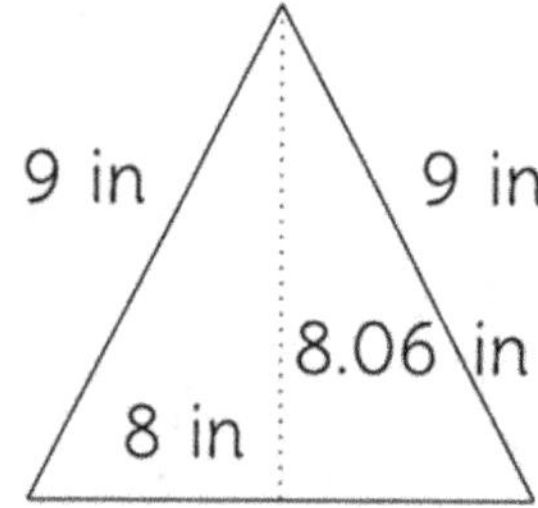

$$A = \frac{1}{2} \times base \times height$$

$$A = \frac{1}{2} \times 8 \times 8$$

$$A = \frac{1}{2} \times 64$$

$$A = 32$$

Perimeter of Isosceles Triangle

The perimeter of a triangle is the total length of its three sides. To find the perimeter, we simply add the lengths of all three sides together:

$$P = side1 + side2 + side3$$

$$P = 9 + 9 + 8$$

$$P = 26$$

Area and Circumference of circles

To find the area (*A*) and circumference (*C*) of a circle, we use the following formulas:

1. Area of a Circle (*A*) = $\pi \times (radius)^2$
   - where π (pi) is a constant with value of (3.14). It is a ratio of the circumference of a circle to its diameter,
   - the radius (r) is the distance from the center of the circle.
2. Circumference of a Circle (*C*) = $2 \times \pi \times radius$

Let's solve an example: suppose a swimming pool has a radius of 11 meters, we are required to calculate its Area and Circumference:

$$\text{Area } (A) = \pi \times (radius)^2$$

$$A = 3.14 \times 11^2$$

$$A = 3.14 \times 121$$

$$A = 379.94 \text{ square meters}$$

$$\text{Circumference } (C) = 2 \times \pi \times radius$$

$$C = 2 \times 3.14 \times 11$$

$$C = 69.08 \text{ square meters}$$

Angles

Types of Angles: Angles can be classified based on their measures:

- **Acute Angle:** An angle less than 90°.

- **Right Angle:** An angle exactly equal to 90°.

- **Obtuse Angle:** An angle greater than 90° and less than 180°.

- **Straight Angle:** An angle exactly equal to 180°.

- **Reflex Angle:** An angle greater than 180° and less than 360°.

- **Full Angle:** An angle equal to 360°.

Measure angles with a protractor. It looks like a semicircle or a half-disc with degree markings from 0° to 180°.To measure an angle using a protractor, we place the center of the protractor at the vertex of the angle, align one side of the angle with the zero mark on the protractor, and read the degree measure where the other side intersects the protractor.

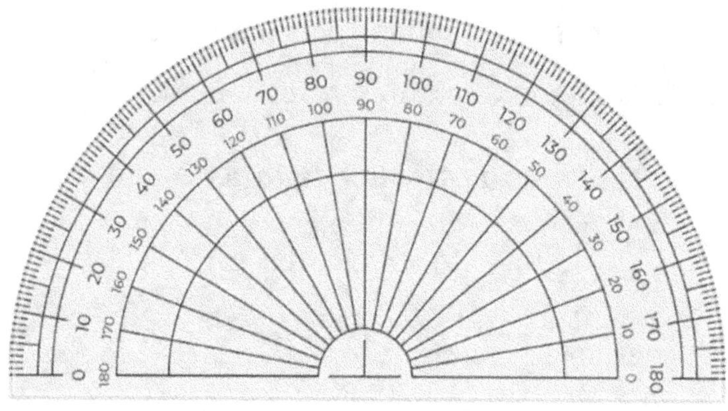

Image: Protector

For example, let's measure the following angle.

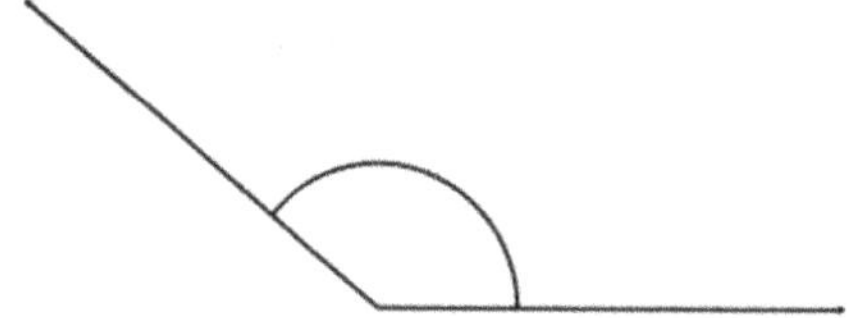

The angle is 140°.

We also know that the angle is greater than 90° and less than 180°, so this is an Obtuse angle.

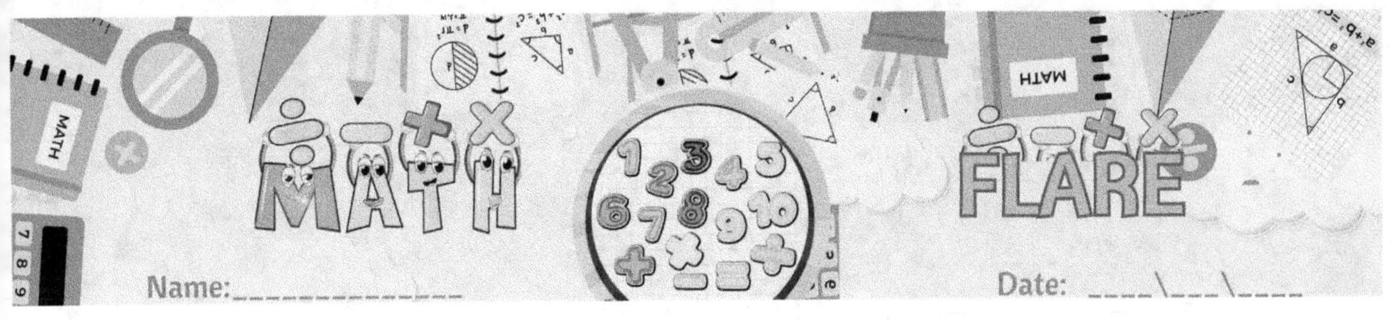

Area and Perimeter: Rectangles and Triangles

1)
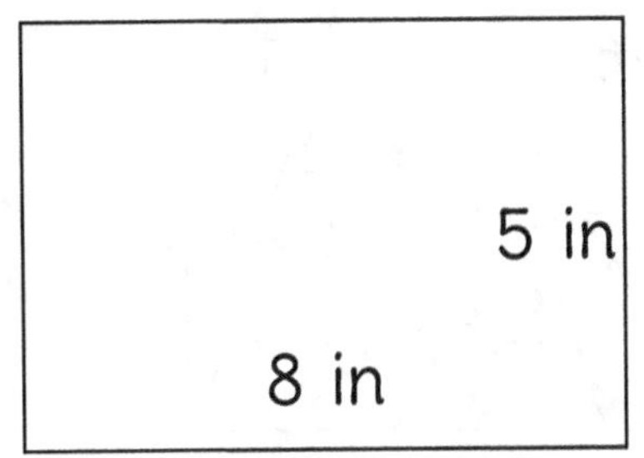

P = 26 in A = 40 in²

2)
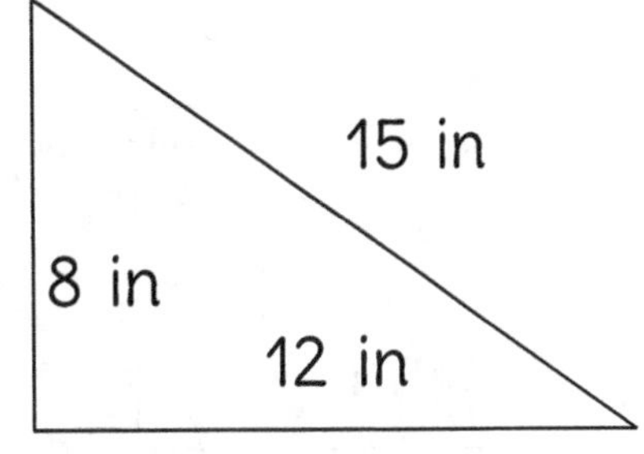

P = 35 in A = 48 in²

3)
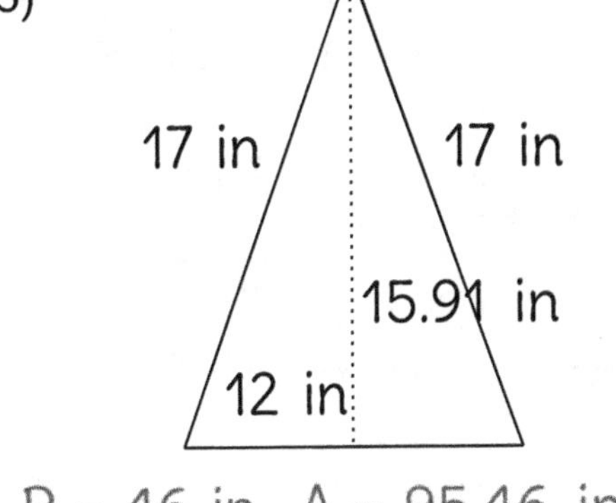

P = 46 in A = 95.46 in²

4)
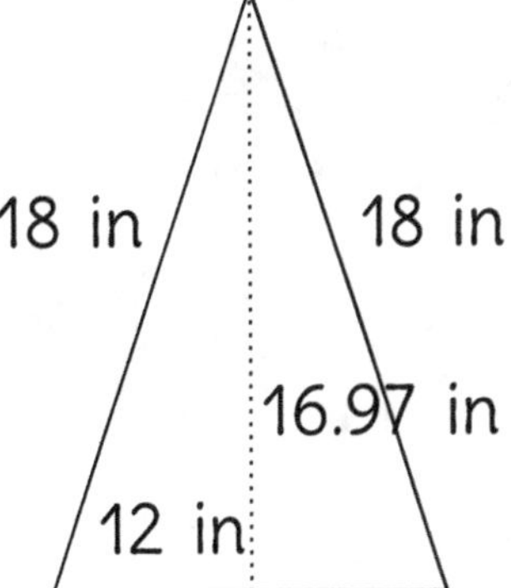

Name:
Date:
MATH
FLARE

5)

18 in
15 in

6)

16 in
16 in
15.20 in
10 in

7)

16 in
12 in
11 in

8)

7 in
9 in

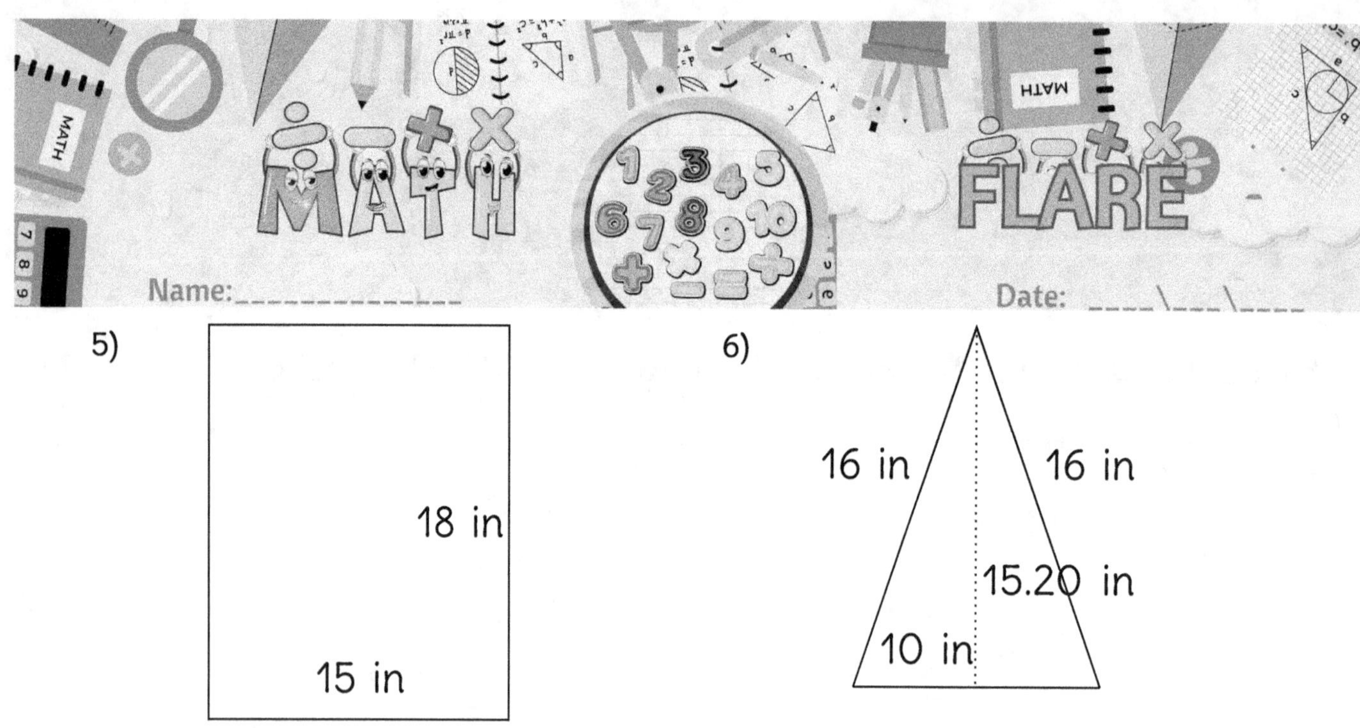

MATH
FLARE
Name:
Date:

9)

21 in
13 in
17 in

10)

13 in
15 in

11)

18 in
14 in
11 in

12)

10 in
8 in

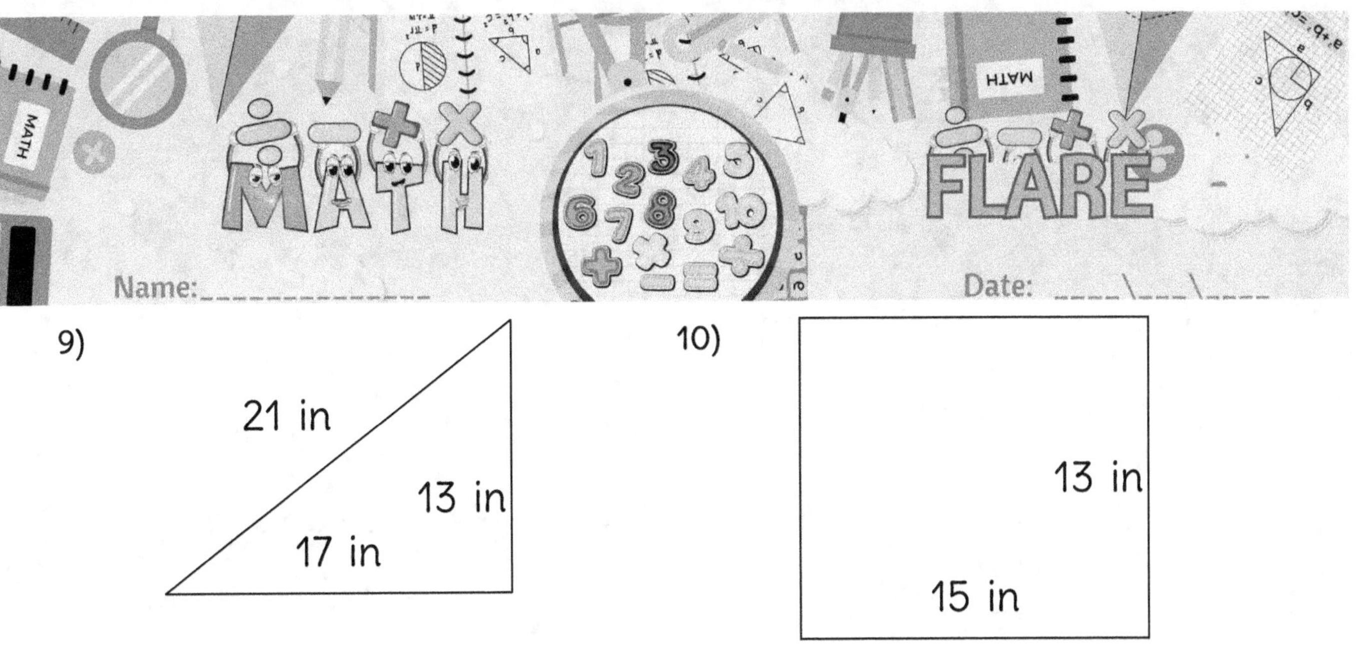

MATH
FLARE
Name:_______________
Date: ______________

13)

15 in
11 in
10 in

14)

7 in
7 in
6.062 in
7 in

15)

15 in
12 in
9 in

16)

19 in
15 in
13 in

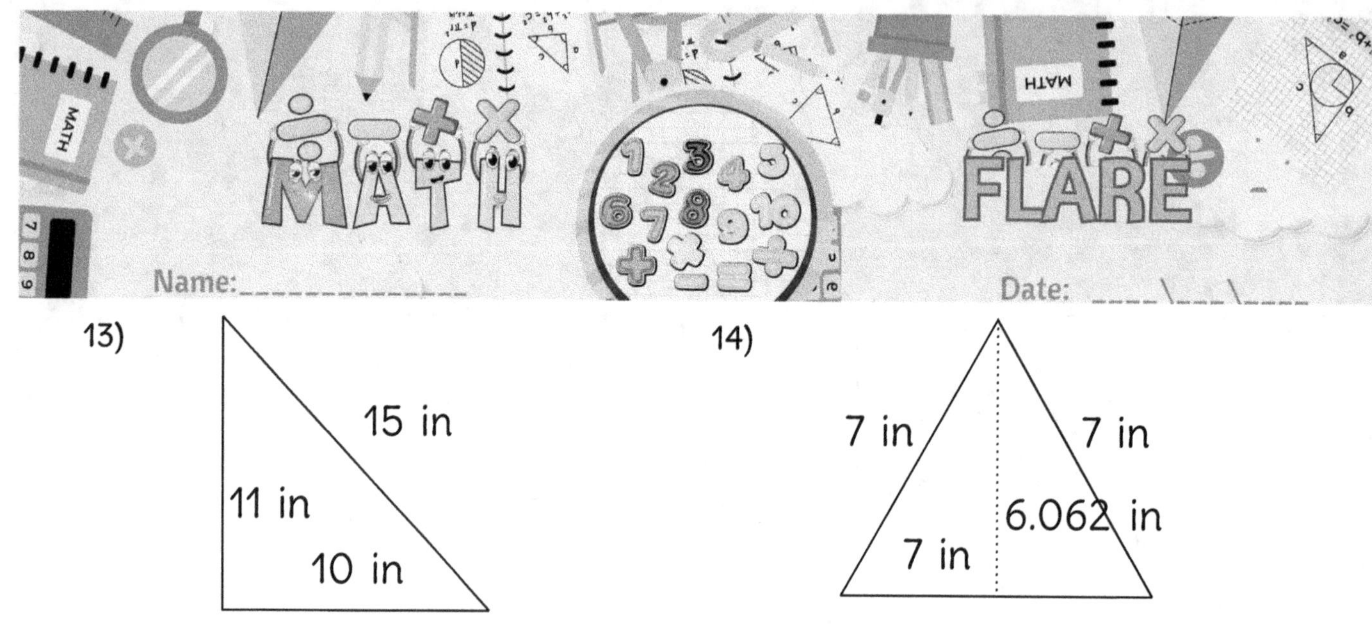

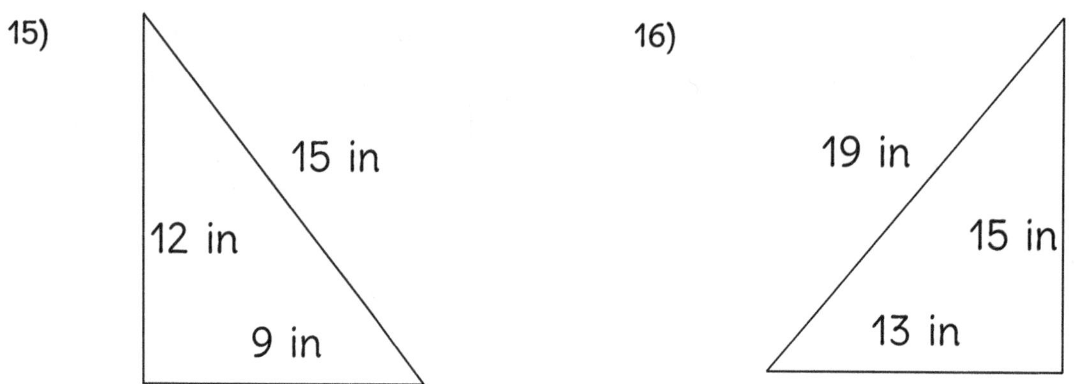

17)

25 in
18 in
18 in

18)

8 in
8 in
8 in
6.928 in

19)

12 in
12 in
10.39 in
12 in

20)

10 in
10 in
8.93 in
9 in

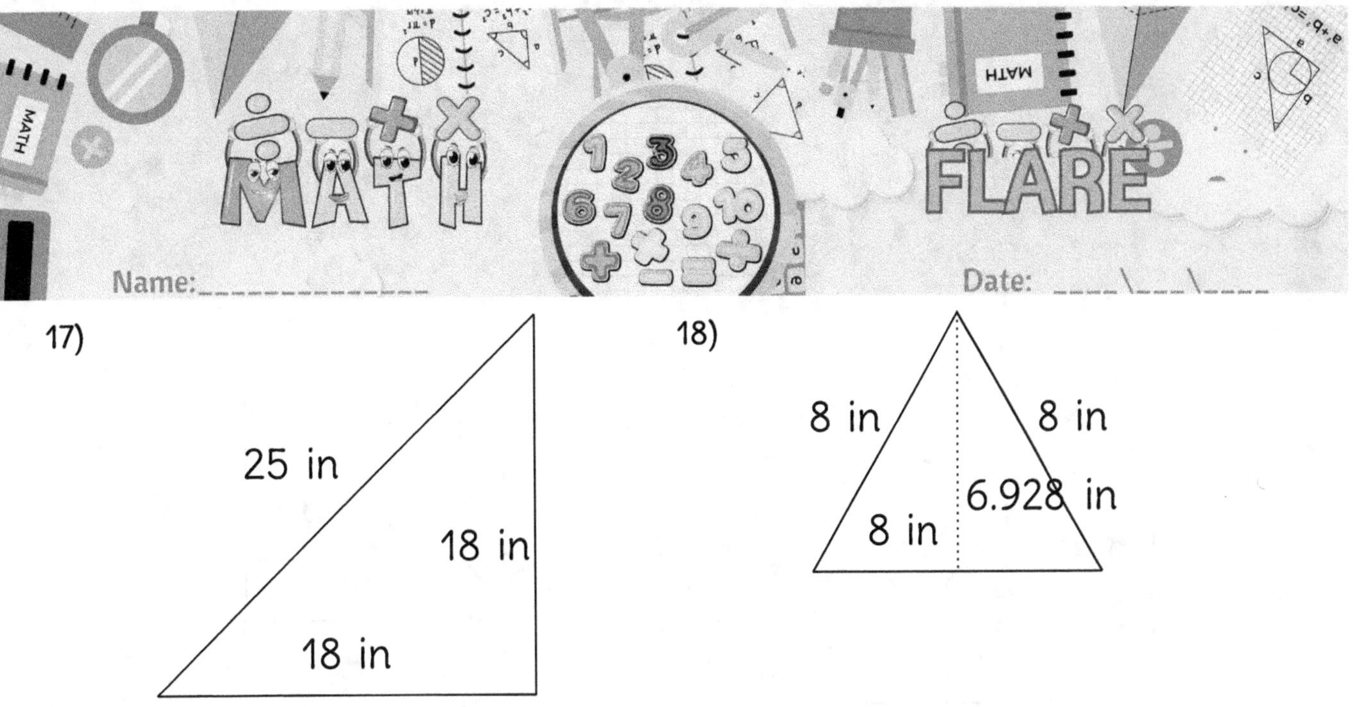

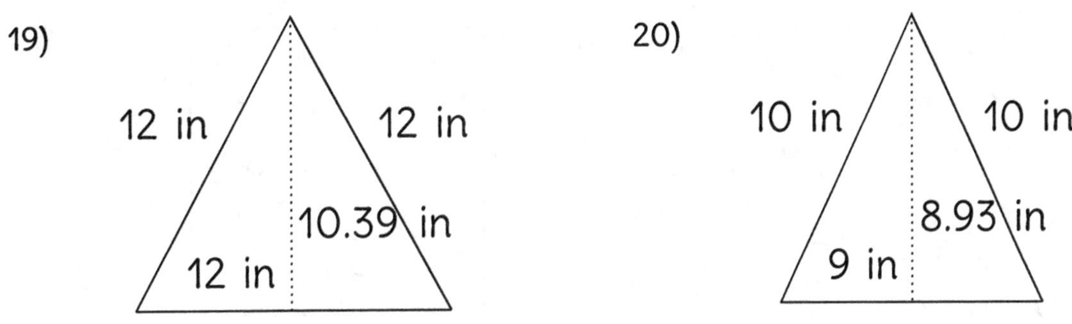

Name:
Date:

21)

21 in
16 in
13 in

22)

17 in
13 in
11 in

23)

17 in
17 in
14.72 in
17 in

24)

9 in
9 in

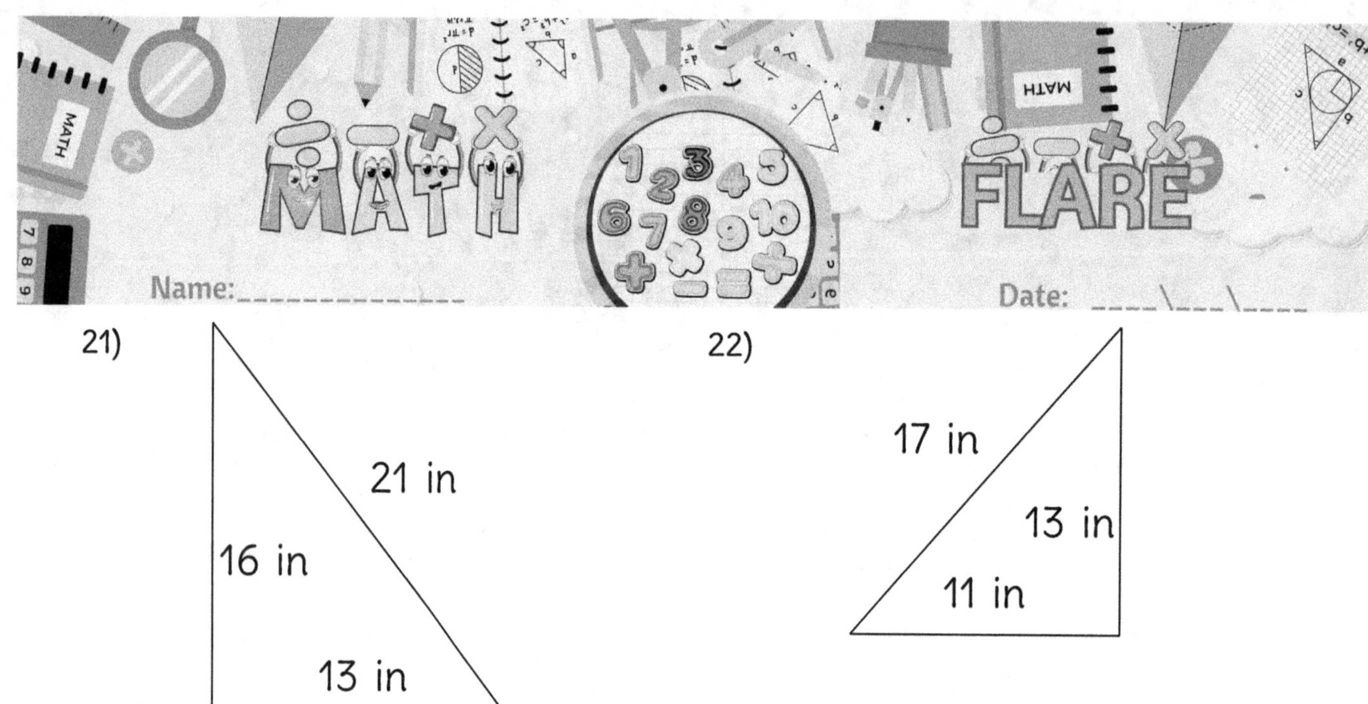

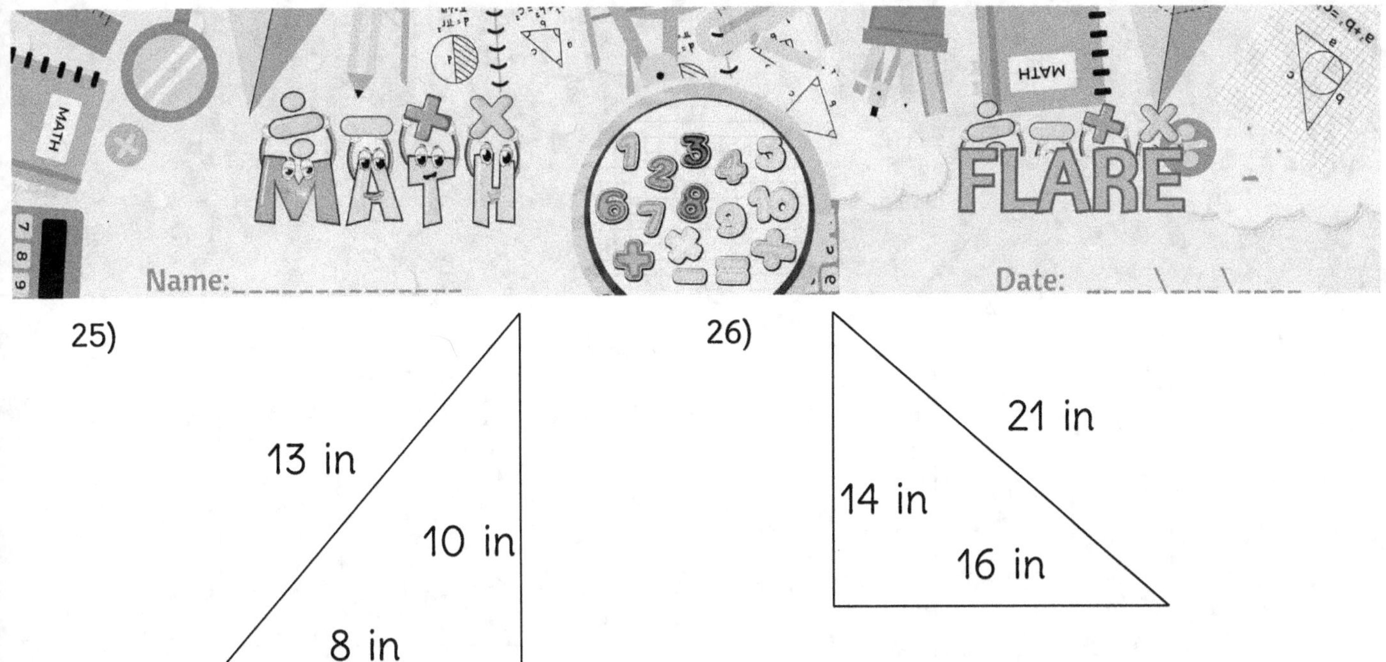

25)

13 in
10 in
8 in

26)

21 in
14 in
16 in

27)

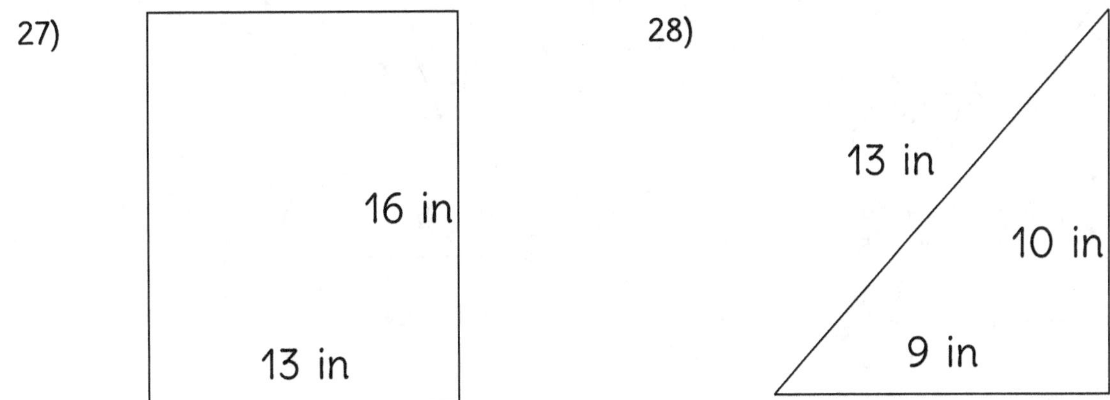

28)

13 in
10 in
9 in

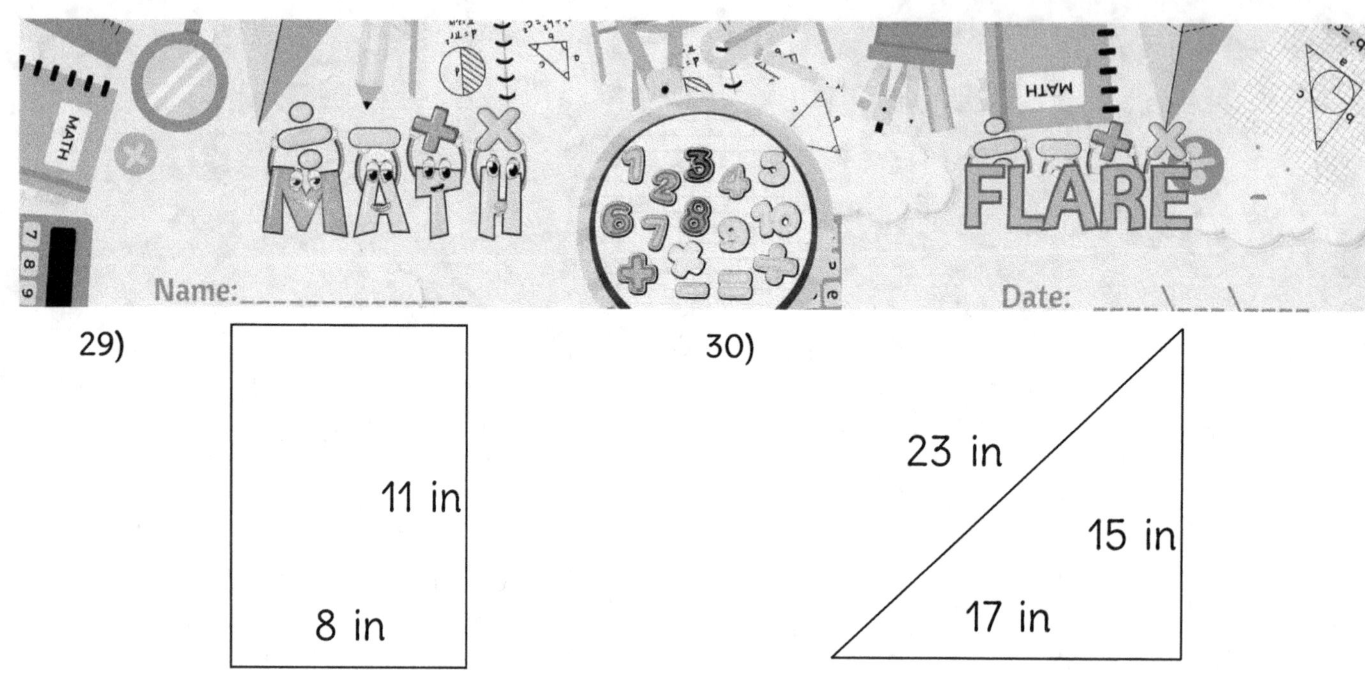

29)

11 in

8 in

30)

23 in

15 in

17 in

31)

20 in

16 in

12 in

32)

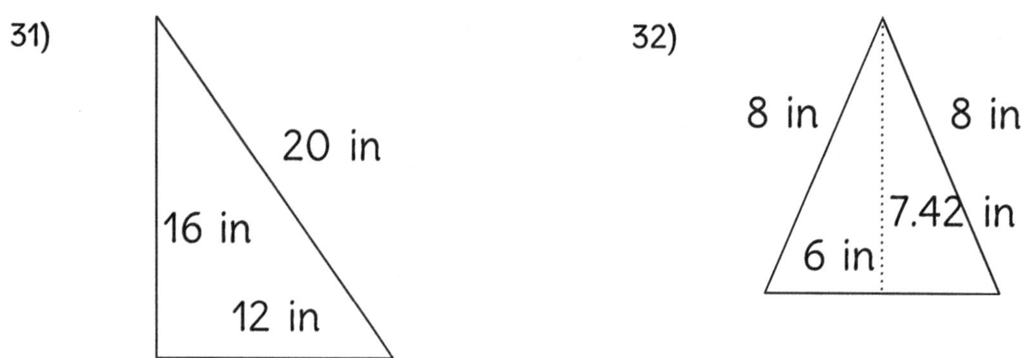

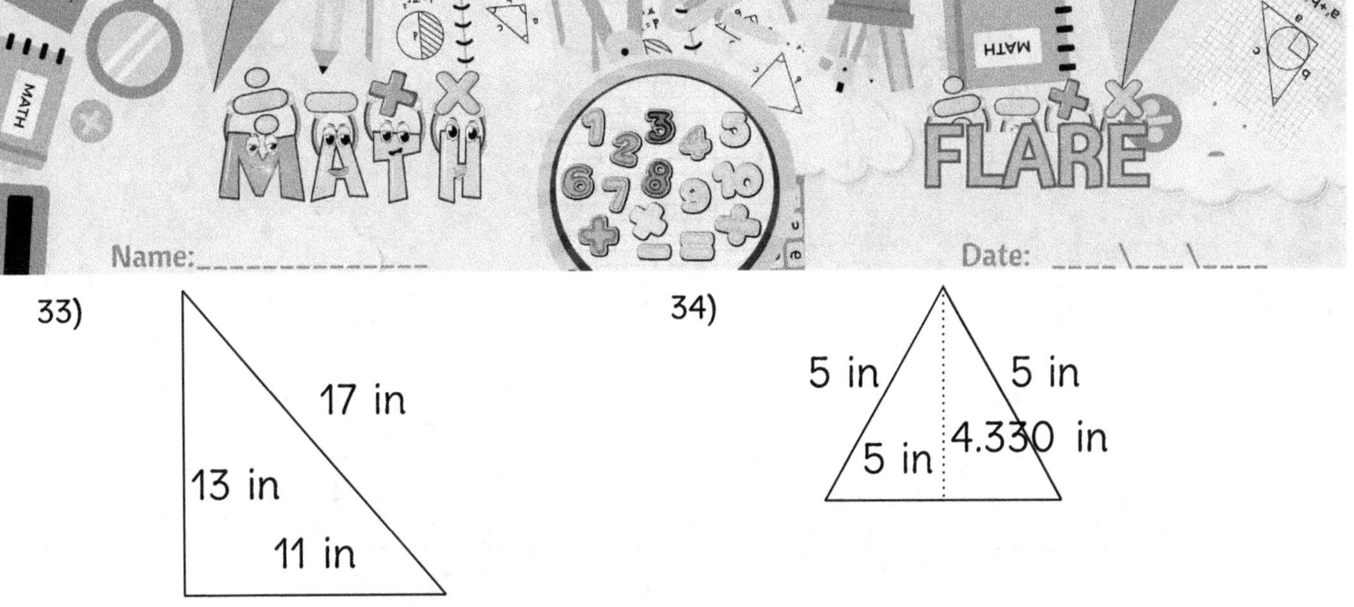

33)

17 in
13 in
11 in

34)

5 in
5 in
5 in
4.330 in

35)

17 in
14 in
10 in

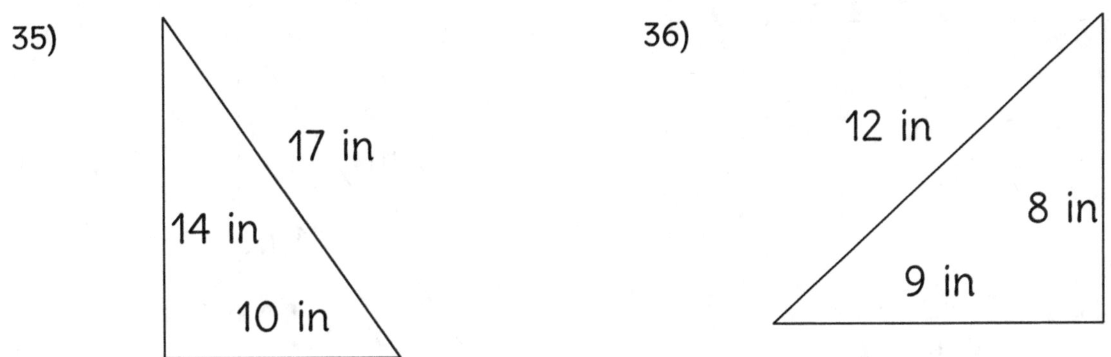

36)

Name:
Date:

37)

11 in
11 in
10.25 in
8 in

38)

15 in
15 in
13.75 in
12 in

39)

11 in
12 in

40)

13 in
11 in
8 in

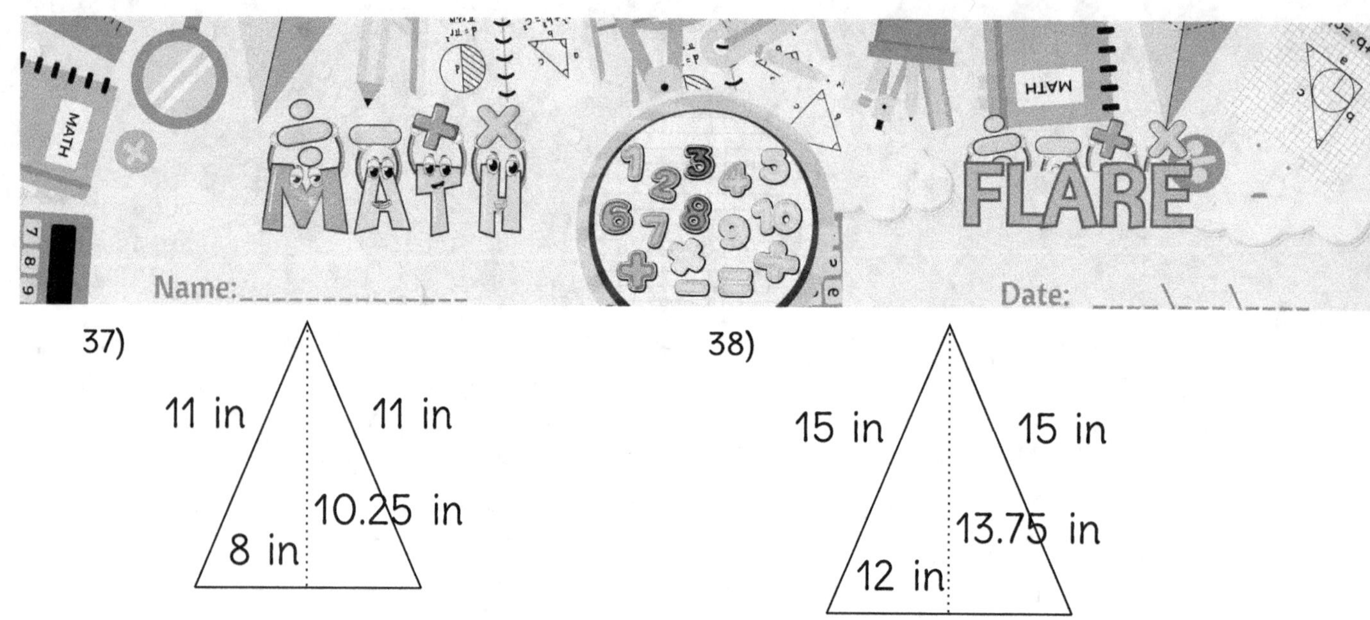

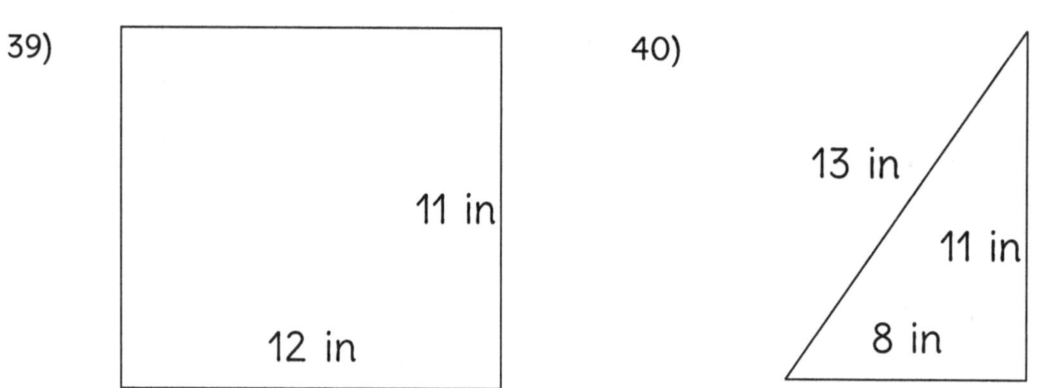

MATH
FLARE
Name:
Date:

41)

16 in
16 in
13.856 in
16 in

42)

14 in
13 in

43)

10 in
10 in
8.660 in
10 in

44)

13 in
13 in
12 in
10 in

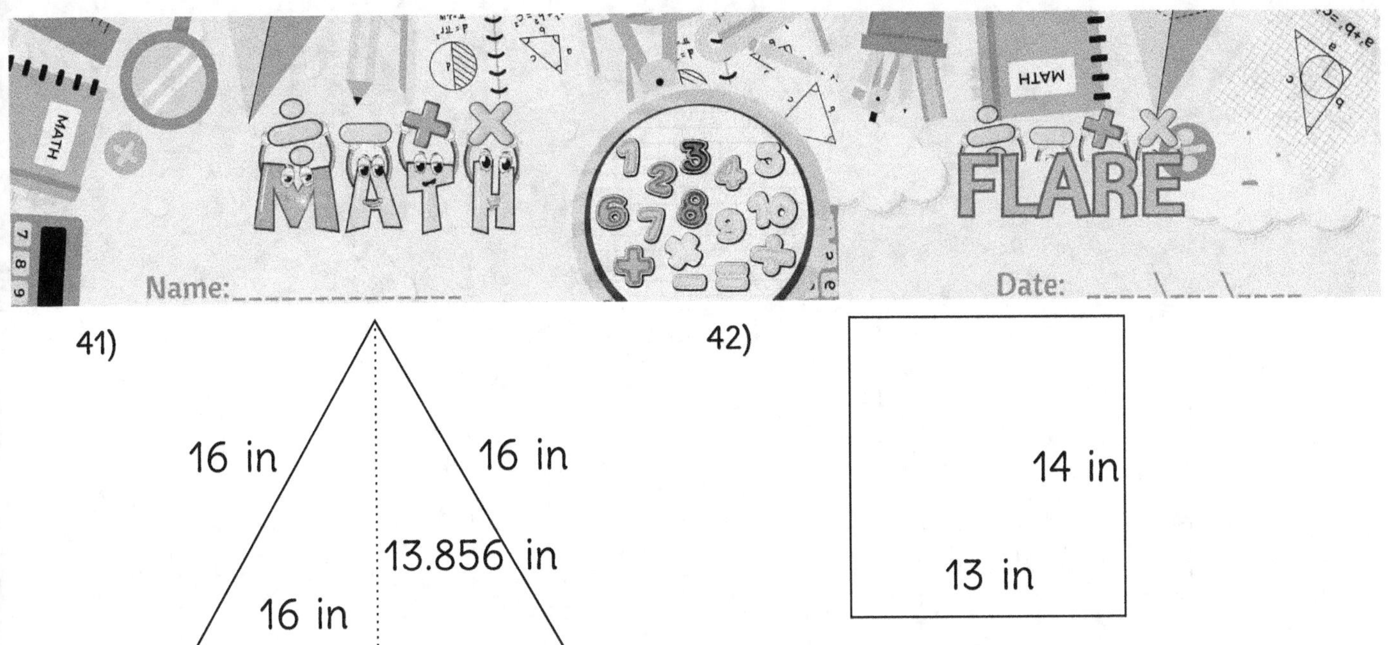

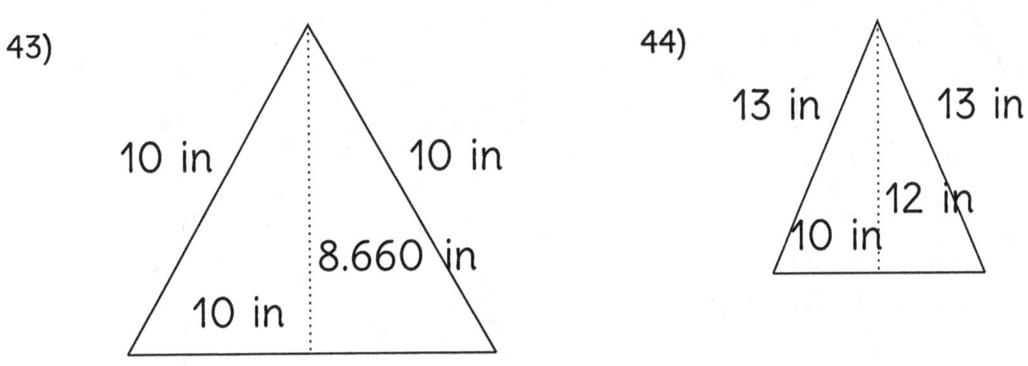

MATH
FLARE
Name:
Date:

45)

7 in
8 in

46)

19 in
14 in
13 in

47)

14 in
14 in
12.124 in
14 in

48)

16 in
12 in
10 in

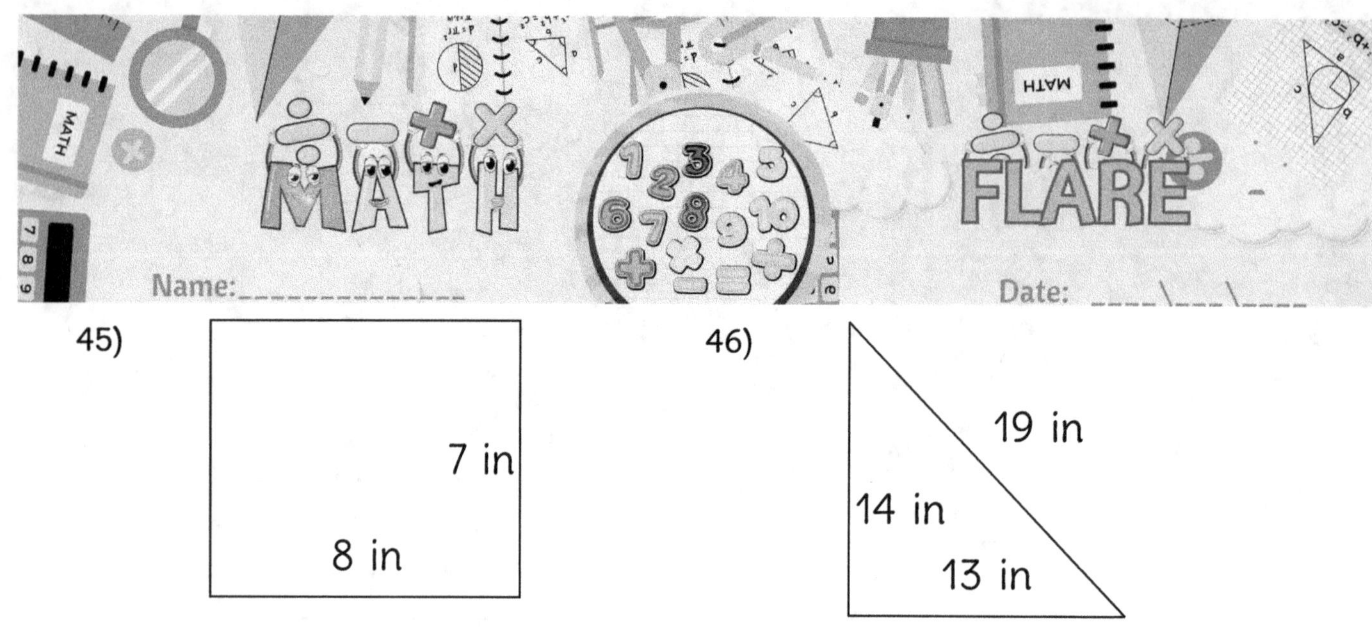

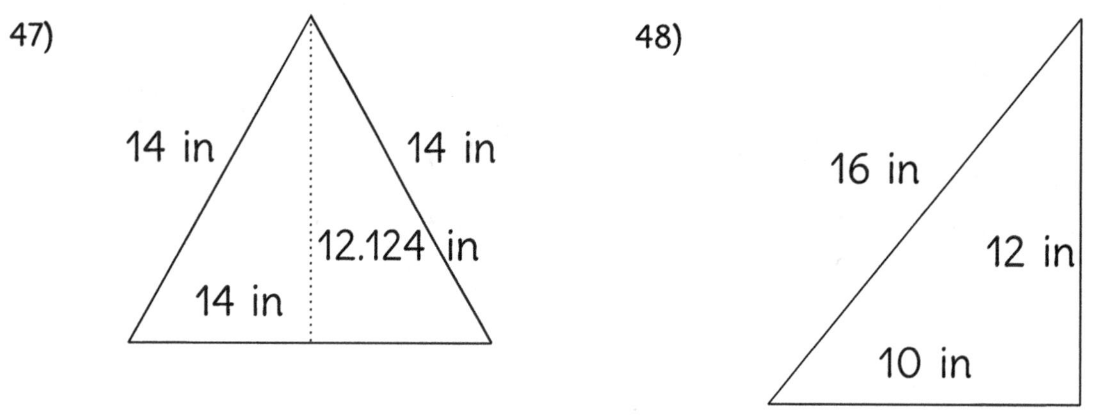

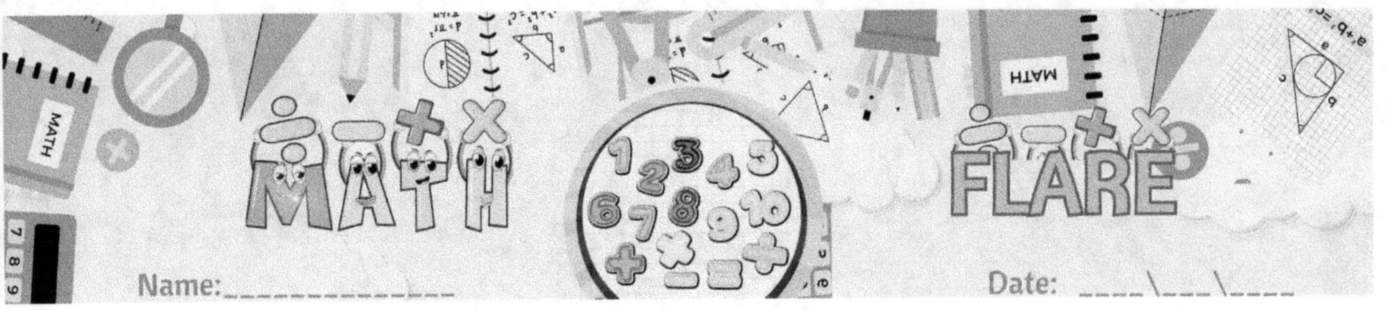

Area and Circumference

Calculate the circumference of each circle. Pi Value = 3.14

1)
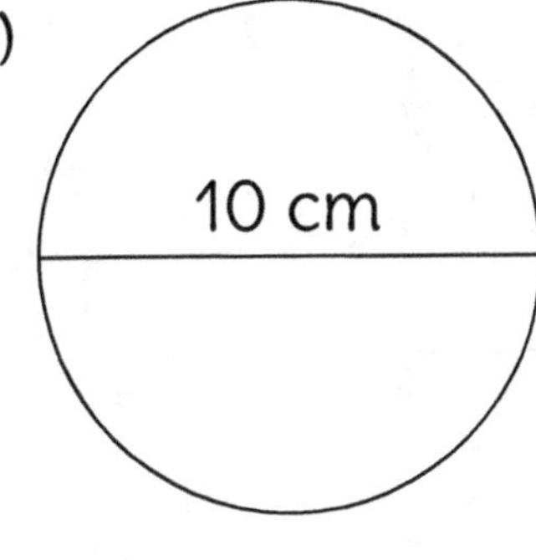

____

____

2)
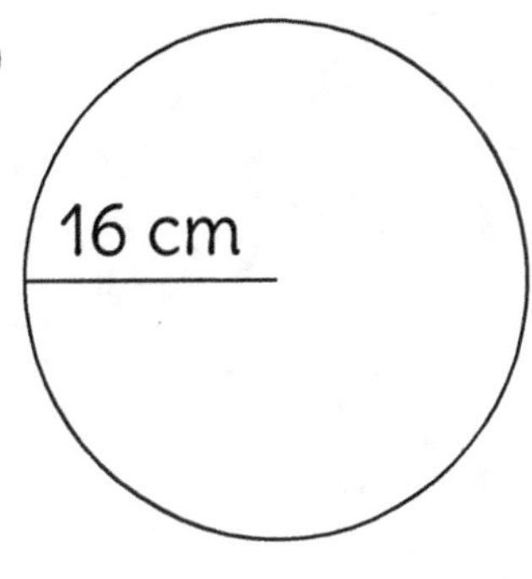

____

____

3)
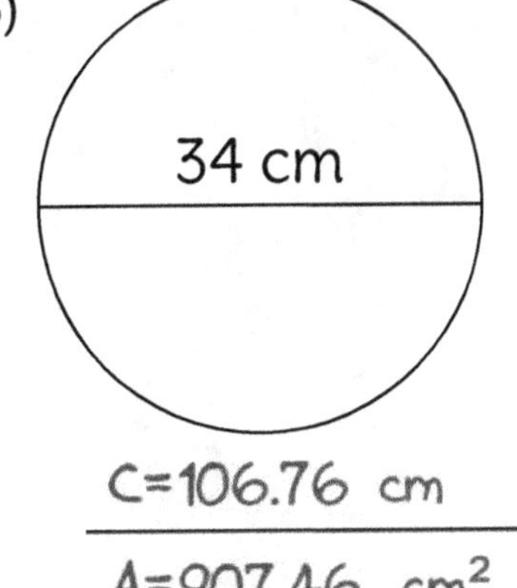

C=106.76 cm

A=907.46 cm^2

4)
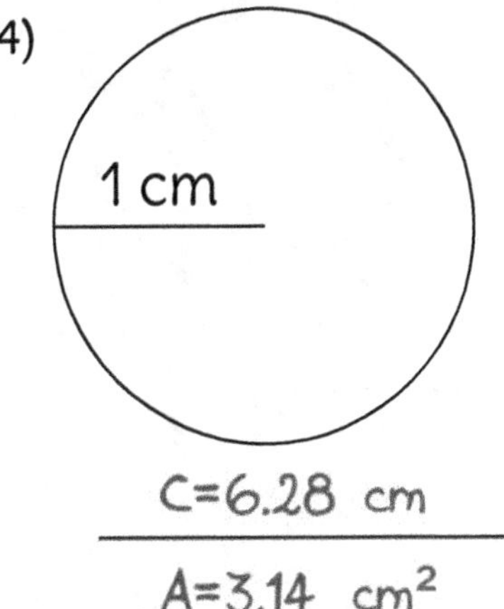

C=6.28 cm

A=3.14 cm^2

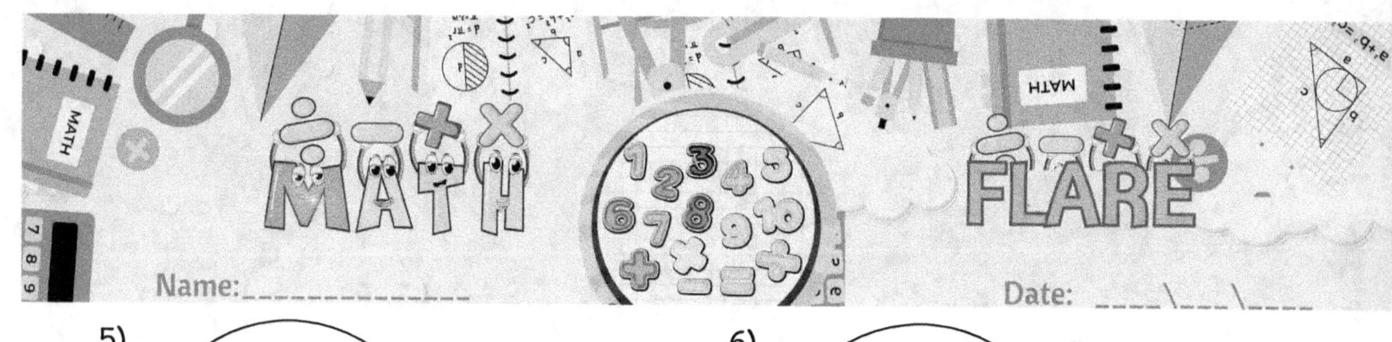

5)

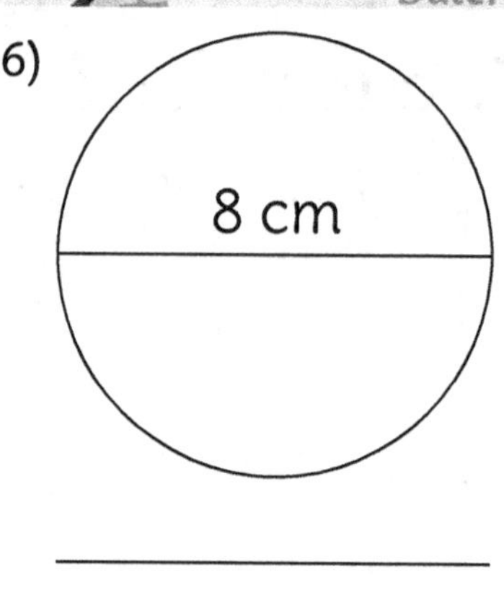

____

____

6)

8 cm

____

____

7)

2 cm

____

____

8)

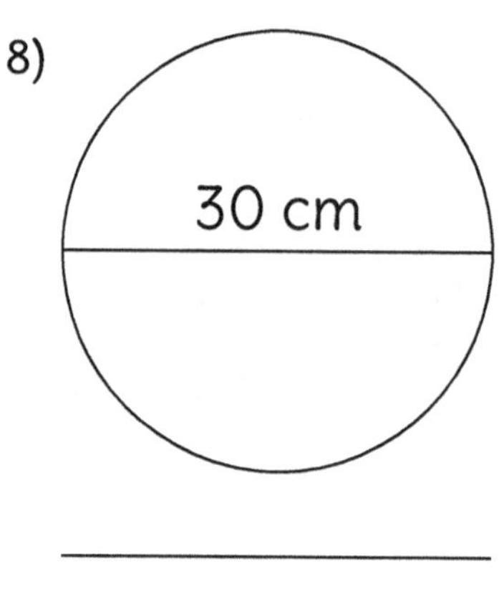

____

____

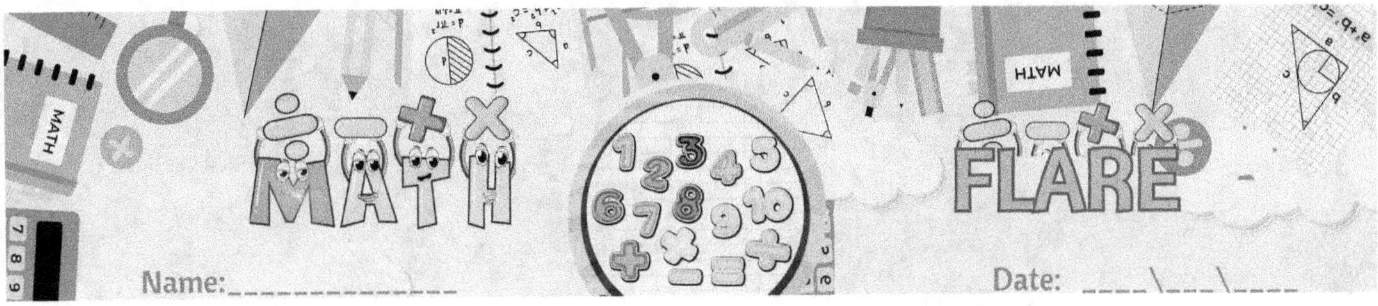

9)

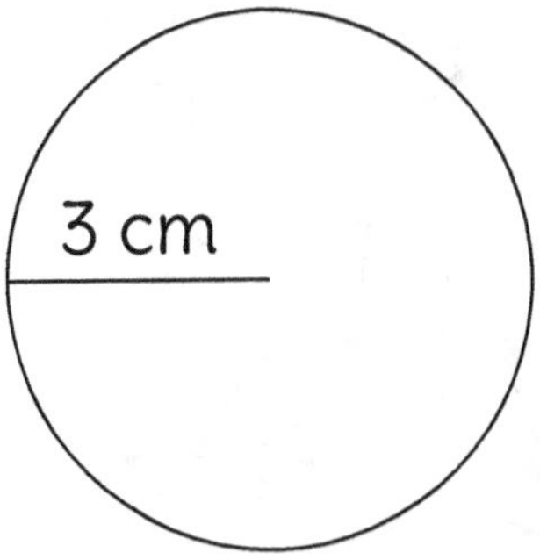

3 cm

____

____

10)

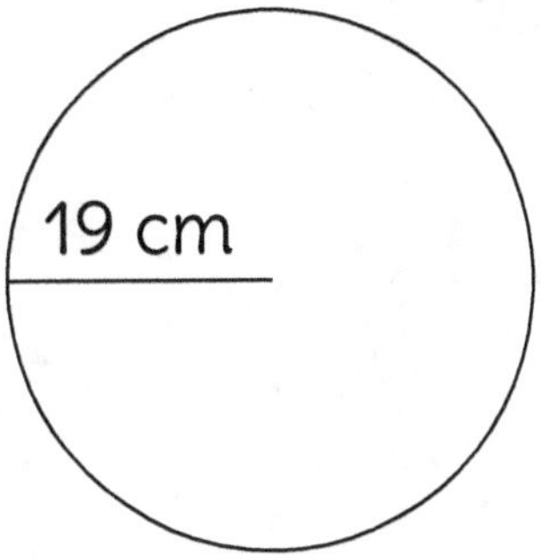

19 cm

____

____

11)

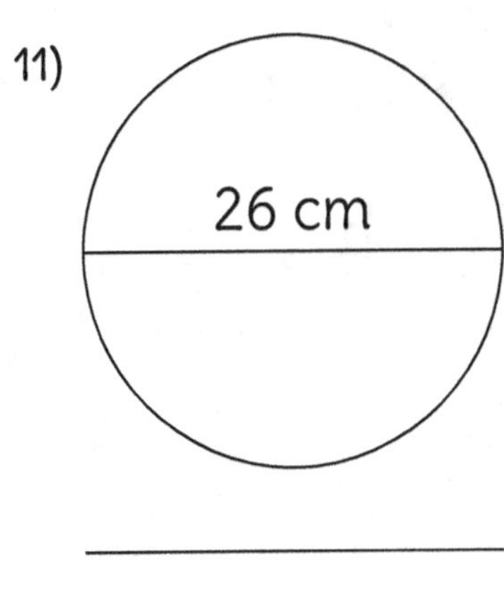

26 cm

____

____

12)

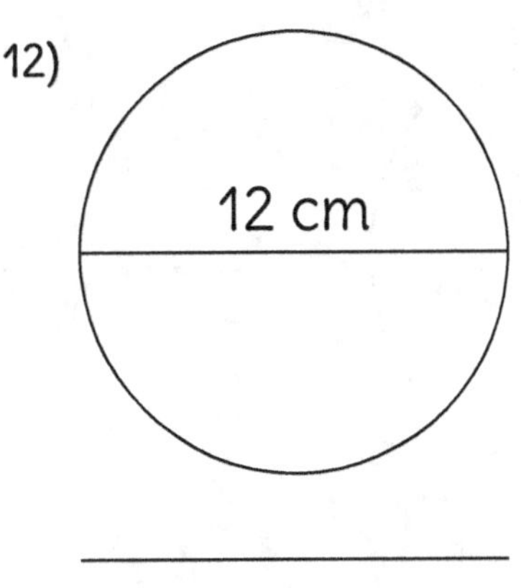

12 cm

____

____

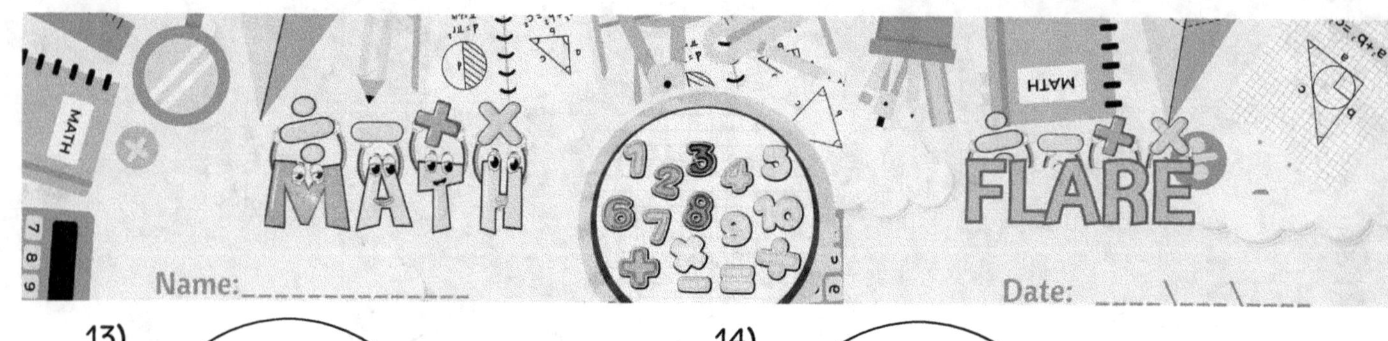

13)

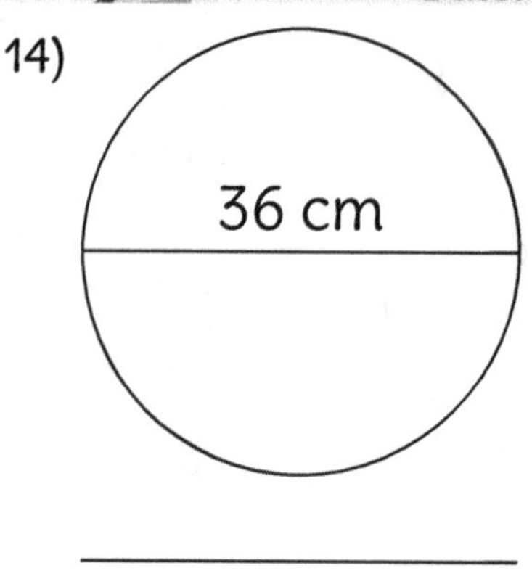

____

____

14)

____

____

15)

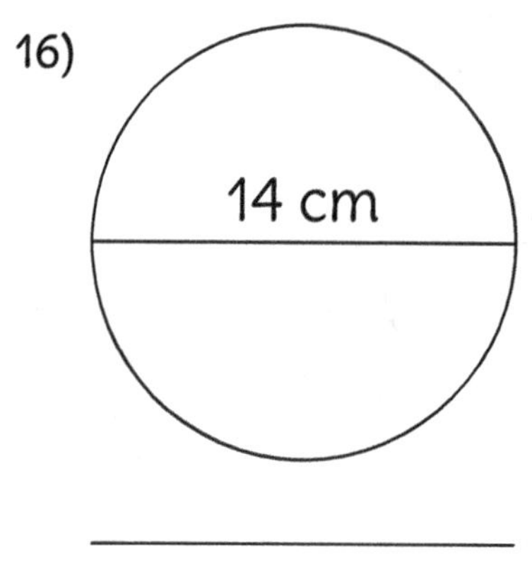

____

____

16)

____

____

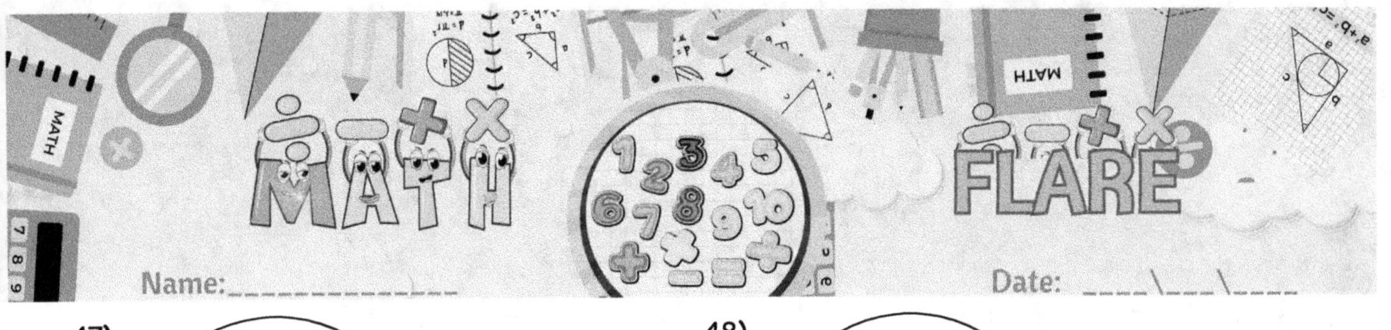

17)

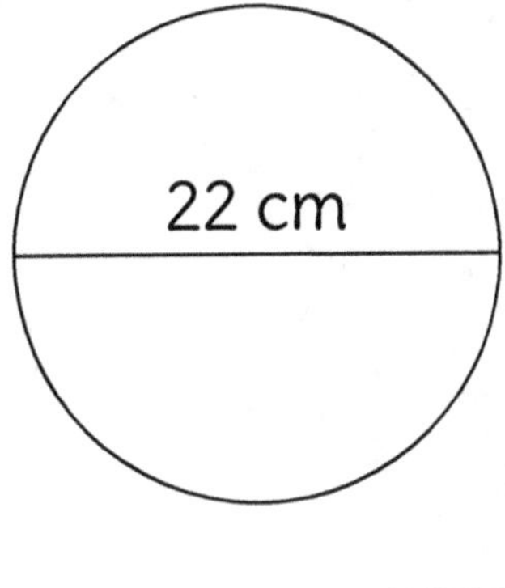

____
____

18)

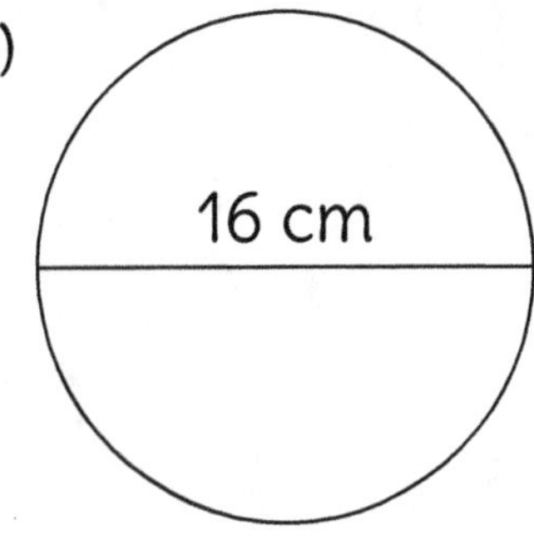

____
____

19)

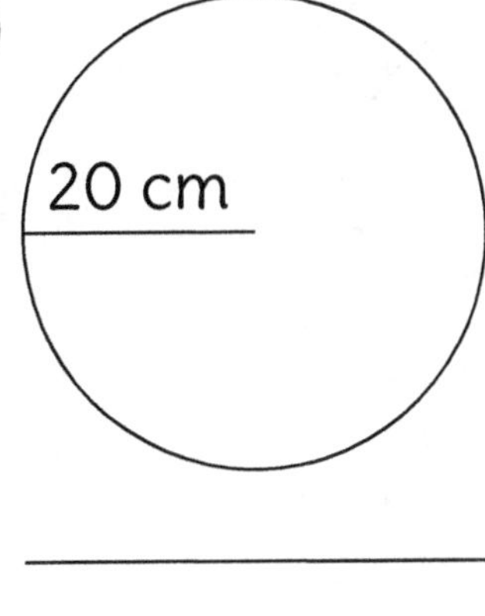

____
____

20)

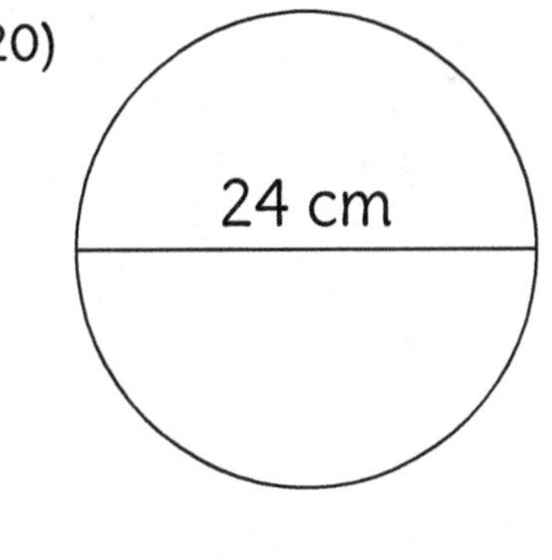

____
____

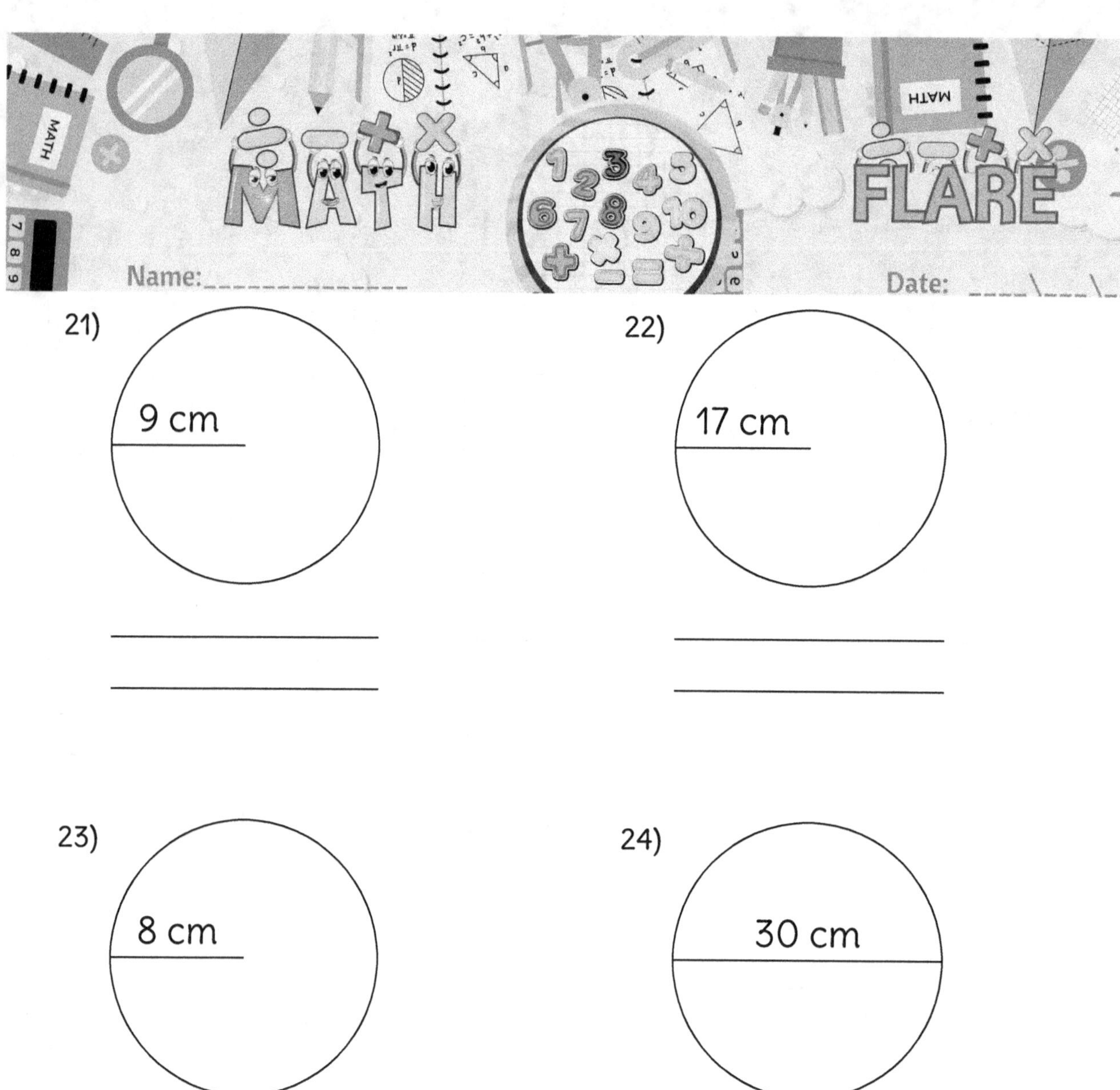
21)
9 cm

22)
17 cm

23)
8 cm

24)
30 cm

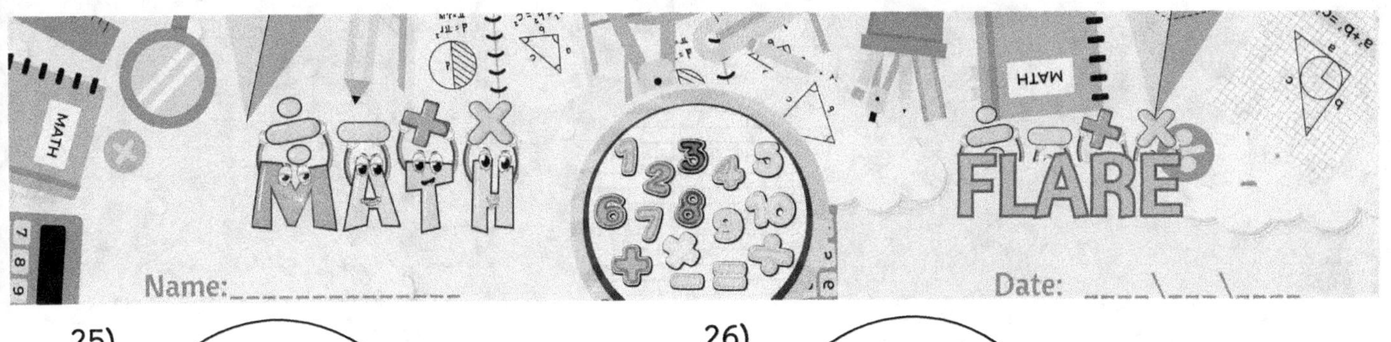

25)

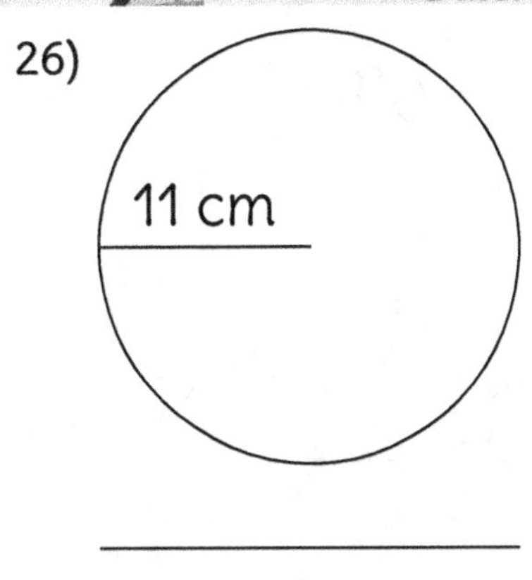

____
____

26)

11 cm

____
____

27)

6 cm

____
____

28)

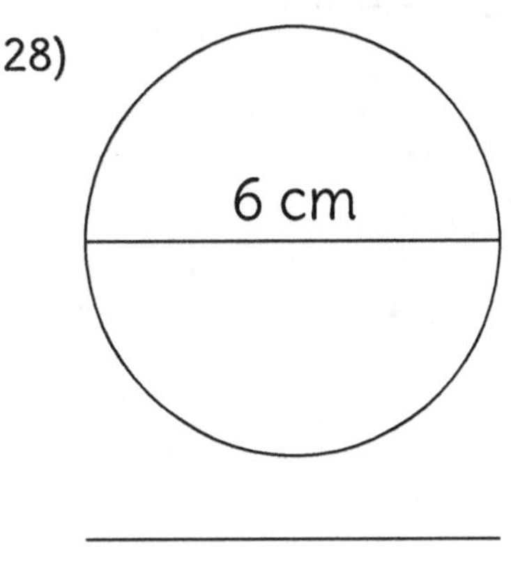

____
____

Measuring Angles

1)

140o

2)

3)

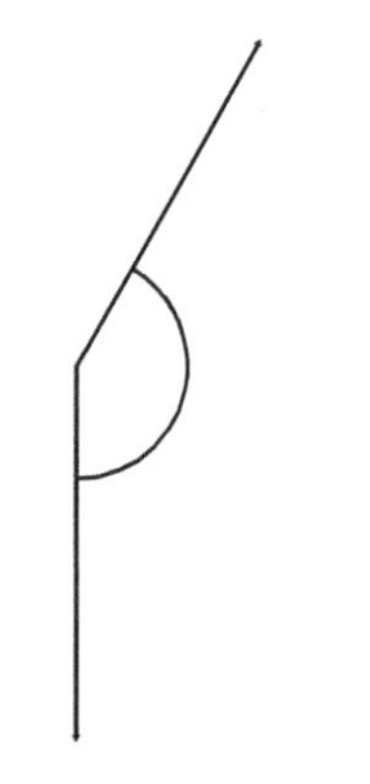

4)

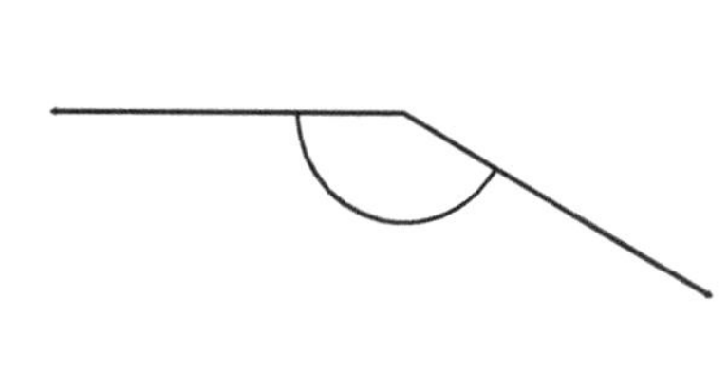

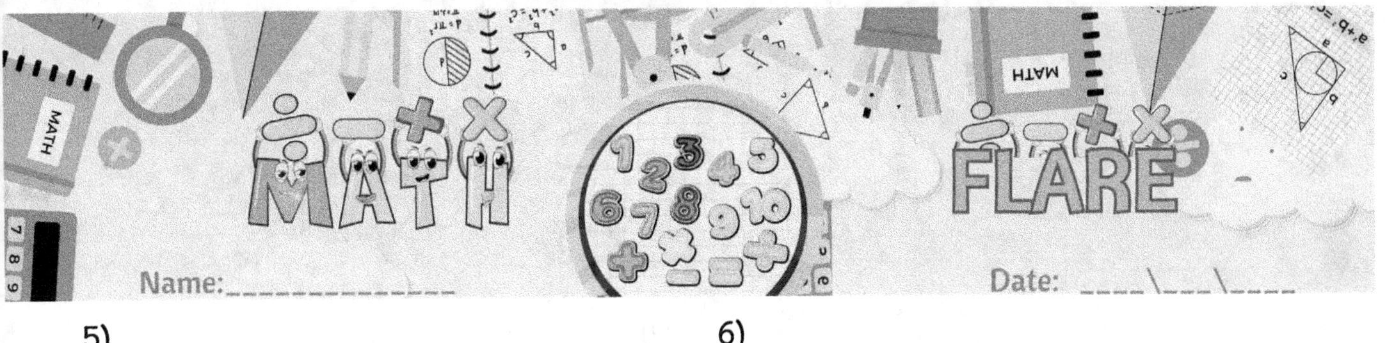

5)

6)

7)

8)

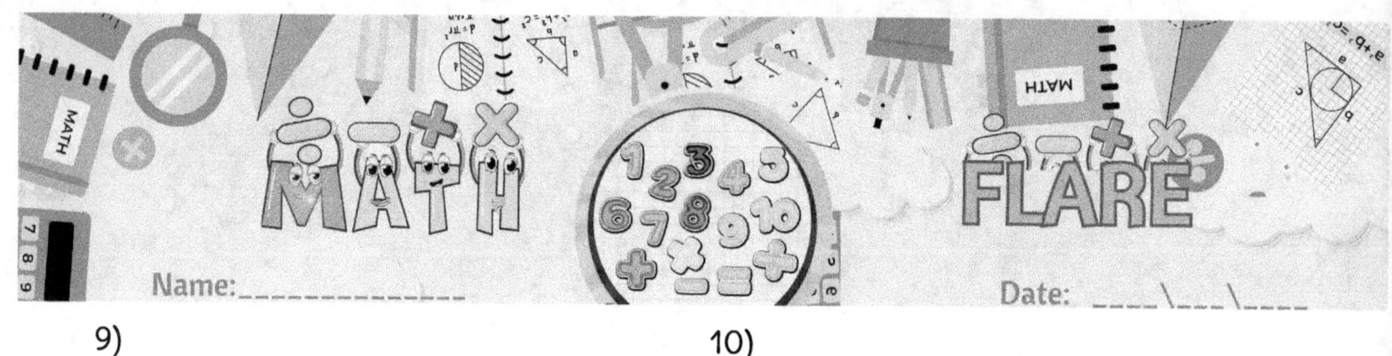

Name:_________________   Date: ______________

9)

10)

11)

12)

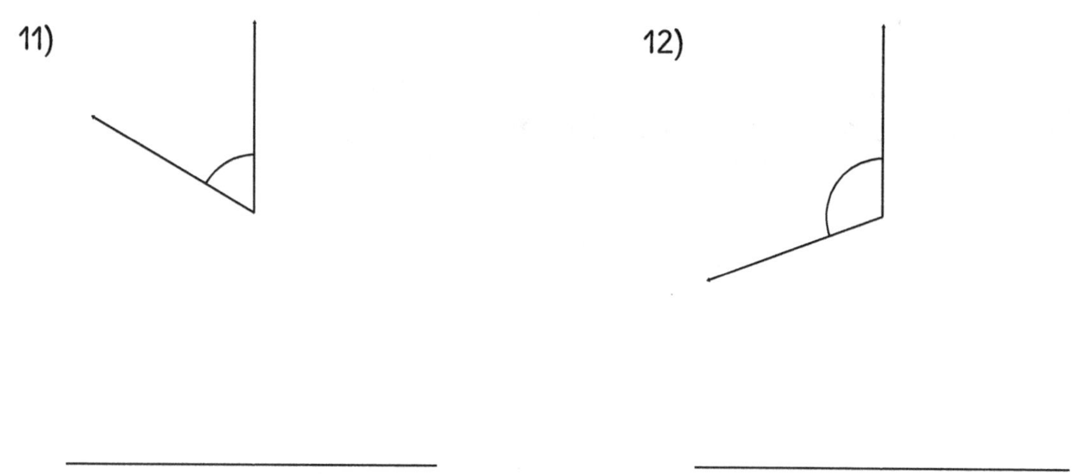

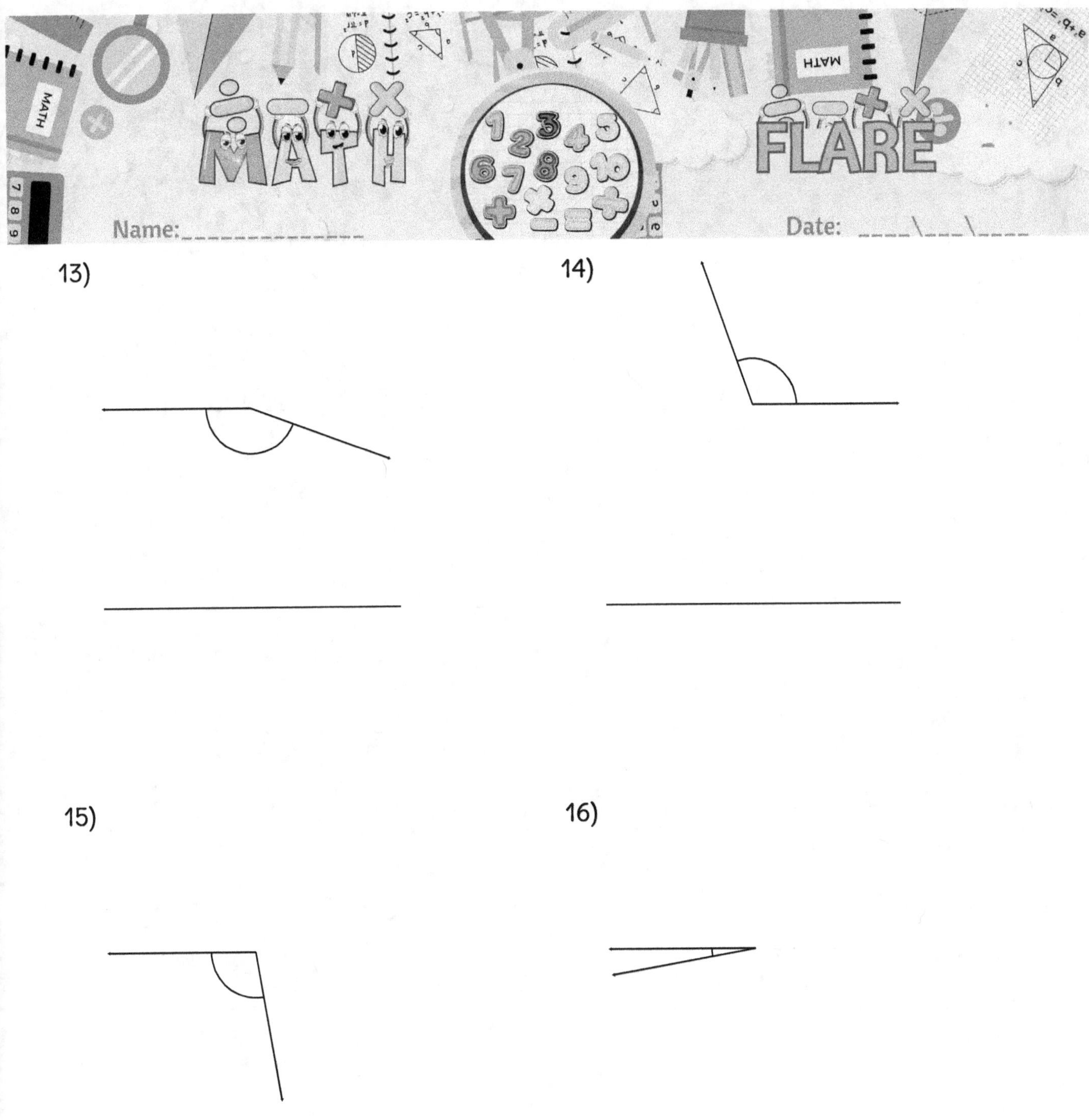

Name:
Date:
13)
14)
15)
16)

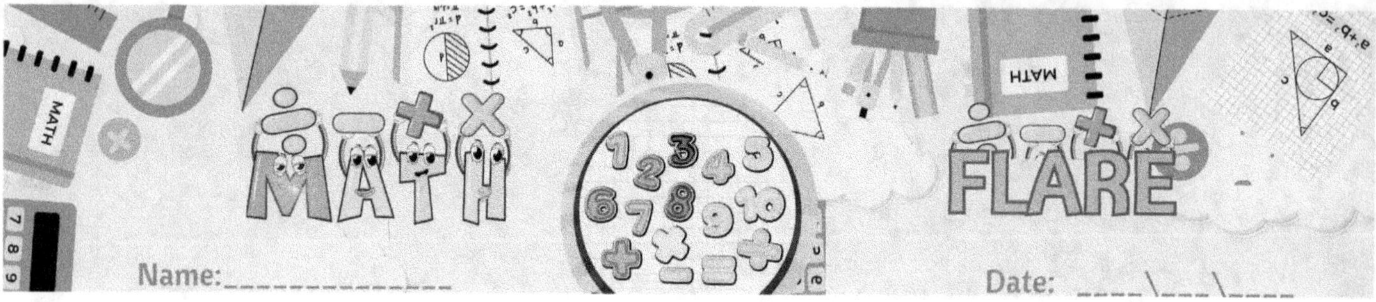

17)

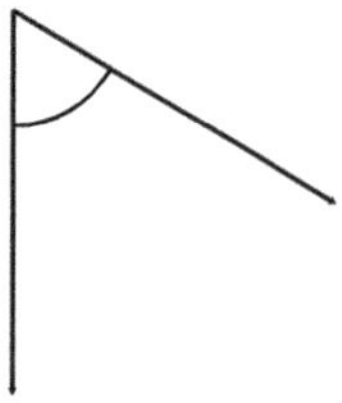

18)

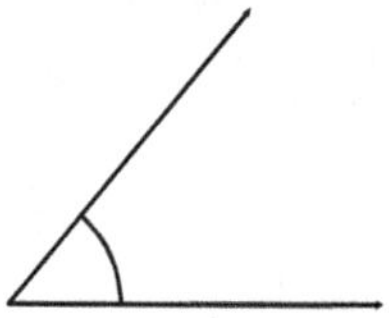

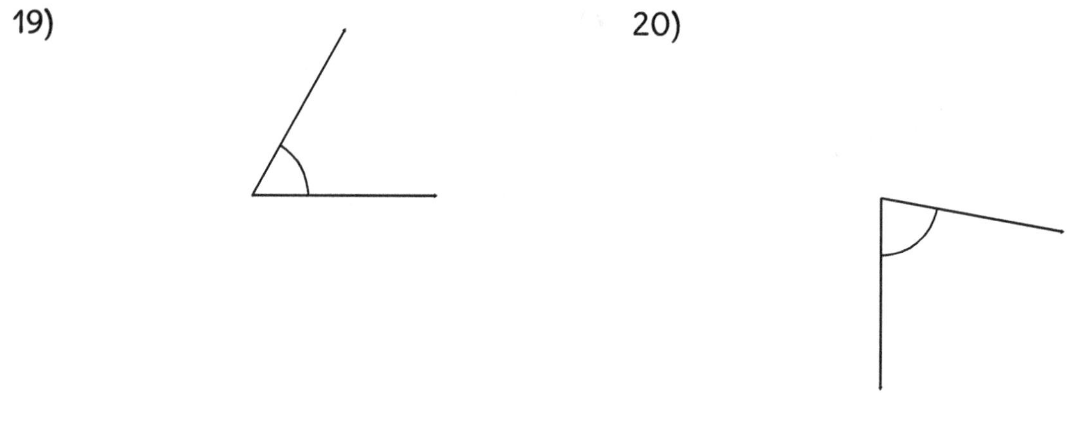

19)

20)

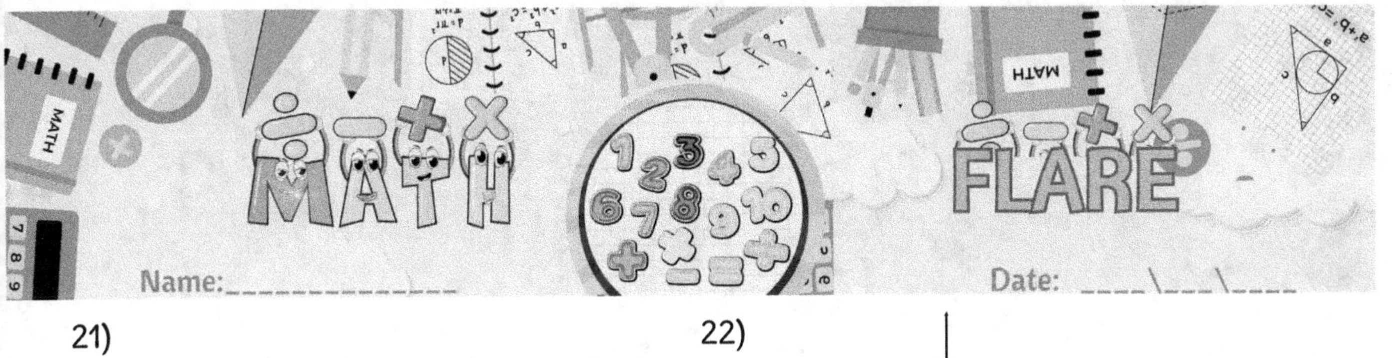

21)

____

22)

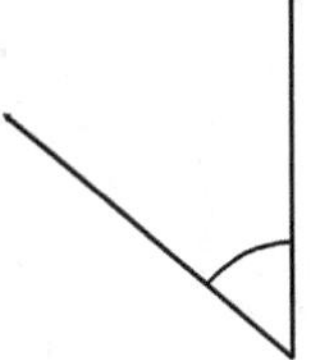

____

23)

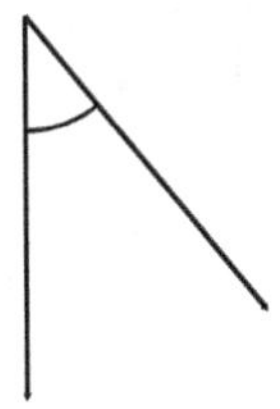

____

24)

____

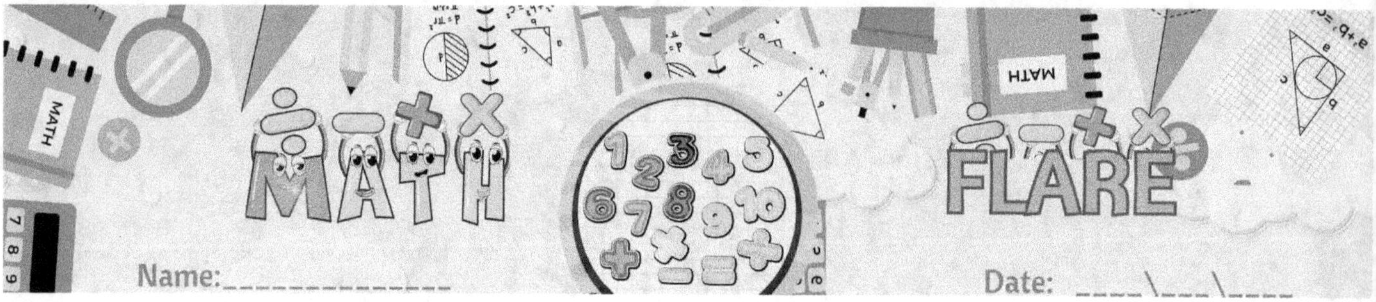

25)

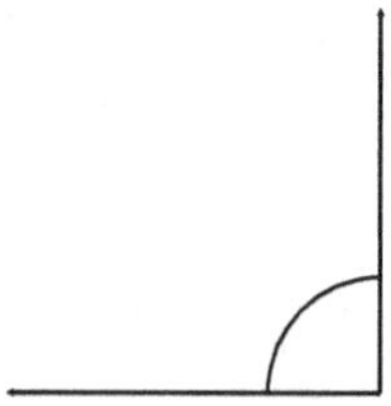

26)

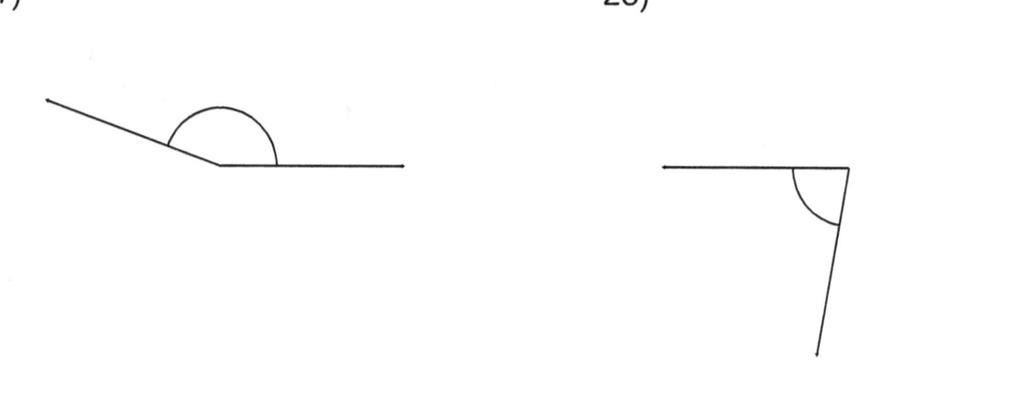

27)

28)

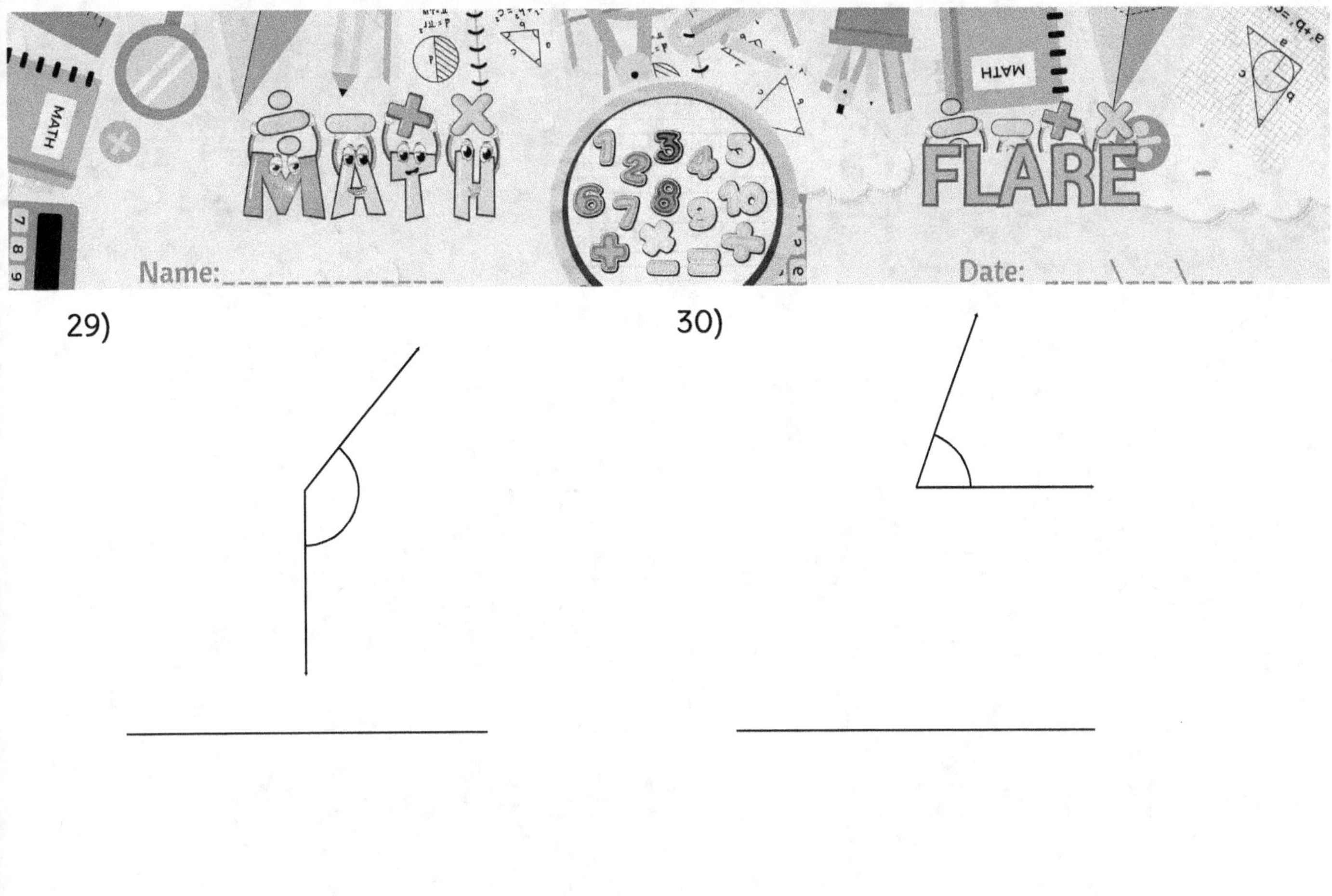

29)

30)

31)

32)

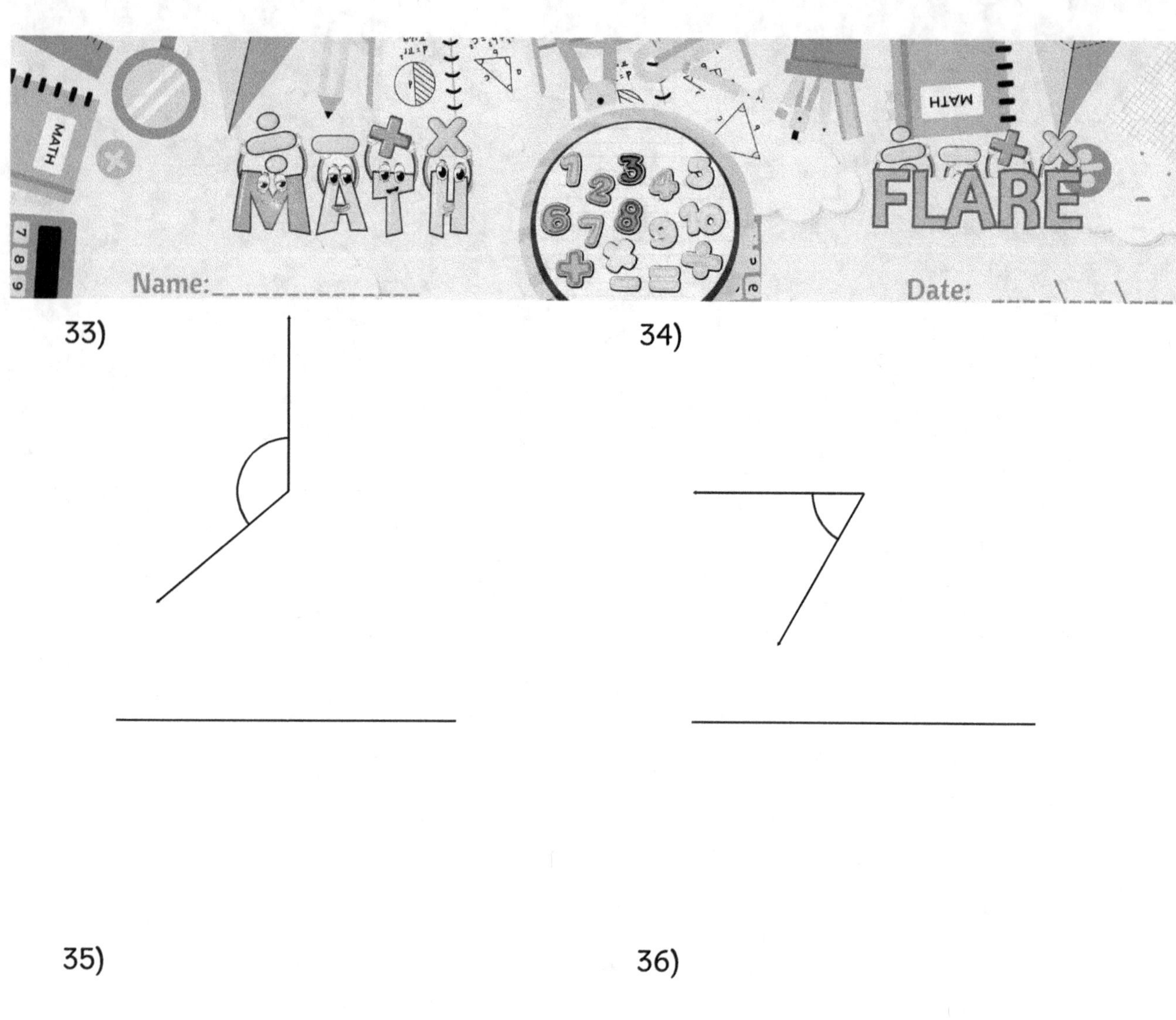

33)

34)

35)

36)

37)

38)

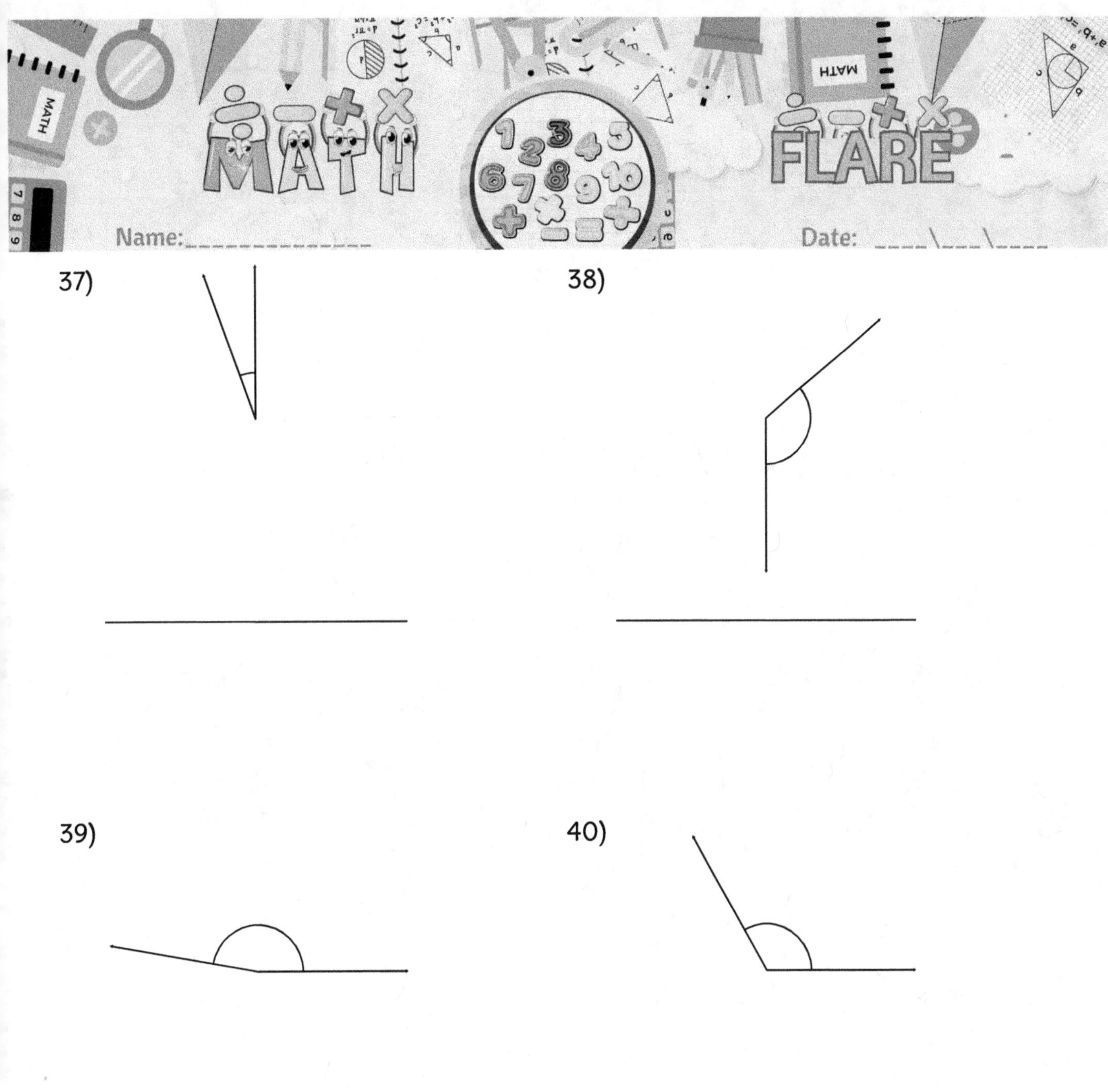

39)

40)

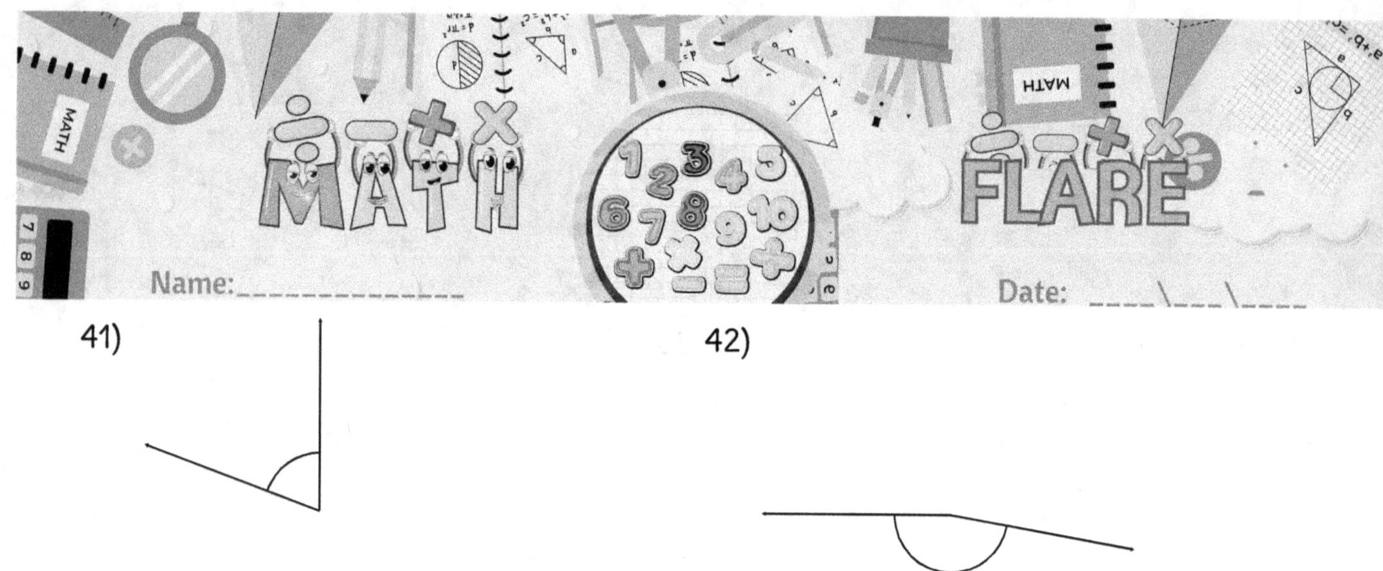

41)

42)

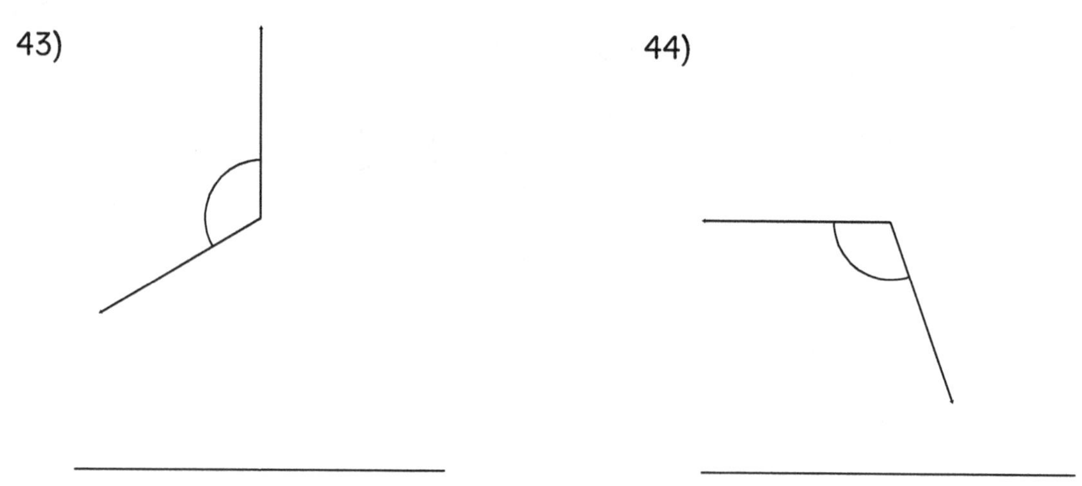

43)

44)

Chapter. 06

Unit Conversion

Metric Conversion
1 meter (m) = 100 centimeters (cm)
1 meter (m) = 1000 millimeters (mm)
1 kilometer (km) = 1000 meters (m)
1 hectare (ha) = 10000 square meters (m^2)
1 square meter (m^2) = 10000 square centimeters (cm^2)
1 cubic meter (m^3) = 1000 liters (L)

Weights and Measures
1 kilogram (kg) = 1000 grams (g)
1 liter (L) = 1000 milliliters (mL)
1 tonne (t) = 1000 kilograms (kg)
1 centimeter (cm) = 10 millimeters (mm)
1 gram (g) = 1000 milligrams (mg)
1 kilometer (km) = 100000 centimeters (cm)

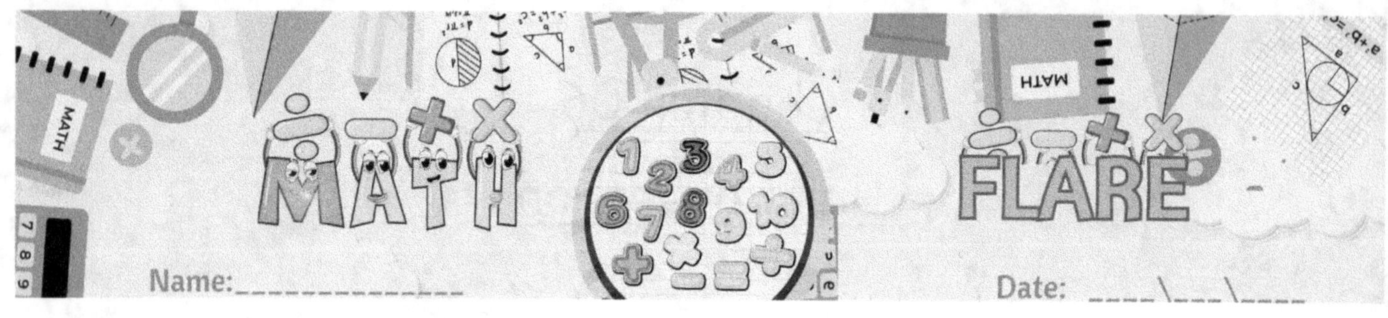

Metric Conversion

Convert the given measures.

1) 1 kl = _____264.172_____ gal

2) 6 kg = _____0.007_____ t

3) 4 g = _____________ t

4) 4 kg = _____________ t

5) 1 g = _____________ t

6) 7 kl = _____________ gal

7) 8 kg = _____________ lb

8) 2 l = _____________ gal

9) 4 kg = _____________ lb

10) 3 kg = _____________ lb

11) 7 g = _____________ lb

12) 6 l = _____________ gal

13) 7 l = _____________ gal

14) 9 km = _____________ mi

15) 9 g = _____________ lb

16) 8 g = _____________ t

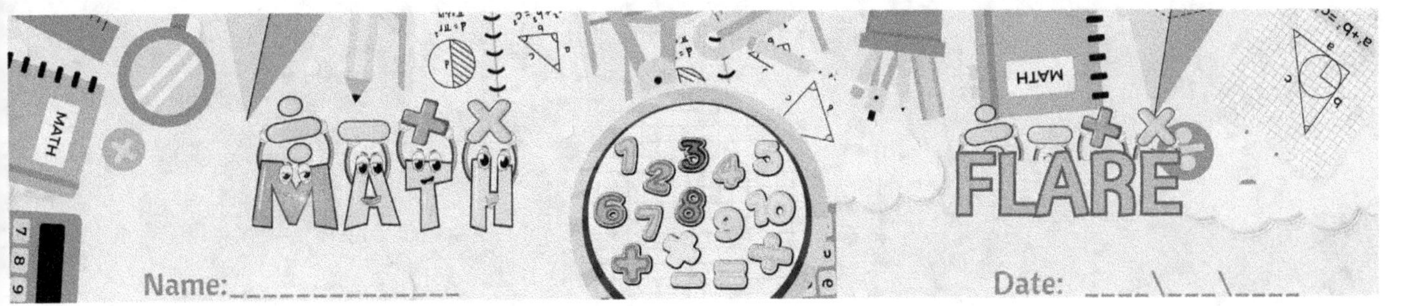

17) 3 l = _________________ gal

18) 5 l = _________________ gal

19) 9 km = _________________ mi

20) 1 kg = _________________ lb

21) 7 kl = _________________ gal

22) 8 m = _________________ mi

23) 8 l = _________________ gal

24) 5 km = _________________ mi

25) 4 kl = _________________ gal

26) 3 km = _________________ mi

27) 2 g = _________________ t

28) 8 kg = _________________ lb

29) 8 l = _________________ gal

30) 1 g = _________________ t

31) 6 kg = _________________ t

32) 7 km = _________________ mi

33) 7 kg = _________________ lb

34) 2 m = _________________ mi

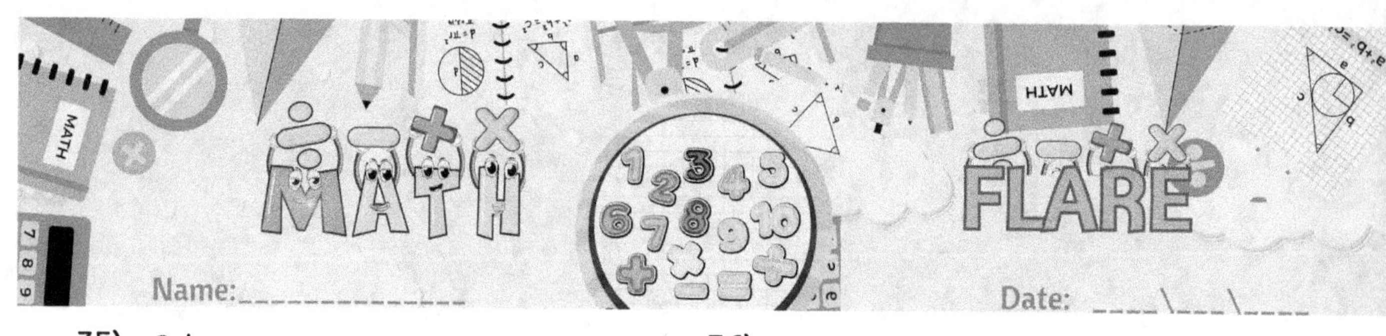

35) 2 km = _____________ mi   36) 1 kg = _____________ t

37) 3 kl = _____________ gal   38) 7 kg = _____________ lb

39) 6 l = _____________ gal   40) 6 m = _____________ mi

41) 5 g = _____________ t   42) 2 kl = _____________ gal

43) 4 g = _____________ t   44) 9 g = _____________ t

45) 1 l = _____________ gal   46) 7 m = _____________ mi

47) 5 kg = _____________ lb   48) 8 l = _____________ gal

49) 7 kl = _____________ gal   50) 4 m = _____________ mi

51) 7 l = _____________ gal   52) 6 g = _____________ t

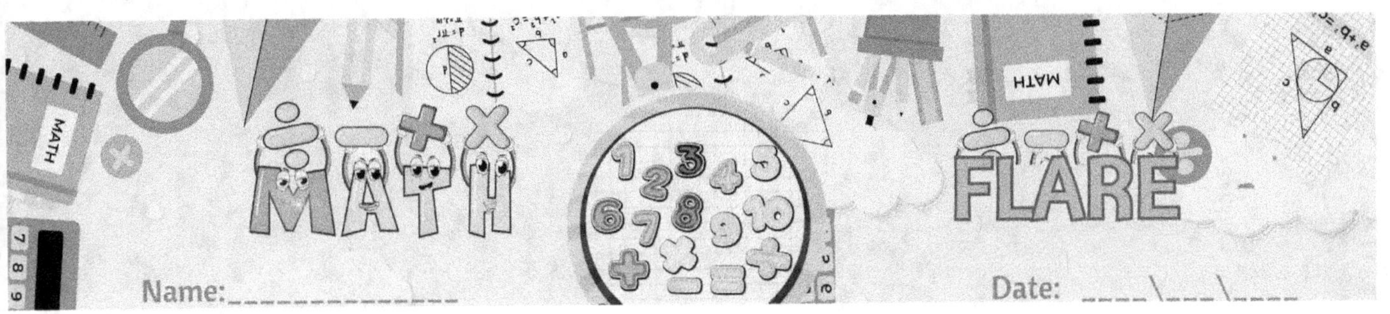

53) 8 kl = _________________ gal   54) 2 kg = _________________ t

55) 5 kg = _________________ lb   56) 2 l = _________________ gal

57) 7 g = _________________ t   58) 7 kg = _________________ t

59) 1 kg = _________________ lb   60) 8 kg = _________________ lb

61) 6 kg = _________________ t   62) 1 kl = _________________ gal

63) 3 m = _________________ mi   64) 4 l = _________________ gal

65) 6 km = _________________ mi   66) 1 g = _________________ t

67) 7 kg = _________________ lb   68) 6 g = _________________ lb

69) 8 kl = _________________ gal   70) 9 kg = _________________ lb

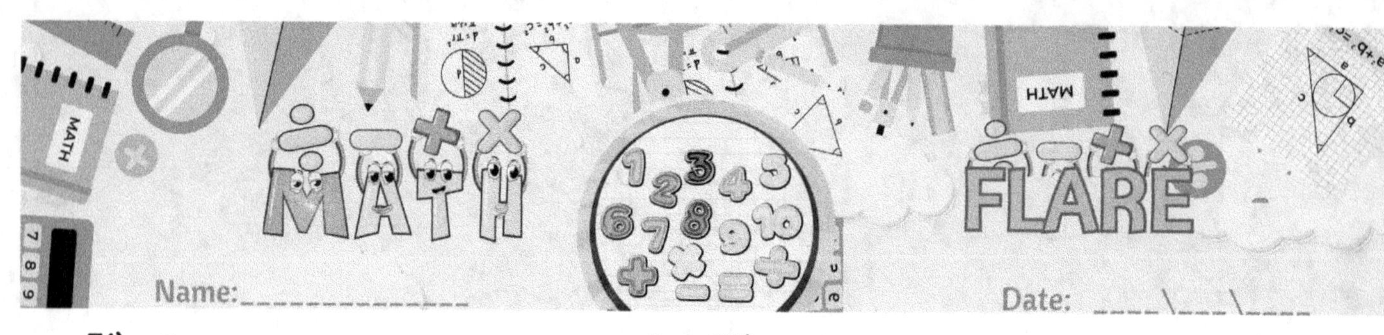

71) 6 g = _____________ lb   72) 6 kg = _____________ t

73) 8 kl = _____________ gal   74) 3 km = _____________ mi

75) 5 l = _____________ gal   76) 5 kl = _____________ gal

77) 5 g = _____________ t   78) 8 kg = _____________ t

79) 5 kg = _____________ lb   80) 6 kl = _____________ gal

81) 7 g = _____________ lb   82) 3 l = _____________ gal

83) 2 g = _____________ t   84) 6 g = _____________ lb

85) 3 l = _____________ gal   86) 1 g = _____________ lb

87) 7 km = _____________ mi   88) 6 m = _____________ mi

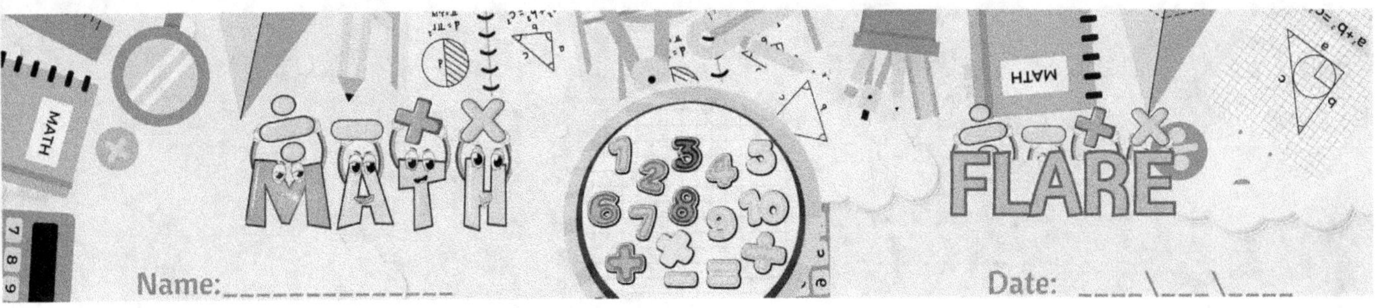

Metric Weights and Measures

Convert the given measures to new units.

1) 66 kL = _66,000_ L

2) 15 kg = __________ t

3) 34 kL = __________ L

4) 50 kg = __________ t

5) 74 L = __________ kL

6) 78 kL = __________ L

7) 11 L = __________ kL

8) 57 km = __________ m

9) 93 kL = __________ L

10) 96 L = __________ kL

11) 40 L = __________ kL

12) 13 t = __________ kg

13) 93 L = __________ kL

14) 92 L = __________ kL

15) 80 L = __________ kL

16) 69 m = __________ km

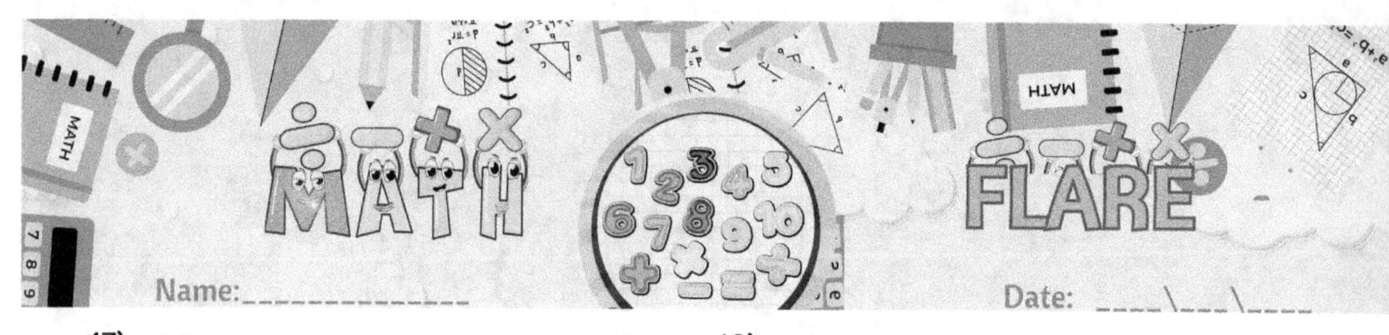

17) 27 m = _____________ km

18) 76 km = _____________ m

19) 67 km = _____________ m

20) 66 t = _____________ kg

21) 98 km = _____________ m

22) 60 km = _____________ m

23) 89 L = _____________ kL

24) 40 kL = _____________ L

25) 48 km = _____________ m

26) 23 L = _____________ kL

27) 42 t = _____________ kg

28) 68 t = _____________ kg

29) 20 kg = _____________ t

30) 63 kL = _____________ L

31) 31 kL = _____________ L

32) 22 m = _____________ km

33) 96 km = _____________ m

34) 78 L = _____________ kL

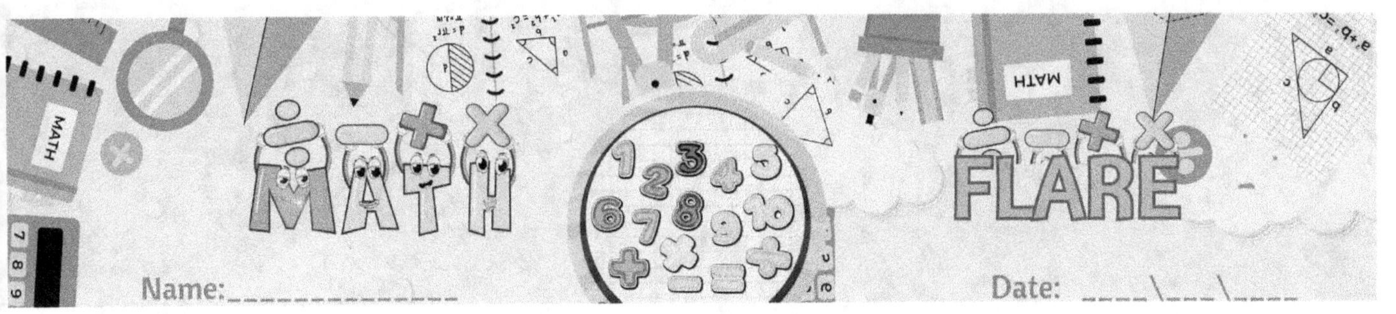

35) 72 t = _____________ kg   36) 28 kg = _____________ t

37) 85 m = _____________ km   38) 17 kg = _____________ t

39) 98 L = _____________ kL   40) 64 L = _____________ kL

41) 63 kg = _____________ t   42) 54 t = _____________ kg

43) 49 kg = _____________ t   44) 70 kL = _____________ L

45) 78 t = _____________ kg   46) 34 t = _____________ kg

47) 37 kL = _____________ L   48) 92 kL = _____________ L

49) 18 km = _____________ m   50) 38 m = _____________ km

51) 13 L = _____________ kL   52) 67 kg = _____________ t

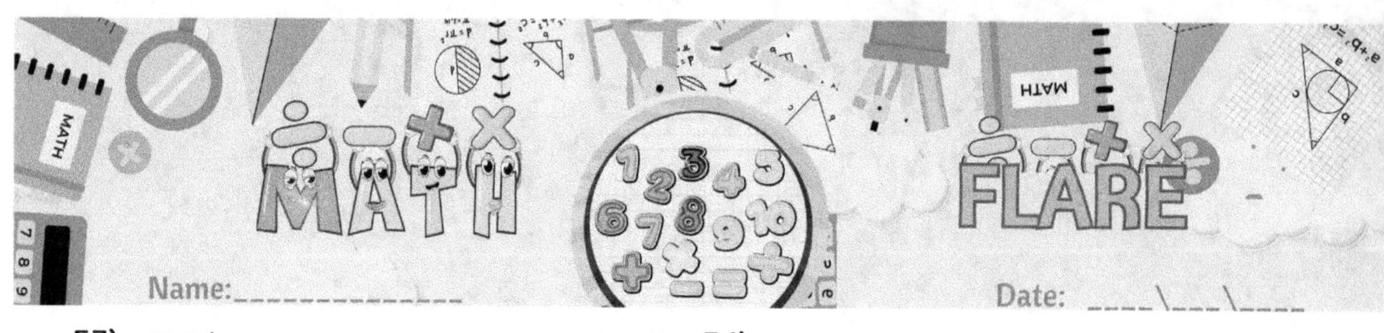

53) 54 kg = _______________ t

54) 44 m = _______________ km

55) 21 t = _______________ kg

56) 37 t = _______________ kg

57) 65 m = _______________ km

58) 68 kL = _______________ L

59) 63 L = _______________ kL

60) 35 km = _______________ m

61) 86 km = _______________ m

62) 81 kL = _______________ L

63) 81 kg = _______________ t

64) 95 m = _______________ km

65) 33 km = _______________ m

66) 18 t = _______________ kg

67) 51 t = _______________ kg

68) 41 t = _______________ kg

69) 70 kg = _______________ t

70) 43 kL = _______________ L

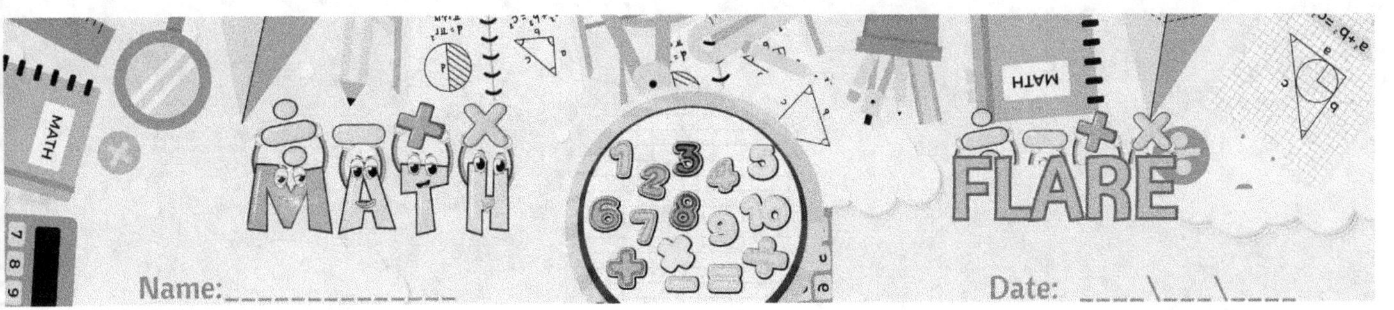

71) 67 kL = _______________ L   72) 44 km = _______________ m

73) 96 m = _______________ km   74) 45 L = _______________ kL

75) 89 kL = _______________ L   76) 77 km = _______________ m

77) 19 kg = _______________ t   78) 66 kg = _______________ t

79) 75 m = _______________ km   80) 12 t = _______________ kg

81) 35 t = _______________ kg   82) 20 km = _______________ m

83) 40 kg = _______________ t   84) 34 L = _______________ kL

85) 38 kL = _______________ L   86) 18 kL = _______________ L

87) 58 t = _______________ kg   88) 51 kg = _______________ t

ANSWERS

Page 1:   Long Division

1. 8,464.6	2. 8,671	3. 9,286.5	4. 9,924.2	5. 7,393.5
6. 20,459.8	7. 19,379.7	8. 7,607.7	9. 9,272.6	10. 22,974.3
11. 10,069	12. 12,650.3	13. 16,495.3	14. 4,649.8	15. 9,838.7
16. 10,374	17. 6,793	18. 12,854.2	19. 32,455.3	20. 4,678.6
21. 4,005	22. 4,791.6	23. 8,961.2	24. 12,287.6	25. 4,174.6
26. 3,479.7	27. 3,540.4	28. 10,043.3	29. 10,542.7	30. 3,642.9

Page 6:   Long Division: Remainders

1. 4,015 R0	2. 3,183 R13	3. 17,789 R0	4. 3,563 R8
5. 8,833 R9	6. 22,211 R0	7. 8,472 R4	8. 14,223 R0
9. 4,266 R2	10. 6,776 R3	11. 6,886 R5	12. 620 R9
13. 6,058 R1	14. 5,653 R14	15. 3,859 R3	16. 6,073 R5
17. 4,717 R5	18. 1,994 R3	19. 2,232 R15	20. 1,456 R16
21. 1,649 R8	22. 654 R9	23. 3,898 R2	24. 13,550 R4
25. 1,342 R12	26. 8,200 R0	27. 8,466 R8	28. 6,159 R5

Page 13:   Multi Digit Multiplication

1. 70,493,595	2. 32,515,728	3. 13,270,139	4. 58,377,642
5. 18,860,361	6. 55,169,920	7. 85,621,256	8. 65,465,325
9. 6,554,074	10. 11,400,600	11. 13,055,661	12. 3,530,058
13. 11,827,664	14. 20,144,243	15. 45,767,735	16. 18,343,694

17. 7,713,096   18. 9,415,399   19. 80,908,825   20. 31,870,356

21. 33,425,756   22. 12,105,738   23. 49,415,352   24. 15,270,800

25. 3,365,024   26. 9,418,285   27. 23,242,138   28. 61,378,260

29. 56,645,320   30. 12,309,456   31. 15,257,780   32. 11,754,606

33. 6,671,208   34. 60,343,574   35. 32,447,604   36. 47,134,360

Page 17: Multiplication Word Problems

1. 100   2. 162   3. 96   4. 60   5. 21   6. 143   7. 95

8. 120   9. 99   10. 72   11. 42   12. 170   13. 144   14. 221

15. 132   16. 105   17. 144   18. 63   19. 221   20. 216   21. 54

22. 90   23. 9   24. 32   25. 24   26. 153   27. 266   28. 95

29. 36   30. 340

Page 25: Division Word Problems

1. 7   2. 77   3. 66   4. 26   5. 97   6. 68   7. 24   8. 5

9. 438   10. 60   11. 34   12. 87   13. 18   14. 65   15. 35   16. 42

17. 79   18. 72   19. 74   20. 52   21. 17   22. 29   23. 85   24. 88

Page 32: Place Value

1. 6 tens

2. 8 hundreds

3. 5 hundred thousandths

4. 3 thousands

5. 6 hundredths

6. 3 tens

7. 7 ten thousands

8. 6 ten millions

9. 4 ten thousands

10. 4 tens

11. 8 tens

12. 1 hundred million

13. 9 tenths

14. 7 tens

15. 5 ones

16. 5 millions

17. 4 hundred thousands

18. 7 tens

19. 3 hundred thousands

20. 7 tens

21. 9 thousandths

22. 5 hundreds

23. 4 hundreds

24. 1 ten thousand

25. 7 millions

26. 3 thousandths

27. 8 ten thousands

28. 8 thousandths

29. 0 thousandths

30. 7 millions

Page 36: Place Value and Expanded Notation

1. 442,218.932

2. 684,311,174

3. 158,391.510

4. 511,801,600

5. 882,776.891

6. 47,223,611.7

7. 65,914,139.5

8. 899,983.666

9. 737,907,851

10. 923,095.051

11. 8,279,880.51

12. 57,647,893.7

13. 31,714,091.6

14. 1,371,452.06

15. 9,996,044.05

16. 964,682,936

17. 542,460.824

18. 3,542,045.86

19. 745,704,585

20. 45,006,840.1

21. 9,201,079.20

22. 94,457,437.8

23. 868,840,718

24. 2,215,510.28

25. 535,939,836

26. 19,654,469.7

27. 802,493.461

28. 25,782,945.6

29. 1,335,266.92

30. 9,565,248.58

Page 43: Place Value and Expanded Notation

1. 81,315,897.3
2. 87,670,936.4
3. 29,708,700.8
4. 513,734.354
5. 47,683,991.7
6. 442,167,605
7. 77,253,035.4
8. 80,115,665.5
9. 76,406,309.8
10. 64,424,637.1
11. 958,126.642
12. 822,936,805
13. 342,379,969
14. 681,908,843
15. 589,520,211
16. 123,896.800
17. 2,346,654.10
18. 144,033.881
19. 59,389,049.0
20. 89,648,432.3
21. 6,092,622.64
22. 6,243,222.99
23. 2,537,365.29
24. 748,383.020
25. 212,834,641
26. 4,976,445.52
27. 81,547,045.5
28. 9,368,404.82
29. 975,861,763
30. 786,232,194
31. 669,742.655

Page 50: Place Value and Expanded Notation

1. 5 ten millions + 1 hundred thousand + 3 ten thousands + 1 thousand + 1 hundred + 9 tens + 3 ones + 9 tenths

2. 8 ten millions + 6 millions + 6 hundred thousands + 4 ten thousands + 5 thousands + 6 hundreds + 9 tens + 7 ones + 4 tenths

3. 7 hundred thousands + 8 ten thousands + 1 thousand + 3 hundreds + 8 tens + 2 ones + 9 tenths + 9 hundredths + 2 thousandths

4. 2 hundred thousands + 9 thousands + 9 hundreds + 3 tens + 6 ones + 7 hundredths + 8 thousandths

5. 9 hundred millions + 5 ten millions + 1 million + 2 hundred thousands + 7 ten thousands + 8 thousands + 6 hundreds + 8 tens + 6 ones

6. 3 millions + 7 hundred thousands + 9 ten thousands + 3 thousands + 9 hundreds + 1 ten + 9 ones + 2 tenths + 8 hundredths

7. 8 millions + 3 ten thousands + 4 thousands + 6 tens + 5 ones + 6 tenths + 2 hundredths

8. 6 hundred millions + 6 ten millions + 3 hundred thousands + 5 thousands + 2 hundreds + 8 tens + 8 ones

9. 6 millions + 5 hundred thousands + 7 ten thousands + 4 thousands + 3 hundreds + 6 tens + 8 ones

10. 2 ten millions + 9 millions + 2 hundred thousands + 1 ten thousand + 5 thousands + 2 hundreds + 5 tens + 8 ones + 1 tenth

11. 7 ten millions + 4 millions + 1 hundred thousand + 3 ten thousands + 4 hundreds + 1 ten + 6 ones + 8 tenths

12. 5 hundred thousands + 9 ten thousands + 1 hundred + 4 tens + 1 one + 4 tenths + 8 hundredths + 8 thousandths

13. 2 millions + 1 ten thousand + 4 thousands + 5 hundreds + 8 tens + 2 ones + 1 tenth + 3 hundredths

14. 4 millions + 9 hundred thousands + 1 ten thousand + 9 thousands + 4 hundreds + 1 ten + 7 ones + 5 tenths + 8 hundredths

15. 1 hundred million + 9 ten millions + 7 millions + 1 hundred thousand + 7 ten thousands + 1 thousand + 1 hundred + 1 ten + 5 ones

16. 7 millions + 2 ten thousands + 1 thousand + 9 hundreds + 4 tens + 4 ones + 1 tenth

17. 2 hundred millions + 8 ten millions + 6 millions + 9 hundred thousands + 3 ten thousands + 1 thousand + 8 hundreds + 7 tens + 5 ones

18. 6 hundred millions + 3 ten millions + 2 millions + 3 ten thousands + 8 hundreds + 1 ten + 6 ones

19. 5 ten millions + 1 million + 2 hundred thousands + 4 thousands + 3 hundreds + 3 ones + 7 tenths

20. 9 millions + 6 hundred thousands + 1 ten thousand + 8 thousands + 7 hundreds + 9 tens + 2 ones + 8 tenths + 6 hundredths

21. 7 ten millions + 5 millions + 8 hundred thousands + 4 ten thousands + 5 thousands + 9 hundreds + 5 tens + 8 ones

22. 6 ten millions + 6 millions + 3 hundred thousands + 9 ten thousands + 3 thousands + 8 hundreds + 9 tens + 6 ones + 6 tenths

23. 2 ten millions + 3 millions + 7 hundred thousands + 4 thousands + 2 hundreds + 3 tens + 6 ones + 7 tenths

24. 4 millions + 4 hundred thousands + 7 ten thousands + 2 thousands + 6 hundreds + 2 tens + 5 ones + 9 tenths + 4 hundredths

25. 2 millions + 8 hundred thousands + 8 ten thousands + 8 thousands + 3 hundreds + 6 tens + 6 ones + 7 tenths + 4 hundredths

26. 7 millions + 2 hundred thousands + 2 ten thousands + 9 thousands + 7 hundreds + 2 tens + 8 ones + 3 tenths + 5 hundredths

27. 5 millions + 4 hundred thousands + 8 ten thousands + 7 thousands + 3 tens + 9 ones + 8 tenths + 7 hundredths

28. 4 millions + 8 thousands + 9 hundreds + 9 tens + 7 ones + 1 tenth + 3 hundredths

29. 9 millions + 7 hundred thousands + 9 ten thousands + 1 thousand + 9 hundreds + 5 tens + 3 ones + 6 tenths + 4 hundredths

30. 6 hundred thousands + 2 ten thousands + 6 thousands + 6 hundreds + 9 tens + 7 ones + 1 tenth + 4 hundredths + 8 thousandths

Page 56: Adding Decimals

1. 1,660.97	2. 1,952.31	3. 1,513.28	4. 1,132.96	5. 1,382.74
6. 914.98	7. 1,640.77	8. 1,002.13	9. 508.72	10. 911.10
11. 1,033.34	12. 1,388.15	13. 1,748.63	14. 1,163.53	15. 1,249.39
16. 1,333.18	17. 811.84	18. 1,372.46	19. 839.25	20. 1,175.81
21. 956.15	22. 1,761.31	23. 1,005.34	24. 1,260.19	25. 833.95
26. 962.95	27. 668.97	28. 1,529.03	29. 614.95	30. 882.65
31. 553.94	32. 1,060.80	33. 1,842.55	34. 1,708.32	35. 1,299.81
36. 1,447.18	37. 1,296.27	38. 1,567.82	39. 1,207.29	40. 930.28
41. 506.59	42. 1,621.25	43. 1,296.03	44. 714.63	45. 1,058.15
46. 1,113.36	47. 479.41	48. 1,027.94	49. 847.94	50. 1,555.57
51. 1,393.87	52. 912.19	53. 1,478.14	54. 1,381.20	55. 814.07
56. 785.05	57. 1,486.40	58. 739.91	59. 1,256.48	60. 1,127.71

Page 59: Subtracting Decimals

1. 438.65	2. 201.76	3. 12.77	4. 205.87	5. 287.32
6. 8.68	7. 108.63	8. 34.89	9. 13.30	10. 638.74
11. 307.68	12. 669.11	13. 668.83	14. 258.54	15. 794.45
16. 610.28	17. 608.10	18. 154.47	19. 194.32	20. 250.50
21. 295.21	22. 374.32	23. 0.27	24. 129.74	25. 276.89
26. 217.08	27. 475.96	28. 756.28	29. 332.55	30. 98.68

31. 117.77   32. 38.28   33. 190.38   34. 524.35   35. 243.48

36. 479.56   37. 358.18   38. 295.52   39. 70.58   40. 36.53

41. 351.29   42. 136.83   43. 262.61   44. 458.27   45. 246.76

46. 643.84   47. 144.44   48. 161.85   49. 531.23   50. 503.69

51. 181.17   52. 215.89   53. 67.49   54. 339.27   55. 196.69

56. 522.06   57. 180.34   58. 140.44   59. 328.21   60. 778.93

Page 62: Multiplying Decimals

1. 122.9616   2. 134.9642   3. 494.8800   4. 59.4260

5. 309.3285   6. 472.9036   7. 118.1898   8. 393.6856

9. 562.0992   10. 304.8902   11. 196.4150   12. 432.3189

13. 389.1720   14. 40.2155   15. 245.6215   16. 137.1936

17. 84.5348   18. 122.8304   19. 55.9471   20. 374.1012

21. 197.3720   22. 420.3540   23. 96.5316   24. 123.3408

25. 178.2396   26. 199.0480   27. 30.7824   28. 295.0344

29. 204.2013   30. 278.9754   31. 116.1148   32. 222.6699

33. 55.2624   34. 413.4636   35. 145.3894   36. 709.7568

37. 124.3737   38. 379.8537   39. 129.7990   40. 53.8650

41. 86.9400   42. 716.7864   43. 166.7174   44. 108.2640

45. 556.5260   46. 57.9999   47. 456.9924   48. 553.2736

49. 41.0592   50. 265.7880   51. 533.0538   52. 77.6556

53. 386.2215   54. 334.8169   55. 611.0544   56. 172.2060

57. 604.0242   58. 155.2320   59. 380.5332   60. 108.1200

61. 297.0240   62. 231.1034   63. 85.8568

Page 69: Dividing Decimals

1. 4.567   2. 3.0   3. 10.143   4. 4.722   5. 3.533

6. 5.763   7. 3.2   8. 27.8   9. 4.815   10. 1.924

11. 11.863 12. 6.138   13. 0.638   14. 2.435   15. 14.48

16. 10.025 17. 2.014   18. 15.575   19. 20.3   20. 8.378

21. 4.382   22. 3.59   23. 8.129   24. 2.821   25. 8.7

26. 3.174   27. 3.55   28. 19.275   29. 4.931   30. 4.117

31. 11.363 32. 76.5   33. 1.169   34. 3.906   35. 2.369

36. 2.125   37. 7.267   38. 1.56   39. 2.357   40. 3.52

41. 6.47   42. 8.725

Page 74: Convert Fractions and Decimals

1. 3/6   2. 1/4   3. 0.45   4. 23/25   5. 0.2   6. 18/70

7. 9/18   8. 0.5   9. 8/50   10. 57/60   11. 0.364   12. 1/2

13. 12/15   14. 0.136   15. 0.118   16. 0.211   17. 0.125   18. 25/36

19. 14/23   20. 0.208   21. 0.8   22. 5/11   23. 0.57   24. 0.6

25. 0.778   26. 8/20   27. 3/9   28. 0.571   29. 0.846   30. 0.957

31. 0.743   32. 19/32   33. 1/12   34. 3/5   35. 0.88   36. 0.812

Page 77: Fractions Multiplication

1. 4/25   2. 4/45   3. 4/11   4. 1/8   5. 7/36   6. 2/7

7. 1/6	8. 5/9	9. 3/20	10. 7/9	11. 9/55	12. 4/33
13. 1/28	14. 3/20	15. 5/33	16. 5/8	17. 1/16	18. 3/55
19. 1/3	20. 1/88	21. 9/35	22. 1/5	23. 1/24	24. 6/11
25. 1/20	26. 49/64	27. 8/27	28. 5/99	29. 2/5	30. 11/24
31. 1/6	32. 11/15	33. 2/15	34. 3/44	35. 2/9	36. 5/18
37. 1/4	38. 10/33	39. 3/20	40. 3/22	41. 3/44	42. 10/21
43. 4/15	44. 3/20	45. 4/9	46. 1/12		

Page 81: Fractions Division

1. 1 1/3	2. 15/22	3. 1 13/27	4. 9/10	5. 3/22
6. 1 2/5	7. 1 1/7	8. 9/10	9. 77/108	10. 7/30
11. 5/18	12. 5/6	13. 7/20	14. 1 1/20	15. 1 1/9
16. 1 2/7	17. 8/15	18. 20/63	19. 9/20	20. 1/4
21. 3/8	22. 2/3	23. 1 3/8	24. 1/5	25. 1/9
26. 9/16	27. 9/10	28. 5/12	29. 2/9	30. 18/55
31. 3/4	32. 11/36	33. 1/2	34. 1 7/33	35. 2/7
36. 2 2/5	37. 4/5	38. 3/16	39. 2/3	40. 1
41. 12/35	42. 3/20	43. 3/5	44. 4 13/16	45. 1 1/5
46. 3/4				

Page 85: Mixed Numbers

| 1. 5/2 | 2. 37/6 | 3. 35/4 | 4. 5/2 | 5. 28/5 |
| 6. 99/16 | 7. 14/3 | 8. 8/5 | 9. 49/16 | 10. 37/9 |

11. 19/3   12. 17/2   13. 109/12   14. 17/3   15. 20/7

16. 15/4   17. 73/9   18. 27/4   19. 4/3   20. 52/7

21. 48/5   22. 11/2   23. 28/3   24. 23/10   25. 37/18

26. 7/3   27. 26/3   28. 55/9   29. 45/16   30. 9/2

31. 19/4   32. 9/2   33. 5/4   34. 101/20   35. 28/9

36. 29/14   37. 28/3   38. 47/7   39. 28/3   40. 11/2

41. 63/8   42. 19/5   43. 11/4   44. 20/7   45. 19/2

46. 37/20   47. 53/6   48. 29/10   49. 6/5   50. 5/3

51. 22/3   52. 38/7   53. 55/6   54. 28/3   55. 17/2

56. 13/10

Page 89: Mixed Numbers

1. 2 9/16   2. 8 2/5   3. 1 2/3   4. 1 1/6   5. 3 1/2

6. 8 1/4   7. 2 3/5   8. 6 9/14   9. 9 7/16   10. 5 4/7

11. 2 3/4   12. 5 7/10   13. 1 3/4   14. 6 3/5   15. 1 9/14

16. 7 1/8   17. 8 1/2   18. 7 11/12   19. 3 5/8   20. 1 1/2

21. 7 9/14   22. 1 2/3   23. 6 4/5   24. 9 2/7   25. 7 1/4

26. 5 3/4   27. 3 4/9   28. 2 1/2   29. 1 1/5   30. 4 3/10

31. 1 1/3   32. 1 3/5   33. 8 3/4   34. 3 2/7   35. 8 7/10

36. 4 3/8   37. 4 11/12   38. 8 1/2   39. 7 1/2   40. 2 3/14

41. 8 1/4   42. 9 3/4

Page 92:   Mixed Numbers: Addition and Subtraction

1. 5 7/24
2. 1 5/14
3. 10 5/6
4. 1 3/4
5. 3 23/70

6. 11/15
7. 2 41/90
8. 3 1/4
9. 8 16/63
10. 7/12

11. 4 1/10
12. 3/40
13. 4 1/6
14. 10 11/14
15. 2

16. 1/5
17. 1 1/4
18. 41/63
19. 8 1/6
20. 6 1/14

21. 6 4/15
22. 10 17/20
23. 13 7/18
24. 10 19/21
25. 11 7/15

26. 12 7/8
27. 2 32/45
28. 2 15/28
29. 12
30. 2 1/4

31. 10 7/10
32. 1 26/45
33. 3 5/6
34. 6 31/42
35. 3 1/20

36. 5 3/10
37. 13/18
38. 6 27/28
39. 6 7/15
40. 15 1/4

41. 12 31/70
42. 15
43. 7 17/24
44. 14 2/5
45. 1 17/45

46. 16 11/20
47. 2 4/9
48. 9 11/30
49. 10 3/14
50. 3 17/18

51. 2 26/35
52. 7/10
53. 1 3/4
54. 4
55. 9 67/72

56. 9 19/21
57. 11 11/12
58. 8 69/70
59. 4 43/45
60. 18 5/6

Page 102:   Mixed Numbers: Multiplication and Division

1. 4 3/4
2. 16 1/14
3. 91/240
4. 13/33

5. 15/16
6. 5/8
7. 12 1/7
8. 27

9. 44/177
10. 73 2/3
11. 4 17/70
12. 45 1/3

13. 10 2/9
14. 26 2/5
15. 17/23
16. 54 6/7

17. 5/9
18. 10 5/8
19. 62 5/6
20. 12 3/20

21. 48 3/4
22. 7 2/3
23. 42 19/21
24. 1 17/125

25. 1 71/76
26. 17 5/8
27. 58 1/3
28. 62 5/6

29. 19 5/7   30. 42/89   31. 24   32. 135/332

33. 13/15   34. 40 10/21   35. 16/39   36. 32/85

37. 22   38. 200/351   39. 5 5/6   40. 29/60

41. 8 4/15   42. 9/11   43. 10 27/35   44. 49 22/25

45. 3 2/3   46. 2 6/7   47. 8/33   48. 51 17/18

49. 2 1/47   50. 6 17/28   51. 39 1/9   52. 10 1/3

53. 34 4/7   54. 44 1/5   55. 1 43/102   56. 44/45

57. 15/44   58. 81/518   59. 85/98   60. 57

Page 112: Area and Perimeter: Rectangles and Triangles

1. P=26 A=40   2. P=35 A=48   3. P=46 A=95.46

4. P=48 A=101.82   5. P=66 A=270   6. P=42 A=76

7. P=39 A=66   8. P=32 A=63   9. P=51 A=110.5

10. P=56 A=195   11. P=43 A=77   12. P=36 A=80

13. P=36 A=55   14. P=21 A=21.22   15. P=36 A=54

16. P=47 A=97.5   17. P=61 A=162   18. P=24 A=27.71

19. P=36 A=62.34   20. P=29 A=40.18   21. P=50 A=104

22. P=41 A=71.5   23. P=51 A=125.12   24. P=36 A=81

25. P=31 A=40   26. P=51 A=112   27. P=58 A=208

28. P=32 A=45   29. P=38 A=88   30. P=55 A=127.5

31. P=48 A=96   32. P=22 A=22.26   33. P=41 A=71.5

34. P=15 A=10.82   35. P=41 A=70   36. P=29 A=36

37. P=30 A=41 38. P=42 A=82.5 39. P=46 A=132

40. P=32 A=44 41. P=48 A=110.85 42. P=54 A=182

43. P=30 A=43.3 44. P=36 A=60 45. P=30 A=56

46. P=46 A=91 47. P=42 A=84.87 48. P=38 A=60

Page 124: Area and Circumference

1. C=31.40 cm A=78.50 cm²
2. C=100.48 cm A=803.84 cm²

3. C=106.76 cm A=907.46 cm²
4. C=6.28 cm A=3.14 cm²

5. C=87.92 cm A=615.44 cm²
6. C=25.12 cm A=50.24 cm²

7. C=12.56 cm A=12.56 cm²
8. C=94.20 cm A=706.50 cm²

9. C=18.84 cm A=28.26 cm²
10. C=119.32 cm A=1,133.54 cm²

11. C=81.64 cm A=530.66 cm²
12. C=37.68 cm A=113.04 cm²

13. C=62.80 cm A=314.00 cm²
14. C=113.04 cm A=1,017.36 cm²

15. C=56.52 cm A=254.34 cm²
16. C=43.96 cm A=153.86 cm²

17. C=69.08 cm A=379.94 cm²
18. C=50.24 cm A=200.96 cm²

19. C=125.60 cm A=1,256.00 cm²
20. C=75.36 cm A=452.16 cm²

21. C=56.52 cm A=254.34 cm²
22. C=106.76 cm A=907.46 cm²

23. C=50.24 cm A=200.96 cm²
24. C=94.20 cm A=706.50 cm²

25. C=125.60 cm A=1,256.00 cm²
26. C=69.08 cm A=379.94 cm²

27. C=18.84 cm A=28.26 cm²
28. C=18.84 cm A=28.26 cm²

Page 131: Measuring Angles

1. 140° 2. 130° 3. 150° 4. 150° 5. 30° 6. 90° 7. 120°

8. 100°   9. 10°   10. 110°   11. 60°   12. 110°   13. 160°   14. 110°

15. 100°   16. 10°   17. 60°   18. 50°   19. 60°   20. 80°   21. 40°

22. 50°   23. 40°   24. 150°   25. 90°   26. 10°   27. 160°   28. 80°

29. 140°   30. 70°   31. 120°   32. 30°   33. 130°   34. 60°   35. 20°

36. 140°   37. 20°   38. 130°   39. 170°   40. 120°   41. 70°   42. 170°

43. 120°   44. 110°

Page 142:   Metric Conversion

1. 264.172   2. 0.007   3. 0.000   4. 0.004

5. 0.000   6. 1,849.204   7. 17.637   8. 0.528

9. 8.818   10. 6.614   11. 0.015   12. 1.585

13. 1.849   14. 5.592   15. 0.020   16. 0.000

17. 0.793   18. 1.321   19. 5.592   20. 2.205

21. 1,849.204   22. 0.005   23. 2.113   24. 3.107

25. 1,056.688   26. 1.864   27. 0.000   28. 17.637

29. 2.113   30. 0.000   31. 0.007   32. 4.350

33. 15.432   34. 0.001   35. 1.243   36. 0.001

37. 792.516   38. 15.432   39. 1.585   40. 0.004

41. 0.000   42. 528.344   43. 0.000   44. 0.000

45. 0.264   46. 0.004   47. 11.023   48. 2.113

49. 1,849.204   50. 0.002   51. 1.849   52. 0.000

53. 2,113.376   54. 0.002   55. 11.023   56. 0.528

57. 0.000   58. 0.008   59. 2.205   60. 17.637

61. 0.007   62. 264.172   63. 0.002   64. 1.057

65. 3.728   66. 0.000   67. 15.432   68. 0.013

69. 2,113.376   70. 19.842   71. 0.013   72. 0.007

73. 2,113.376   74. 1.864   75. 1.321   76. 1,320.860

77. 0.000   78. 0.009   79. 11.023   80. 1,585.032

81. 0.015   82. 0.793   83. 0.000   84. 0.013

85. 0.793   86. 0.002   87. 4.350   88. 0.004

Page 147: Metric Weights and Measures

1. 66,000   2. 0.015   3. 34,000   4. 0.050   5. 0.074

6. 78,000   7. 0.011   8. 57,000   9. 93,000   10. 0.096

11. 0.040   12. 13,000   13. 0.093   14. 0.092   15. 0.080

16. 0.069   17. 0.027   18. 76,000   19. 67,000   20. 66,000

21. 98,000   22. 60,000   23. 0.089   24. 40,000   25. 48,000

26. 0.023   27. 42,000   28. 68,000   29. 0.020   30. 63,000

31. 31,000   32. 0.022   33. 96,000   34. 0.078   35. 72,000

36. 0.028   37. 0.085   38. 0.017   39. 0.098   40. 0.064

41. 0.063   42. 54,000   43. 0.049   44. 70,000   45. 78,000

46. 34,000   47. 37,000   48. 92,000   49. 18,000   50. 0.038

51. 0.013   52. 0.067   53. 0.054   54. 0.044   55. 21,000

56. 37,000   57. 0.065   58. 68,000   59. 0.063   60. 35,000

61. 86,000   62. 81,000   63. 0.081   64. 0.095   65. 33,000

66. 18,000   67. 51,000   68. 41,000   69. 0.070   70. 43,000

71. 67,000   72. 44,000   73. 0.096   74. 0.045   75. 89,000

76. 77,000   77. 0.019   78. 0.066   79. 0.075   80. 12,000

81. 35,000   82. 20,000   83. 0.040   84. 0.034   85. 38,000

86. 18,000   87. 58,000   88. 0.051